Real Options and Option-Embedded Securities

William T. Moore

John Wiley & Sons, Inc.
New York ▪ Chichester ▪ Weinheim ▪ Brisbane ▪ Singapore ▪ Toronto

For Linda

Library of Congress Cataloging in Publication Data:

ISBN 0-471-21659-3

Printed in the United States of America.

10 9 8 7 6 5 4 3 2 1

Table of Contents

About the Author

William T. Moore is Professor of Finance, and holder of the David & Esther Berlinberg Chair at the Moore School of Business, University of South Carolina. He is presently the Editor of the *Journal of Financial Research*, a scholarly publication produced quarterly. He was awarded a Ph.D. degree from Virginia Polytechnic Institute in 1982 with fields in finance and statistics. Dr. Moore's research interests have included capital investment analysis, risk measurement, asset pricing, capital and organizational structure, dividend policy, and financial distress and reorganization. He has been recognized for teaching excellence throughout his academic career. Before entering the academic profession, Dr. Moore was a U.S. Army officer and served as an infantry lieutenant in Vietnam.

Preface

This book is about applying what we know about financial options to many everyday decisions that arise in business finance. The insights developed and explained herein are not new for the most part, but are rather the product of numerous important intellectual advances brought to us by scholars over the past few decades.

There are several fine books on options and other derivatives written for students of investment. These books cover strategic use of options in managing risk, as well as theoretical valuation of options. Similarly, there are some excellent and recent books about applications of option analytic methods to firms' capital investment decisions. Moreover, one can now find books specializing in designing and valuing corporate securities such as callable bonds, putable notes, convertibles, and warrants. This book is designed to encompass all three aspects of options: (1) strategic use of options in corporate risk management; (2) application of option analytic techniques in capital investment decisions; and (3) valuation and design of securities using modern option pricing theory.

The book is targeted to students in graduate business programs as well as practitioners in financial institutions, industrial corporations, and consulting firms. Following each chapter are questions and problems, and solutions are provided in the back of the book.

In the first four chapters we visit options markets around the world, explore strategic applications of financial options for managing and controlling risk, and develop theoretical pricing models. We survey exchange-traded options such as calls and puts on stocks, interest rate options, options on futures, and index options.

In Chapter 5 we explain how options arise metaphorically in virtually all aspects of firms' capital investment and financing decisions. Valuation methods for option-embedded securities are presented in Chapters 6, 7, and 8. Here we determine how to value warrants, rights, callable bonds, convertibles, and other option-embedded securities using state-of-the art methods. We explore principles of designing securities to accomplish various strategic objectives, and we survey increasingly popular financing instruments such as structured convertibles — for example, PERCS, LYONS, ACES, and ELKS.

The option metaphor is applied to capital investment decisions in Chapters 9, 10, and 11. These decisions often involve capital projects that contain flexibility — managers may modify the projects after they have been undertaken. Such flexibility has value and it may be analyzed using options. We'll see that many capital projects have implicit options to expand, reduce scale, abandon, or switch modes of production, and we now know how to assess the values of these features. Finally, in Chapter 12 we explore application of options in corporate risk management. We will see that options may be tailored to firms' needs to limit losses from operations and to control financial risk. We will survey second generation options such as cylinders, digital and binary options, knock-in and knock-out options, and lookback options

The many fine students who have offered suggestions and criticisms have my sincere appreciation and utmost respect. The generous support of the Moore School of Business of the University of South Carolina is gratefully acknowledged, as well as the excellent support through the David and Esther Berlinberg Professorship established by my friend Dr. Frederick M. Weissman. I offer special thanks to Ellen Roueche and Michelle Cook for their expert help in preparing the manuscript, to Megan Orem for her skilled editing and typesetting, and to Frank Fabozzi for his generous and helpful guidance and support throughout the development of the book.

William T. Moore
August 2001

Chapter 1

Introduction to Options

T he following is an excerpt from the *prospectus* of the Merrill Lynch Pacific Fund, Inc., an investment company specializing in equity investment in the Pacific Rim.

> The Fund may write (i.e., sell) covered call options on its portfolio securities, purchase put options on securities and engage in transactions in stock index options, stock index futures and financial futures, and related options on such futures... [April 28, 1995 *Prospectus* of Merrill Lynch Pacific Fund, Inc., p. 13]

The securities mentioned in the excerpt — options, futures contracts, and options on futures — are examples of *derivatives*. These securities derive their values from the values of other assets such as stocks and bonds, hence the name.

In many cases, options arise naturally in capital investment decisions made by firms, and these are often more subtle than options on stocks and bonds. For instance, when a pharmaceutical firm such as Abbott Labs undertakes a research project involving a new drug, the odds against ultimate development of the drug into a profitable prescription product are tremendous. However expenses associated with the research program may be viewed as the cost of an option, the option to develop the drug for medical use in the event it is successfully developed. As we will see, straightforward application of familiar capital investment tools such as net present value (NPV) analysis will result in rejection of many research projects because traditional methods overlook option features. Such projects are appropriately evaluated as options.

This book is about options that arise in financial decision-making. You probably are already familiar with *call* options to buy stocks and their opposites, *put* options to sell stocks. You may know that *convertible* bonds and preferred stocks have embedded call options, that *warrants* and stock purchase *rights* are special types of call options, and that some types of bonds may be surrendered (put) to the issuing firms in exchange for specified cash amounts under certain conditions. Thus, options appear to inhabit much of the financial landscape, even though we must often look hard to find them as they lay hidden in various financial opportunities. For instance, when a firm purchases capital equipment needed for production, it may delay production until economic conditions are more favorable. This means that the ordinary-looking capital investment proposal may have an embedded option, and the value of this option should be taken into account when evaluating the proposal.

If we look hard enough and think carefully enough, we will find call and put options in virtually every aspect of financial decision-making. This includes personal investment decisions such as buying puts and calls, corporate investment decisions involving capital outlays, risk management, and corporate financing decisions involving convertible securities, warrants, and rights.

As you go through this book, you will see that in one sense the scope is limited. We will explore options in depth, but will not concern ourselves to a large extent with the more general category of financial instruments known as *derivatives*. Options are derivatives in that their values derive from values of other securities or assets, but derivatives also include futures contracts and forward contracts, among others.

In another sense, you will see that the scope of the book is broad in that we will find options nearly *everywhere*. Discussion of standard call and put options is found traditionally in textbooks on investment management, and treatment of real options such as the option to delay production is a topic found increasingly in modern courses in corporate financial management. But the treatment here includes employing and evaluating options however they might arise in the corporate setting, and that takes us into areas that traditionally have been in the domains of both investment management and corporate finance.

DEFINITIONS

Let's begin with some important definitions.

Option Contract: An agreement between two parties that assigns the right to buy (call option) or sell (put option) a specified asset at a stipulated price.

Forward Contract: An agreement between two parties stipulating that one shall buy a specified asset from the other at an agreed-upon price at a future date. This sounds like an option, but note that the option involves the *right* to buy or sell, whereas the forward contract involves the *obligation*.

Futures Contract: An agreement between two parties stipulating that one shall buy a specified asset from the other at a future date. An important feature that distinguishes futures from forwards is that futures trading is accomplished using highly standardized contracts. Because they are standardized as to expiration dates and denominations they are easily traded, hence futures markets offer excellent liquidity.

Swap: An agreement between two parties to exchange one series of cash flow obligations for another. For example, one firm may swap fixed interest payments for floating interest payments based on some notional amount. This is an interest rate swap and swaps involving currencies are common as well.

All types of derivatives represent arrangements to buy, sell or exchange some underlying asset at a point in the future. While forward and futures contracts are *obligations* to buy or sell, and swaps are contractual exchanges of assets, options are *rights* to buy or sell. The buyer of a call option, for example, receives the right to buy a specific asset at a particular price. This right is granted by the *seller* (also called the *writer*) of the call, who agrees to sell the asset in the event the call buyer chooses to exercise the right.

WHY OPTIONS EXIST

A natural question that arises in the study of options and derivatives is, Why do they exist? Some might complain that futures, forwards, and options are really just legalized lotteries established for the benefit of the idle rich. And financial catastrophes such as the bankruptcies of Barings PLC and Orange County, California present glaring examples that are used to indict the derivatives industry. But the industry is not a gambling casino and derivatives provide tremendous benefits by allowing efficient sharing and allocation of financial risks.

A simple example will illustrate. Suppose we own common stock presently worth $100. Even if the stock is a "Blue Chip," with a long history and strong reputation, its value is subject to dynamic and unpredictable market forces. In fact, such a stock in the United States will typically fluctuate in value by 20% or more in a given year. In Australia, it is more like 35%.

Suppose you want to invest in the stock but would like to avoid the risk of losing a significant portion of its value. If options did not exist this would simply be impossible. But let's say you can buy a put option on the stock with $100 exercise price and the option costs $4.50. The *exercise price* is the specified price at which the asset (the stock) may be sold by exercising the put. For simplicity, let's say you have 100 shares of the stock valued presently at $100 per share, and the put option is for 100 shares. Its current value is $4.50 per share or $450 for the contract. Now suppose that by the expiration date of the put, the stock price has declined to $90 per share. The shares of stock in your portfolio have now declined in value by $1,000. But the put contract may be exercised; that is, you may sell 100 shares of stock for the exercise price of $100 per share. You could buy 100 more shares at $90, use them to execute the put, which would allow you to clear $10 per share, or $1,000. This happens to offset the loss in the stock in your original portfolio. Is this a free lunch? No — remember you paid $450 for the put contract — but that's the worst of it. As you will see in Chapter 2, you would be out $450 no matter how low the stock goes.

The point is that without well-developed options markets, it would be difficult and costly for us to transfer unwanted risks to those more willing and able to bear them. Because options and other derivatives are used principally to manage risks, these products are analogous to ordinary insurance contracts, whose societal value is abundantly clear.

OPTIONS MARKETS

Stock Options

Let's discuss the markets for call and put options on common stocks first. Here's some brief history. In the United States until the early 1970s, options were traded in an informal network in which there was no uniformity in contracts and no established trading procedure. There were some strides toward organized trading in options before 1973, the year in which the Chicago Board of Trade created the "CBOE," the Chicago Board Options Exchange, which is a modern exchange featuring an "open outcry" auction process (like stock exchanges) and highly standardized option contracts. These are standardized such that those that expire in, say May, expire on the same date in May. Exercise prices are usually specified in $5 increments, and options may be "listed" on the CBOE only if the firms that issue the underlying stocks have been profitable in the recent past, have not defaulted on debt recently, have ample trading volume and a large number of individual shareholders, in addition to other requirements. Think of these as the necessary conditions for listing. Furthermore, a stock will not generally have options listed on the CBOE unless it exhibits a healthy degree of price volatility — options on assets with little fluctuation in value command little investor interest for reasons we'll see in Chapter 2.

Let's consider some puts and calls on stocks. On August 24, 2000, America Online (AOL) had puts and calls listed for trading on the CBOE with exercise prices ranging from $50 to $100 per share — AOL's stock price closed at $60 on that day. Standard option contracts are identified by three features: (1) the underlying stock, (2) the exercise price, and (3) the expiration date. The call option contract with October expiration and $70 exercise (or strike) price was priced at $0.81 per share on this day. Standard contracts are for 100 shares, hence this contract was valued at $81. Expiration is always on the Saturday following the third Friday of the month, so with a calendar we can easily determine the exact expiration date.

On the same day, put options with the same exercise price ($70) and the same expiration (October) were priced at $10.88 per share, or $1,088 per contract. Since the put's exercise price is greater than the stock price, we say the option is "in the money." This means that if we owned this option ($70 exercise), and the stock was priced at $60, and *if* it expired immediately, we would exercise it. This is what determines whether an option is in the money. Notice that the call ($70 exercise price) is "out of the money." That is, if the option was expiring now and the stock price was $60, we would *not* exercise. The price of the option has no bearing on the determination of whether it is in the money.

To get a feel for the profit and loss potential for options, suppose you had bought AOL calls with a $70 exercise price at $0.81 in August and in October, at expiration, the stock price had gone up 20% to $72 per share. Would you exercise? What would be your rate of return? Yes, and your rate of return would be 147%! That is, ($72 − $70 − $0.81)/$0.81 = 1.47. Of course, had the stock declined by 20% to $48, the option would have expired worthless (unexercised) and your rate of return on the option investment would have been −100%. Bear in mind that these dramatic rates of return are possible on a stock that had hypothetical price movements of just 20%. And this is not an unusual example by any means.

In our discussion so far, we might naturally have the impression that expiration of an in-the-money option necessarily entails transfer of ownership of the stock and conveyance of the exercise money. For instance, if we had exercised the AOL call option, we would have given the seller of the contract $7,000 and the seller would have surrendered the stock valued at, say $7,200 in our example. But many investors find these transactions too cumbersome and too costly. Instead of actually exercising the option, the investor may close out the position before the expiration date by executing a purchase or sale to offset a corresponding sale or purchase. For instance, if you had sold (written) a call option that is expiring in the money, you could enter an order to buy that contract, thereby closing your position. This is done through a central organization for CBOE options called the Options Clearing Corporation, and it makes transactions much more efficient. Another way to realize the profit is to settle on a cash basis at expiration. In this example, you would receive the difference between the stock value at expiration, say, $7,200 for 100 shares, and the exercise price of $7,000. Thus you would have $200 transferred to your account and the same amount would be deducted from the account of a writer of the same option. And in most derivatives markets including those for futures and forward contracts, transactions are settled often on a cash basis. Thus, when Hillary Clinton entered into a cattle futures contract in the 1980s, and the value of beef appreciated such that she had made a handsome profit, no cows were actually delivered to her home in Arkansas. Instead, the profit from the transaction was credited to her trading account.

Before we leave this section, here are a few numbers that may help put these various markets in perspective. The CBOE lists call and put options for about 1,300 firms. In the U.S., stock options are also traded on the American Stock Exchange (1,200 firms), the Philadelphia Stock Exchange (nearly 800 firms), and the Pacific Exchange (over 800 firms). A few stock options were traded on the New York Stock Exchange (NYSE) until the late 1990s. No options are traded in Nasdaq, the huge electronic over-the-counter market; however it remains to be seen what effect the 1999 merger between Nasdaq and the American Stock Exchange will have on option trading.

The CBOE also commands most trading volume; 55% of call trades and 70% of put trades in the U.S. are executed on this exchange. The American Stock Exchange accounts for about one-fourth of call volume and 15% of put volume. For the four markets combined, daily trading comes to about 600,000 contracts, or about 40% to 70% of the share volume on the NYSE.

Index Options

Before we proceed to other options markets, in and outside the United States, consider the following quote:

> Twenty-five years ago it was comparatively easy to acquire a sound knowledge of the general investment

field...[but now] the different types of securities have multiplied in number to an almost unlimited extent... [from "Securities Innovations...," by P. Tufano, *J. Applied Corp. Finance*, Winter 1995.]

This quote is from John Moody, founder of *Moody's Investors Services*. Although the quote is from 1910, it is just as applicable now. As we have seen, options on individual common stocks are traded in the U.S. on the CBOE, American Stock Exchange, Pacific Exchange, and the Philadelphia Exchange. There are also options on stock *indices* (e.g., the S&P 500). In the United States there are about 20 indices on which options are written, but only three are actively traded: the S&P 100 and S&P 500 traded on CBOE, and the Major Market Index (MMI) traded on AMEX. The S&P indices are, unlike the Dow Jones indices, weighted by market capitalization. In other words, GM common is contained in the Dow Jones Industrial Average (DJIA) and it is treated equally with IBM. These same stocks are also contained in the S&P indices, but their share prices are multiplied by the numbers of shares outstanding to give a value-weighted index.

Why are there options on indices? Mainly because of their use in portfolio risk management. Remember that a put option can serve essentially as an insurance contract for a common stock. Suppose you hold a large, well-diversified portfolio as many large financial institutions do. If you would like to insure this portfolio you could do so by buying puts on an index that most closely resembles your institution's portfolio — we'll see how in Chapter 2.

You might wonder, Why not simply buy puts and/or calls on the individual stocks? The fact is that you would overpay, even if you ignored transaction costs. The explanation may not be apparent to all, but with your background in finance you may already suspect the reason. Recall that options derive their values from volatility. As we will see in Chapter 3, all else the same, a call or put on a low volatility stock is worth less than one on a high volatility stock. When we add stocks to a portfolio, some of their volatility is diversified away — we remove the unique or unsystematic risk. Consequently, a call or put option written on a portfolio, say the S&P 100, is *not* equivalent in value to a portfolio of calls or puts written on the 100 stocks included in the index. Said differently, if you employed individual stock options to manage the risk of a large portfolio, you would end up paying for reduction in some risks that have already been neutralized through diversification. This is why there exist markets for options on portfolios (indices) as well as individual stocks.

To illustrate index options consider the S&P 100 index options (symbol OEX) trading on the CBOE. On August 24, 2000, the September-expiration index call with strike price of 825 was priced at 14.88. What does this mean? The S&P 100 Index is measured in "points," not dollars, thus we need some method of monetizing the index. The CBOE transforms points to dollars for this contract simply by scaling the number of points by $100. In this case, the exercise price of the S&P 100 call is $100 \times 825 = \$82,500$ per contract. The price of the contract is $100 \times 14.88 = \$1,488$, and the value of the underlying asset, the S&P 500 Index, is $100 \times 825.15 = \$82,515$.

If this option is exercised when the S&P 100 index is, say, 833 points, the buyer of the call will in essence pay $82,500 for an asset worth $83,300 ($100 \times 833$). These contracts are settled on a cash basis, thus the exercise price is not literally transferred to the call writer, and the S&P 500 Index is not literally transferred to the buyer. Instead, the buyer in this case would receive the cash difference between the value of the underlying asset ($83,300) and the contract's exercise price ($82,500), or $800.

The CBOE lists options on a number of other stock indexes, including the Dow Jones Industrial Average, the Dow Jones Utility and Transportation indexes, The Nasdaq 100 Index, the S&P 500 Index, and the Russell 2000 Index. The American Stock Exchange lists options on several specialized indexes such as Hong Kong and Japanese Indexes, an internet index and several indexes formed by Morgan Stanley Dean Witter. The Philadelphia Exchange also lists options on equity indexes as well as indexes on precious metals such as gold and silver.

The CBOE lists options on U.S. government securities. Although the options are written directly on bonds and notes, they are called interest rate options because they are used to hedge interest rate risk. The CBOE lists options on government bonds (long maturity) and government notes (less than 10 years) in denominations of $100,000.

Currency Options

In the United States, options on foreign currencies are traded on a few exchanges. Trading currency options began on the Philadelphia Stock Exchange in British pounds in 1982 and in a few months expanded to Japanese yen, Swiss francs, German marks, and Canadian dollars. Now several major currencies including the Euro have options listed on the Philadelphia Stock Exchange (PHIL-X). Some currency options are also traded on the American Stock Exchange and on the Chicago Mercantile Exchange.

Some options are said to be "European style," while others may be "American style" and these designations have nothing to do with geography. A European-style option may not be exercised until its expiration date, whereas an American-style may be exercised at any time up to expiration. These distinctions apply to any options, not just currencies, and PHIL-X lists both styles of currency options.

Most currency options listed on PHIL-X expire on Friday preceding the third Wednesday of the month of expiration. A few contracts expire at the end of the month (EOM). Remember that exchange-listed stock options expire on Saturdays following the third Friday of the month.

Let's see how currency options work with an example. On August 24, 2000, European-style put and call contracts for 62,500 Euros were listed on PHIL-X, with September expiration, and exercise price of $0.88 per Euro. Put contracts were priced at $.0057 per Euro, or $356.25 per contract. On that day, the spot exchange rate for the Euro was quoted at $0.8989 per Euro, hence the puts were out of the money; that is, the value of the underlying ($0.8989) was greater than the exercise price ($0.88).

If the dollar value of the Euro falls to, say $0.85, and you had bought one put contract on this date, you would exercise and your rate of return would be $(0.88 - 0.85 - 0.0057)/0.0057 = 4.26$, or about 426%! However, remember the very likely possibility that this out-of-the-money put will remain out of the money, in which case your rate of return would be −100%.

Why do currency options exist? For the same reasons that options exist on virtually any other financial assets — risk management and other forms of strategic portfolio management. We will see later that options used strategically in portfolios can be extremely powerful instruments for reducing and controlling risk. Thus, a firm headquartered in the United States, with commercial interests in Germany, can use put and call options on German marks to reduce its currency risk exposure. As we will see, in the limit a firm can remove all of its currency risk if there is a well developed market for currency options.

Futures Options

Up to this point, we have discussed markets for options on stocks, options on stock indices, options on bonds, and options on currencies. Each of these types of securities has its own well developed market structure. There are at least two more: (1) options on futures and (2) options on corporate securities such as those embedded in convertible bonds and preferred stocks. Let's consider options on futures first. Remember that a forward contract is simply a contract to buy or sell a specified asset at a fixed price at some point in the future. For example, a natural way to avoid currency risk on a foreign account receivable is to sell the currency forward. If you have 100,000 Euros receivable in 30 days and the forward rate is, say 90 cents per mark, then you can enter into a contract today to sell the 100,000 Euros for $90,000 in 30 days. In this case the currency risk is removed entirely.

A futures contract is also an agreement to buy or sell an asset on a certain date. So how is it different from a forward? At the end of each trading day the futures contract is "marked to market." This means that changes in the value of the futures contract are reflected in the buyer's and the seller's accounts each day. Suppose the futures price today for delivery of 100,000 Euros next month is 90 cents per Euro, and you buy one contract. Tomorrow, suppose the futures price declines to 89 cents. This means that your account would be debited $1,000 ($0.01 × 100,000) and the account of the seller of the futures contract would be credited by this amount. This process is repeated each day until the contract expires or is closed out. Another way to think of a futures contract is as a succession of forward contracts, whereby each day ends with a contract being closed out and another one being entered.

Options on futures contracts are listed in the U.S. on the Chicago Board of Trade (CBT), Chicago Mercantile Exchange (CME), Kansas City Board of Trade, New York Cotton Exchange, New York Mercantile Exchange, and the New York Coffee, Sugar and Cocoa Exchange. The ones with the greatest economic significance are the Treasury bond futures options traded on the CBT, and the S&P 500 futures options traded on the CME.

You might wonder why we have options on futures. The main reason is that there is often not a well established market in the underlying asset. For instance, consider stock indices such as the S&P 500. This is nothing more than a number representing the value of a portfolio of 500 common stocks. But the index itself does not have a market — you can buy and sell the individual stocks, but not the index directly. Thus an option on a futures contract on the S&P 500 is an option on a fairly liquid asset (the futures contact) as opposed to the relatively illiquid underlying asset (the portfolio of 500 stocks).

Options on S&P 500 futures contracts are traded on the Chicago Mercantile Exchange (CME). On August 24, 2000, calls on the October-expiration S&P 500 futures contract with 1510 exercise price were traded at 55.20.

Values of these options are scaled by $250, thus the exercise price for one contract is $250 \times 1510 = \$377,500$. The price of one call contract was $250 \times 55.20 = \$13,800$, and note that the call is out of the money. Suppose the futures price rises to 1570 and that the call option is exercised. The call buyer receives the cash difference between the futures price (1570) and the exercise price (1510), or 60 scaled by $250 which gives $15,000. This amount comes from the call writer. Moreover, exercise means the call buyer is assigned a long position in the futures contract, which may then be closed or allowed to continue until its expiration. A put option on the futures contract works in much the same way. At exercise, the put holder receives cash in the amount of the difference between the exercise price and the futures price, scaled by $250, and is assigned a short position in the futures contract.

Interest Rate Options

Options are valuable devices for managing interest rate risk. For example, suppose a firm issues a bond with a floating coupon rate such that the rate is tied to the London interbank offer rate (LIBOR). The firm's cost of debt will then vary with this rate, increasing as LIBOR rises. A variety of option products exist that are useful in offsetting these variations.

The firm could use exchange-traded bond futures options listed on the Chicago Board of Trade (CBT). These are calls and puts on Treasury Bond futures also traded on the CBT. By buying puts in our example the firm will benefit if interest rates rise as bond prices decline. The benefit will then offset some of the added cost due to the increased coupon rate on the floating-rate bond issue.

As you will see in Chapter 12 a large market exists for interest rate *caps*, *floors*, and *collars*. These are calls and puts structured by investment banks for their client firms. They are tailor-made option contracts traded over the counter, and as their names reveal they are structured to place upper limits and lower bounds on firms' interest expenses and income.

Corporate Securities

Now consider corporate securities, which as we will see later have embedded options. Often the options are explicit. For example, a corporate bond may be callable by the issuing firm, the same bond may have a put option allowing it to be sold back to the issuing firm, and some bonds and other senior securities may be converted into common stock. Warrants and stock purchase rights, as well as executive and employee stock options, are call options written by firms.

In general, convertible preferred stocks, warrants, and rights are traded on stock exchanges, although not necessarily on the same exchanges on which the underlying common stocks are listed. For instance, Amax, Inc. has common stock listed on the NYSE, a preferred issue listed on the AMEX, and convertible bonds traded on bond markets, e.g., the NYSE bond market.

Corporate bonds increasingly are issued with put features which allow bond investors to sell their securities back to the issuing firm for a fixed price under certain conditions. For instance, "event risk covenants" specify that bonds may be sold (or put) back to the issuing firm for a fixed cash amount if certain events such as takeovers occur. Such an event might otherwise drive down the value of the bond issue, thus such a put feature represents insurance for the bondholder.

Convertibles are interesting (and complex) because they typically contain at least two options. One is obvious — the convertible holder has the option of surrendering the bond or preferred issue for a fixed number of shares of common. This is a call option and the exercise price is the value of the convertible security (what is given up in exchange for the common stock upon conversion). The issuing firm typically has an option, that of calling the convertible security before maturity for redemption. Determining the fair value for these securities is difficult due to the two option features, but the task is still more daunting because the contracts usually allow the call provisions to change over time.

To illustrate, consider Boise Cascade's 7% coupon bond issued in 1986. In the bond's indenture (contract) the terms of call are spelled out. The bond could not be called for three years from the issuance date (i.e., the call provision is deferred and this is typical). Moreover, the call price at which the firm may redeem the bond issue ratchets down each year. For instance, if Boise Cascade had called the bond in 1995, it would have had to pay investors "101.40," or 101.4% of the face value of $50 per bond. By 1996, the call price had dropped to 100.70, and thereafter is was 100% of face value.

The conversion and call options on most convertible bonds and preferred stocks together create a powerful tool for managing capital structure. Here's how it works. Suppose a convertible bond has a *conversion ratio* of 20, meaning that each bond can be converted for 20 shares of common stock. The bond is issued at $1,000 par and the common stock at that time is priced at $40 per share. Thus the *conversion value* is 20 × $40 = $800 (i.e., the value of the common stock into which the issue may be converted). As time passes and, assuming the firm does well, the stock price increases and the conversion value grows. Suppose that the common stock price has now risen to $60 per share. The conversion value is then $1,200 and the bond should be priced at no less than $1,200. (Why?) Suppose the call price is 100, meaning 100% of par value, or $1,000. If the firm exercises its call provision, it effectively tells the convertible bondholders that they must either surrender their bonds for $1,000 (call value) *or* exercise their conversion right and convert for $1,200 of stock. The choice is obvious and the immediate effect on the firm's balance sheet is a dramatic reduction in financial leverage, and there is no immediate outflow of cash. This is referred to as *forced conversion.*

Warrants are also issued by corporations, usually in conjunction with another security (i.e., common stock, bonds or preferred stock). A warrant is a call option on the firm's common stock. It is identical to an ordinary call in that an exercise price is stipulated and an expiration date is set, often five years after issuance. Two key differences are that (1) warrant exercise results in additional common shares outstanding (dilution) and (2) exercise results in a cash inflow to the firm. This is not the case for ordinary call options which are contracts between investors and therefore the issuing firms are not involved. Thus, warrants will be valued in a similar way to call options, but account must be taken of dilution on the firms and the cash inflow.

As we have said, warrants are usually issued in conjunction with bonds or stocks as *units.* Warrants are often added to otherwise straight bonds or preferreds in order to "sweeten" the issues. In other words, if the investment bank that is helping the issuer market the securities feels that the market will not accept them at par, then the firm may be persuaded to add a little inducement. As we will see later, this inducement may be used to help resolve conflicts that naturally arise between bondholders (preferred stockholders) and common stockholders.

Like warrants, rights are options to buy common stocks, thus they are calls. Rights offers represent a method for issuing new common shares. The issuing firm gives its existing shareholders rights to buy newly issued common shares at a fixed (subscription) price during a subscription period that typically lasts three weeks or so. This method of issuance is an alternative to the general cash offer whereby the firm offers shares to the public at large. Investors who do not wish to exercise the rights may sell them to other investors in the market. Rights are usually traded on the same exchange as the firm's common stock.

Nonstandard Options

As we go through this book you will meet a number of nonstandard or *exotic* options. These are usually traded over the counter and not listed on exchanges such as the CBOE or CBT. They are tailor-made by investment banks to solve client firms' risk management problems.

For instance, a firm can manufacture a forward contract using options in order to lock in a future price of a commodity. These *cylinder* options allow for deviations from standard forward contracts in order for firms' specialized needs to be met. You'll also learn about *binary* and *digital* options which pay fixed amounts in the event underlying assets exceed or fall below exercise prices. *Rainbow* options are options to buy or sell multiple assets, or they may be viewed as options on single assets with multiple sources of risk.

You will become familiar with *compound* options — options on options. These include calls on calls, calls on puts, puts on calls and even puts on puts. We may also fashion a contract in which the exercise price is represented by a risky asset rather than a fixed dollar amount. Such an option to exchange one asset for another is at once a call (on the underlying) and a put (on the asset used to exercise the option).

SUMMARY

Options are rights to buy (calls) and sell (puts) underlying assets at specified prices (exercise or strike). The buyer of a call or put receives a right, and the seller or writer incurs an obligation. This makes options different from other financial contracts.

In this chapter, we have focused mostly on financial options (i.e., options for which the underlying assets are financial securities). Calls and puts on stocks are prominent options and these are traded on four exchanges in the United States. Calls and puts on stock indexes such as the S&P 100 are also prominent and serve as convenient vehicles for hedging risk of large portfolios. Similarly, options on bonds, or interest rate options, may be used to control interest rate risk in bond portfolios.

In addition to options on individual stocks and indexes, a well-developed market exists for options on futures contracts. The benefit of such options is that the underlying assets as well as the options themselves have liquid markets. Calls and puts on foreign currencies are also available, and this includes the new Euro. As you will see in Chapter 2, these are useful for managing risk of receivables and payables denominated in foreign currencies.

Corporate securities contain options in many forms. For instance, there are corporate bonds and preferred stocks that may be called by the issuer, many may be converted into common stock, and some may be sold back to the issuer for specified amounts. All these features are implicit options and they are taken into account by the markets in determining their prices. Some corporate securities such as warrants and rights are explicit options, and often these are used for raising capital or used as compensation.

As you will see in Chapter 2, options help us transfer and manage risk. This is their chief societal benefit. Indeed, ordinary insurance is a put option and this insight has led to the development of portfolio insurance widely used by pension funds and other managed portfolios. Options allow us to do things we simply cannot do with ordinary stocks and bonds; hence, options help make the capital markets more complete.

In Chapters 3 and 4 we delve into the intricacies of option pricing. This all-important endeavor is somewhat technical and challenging, but indispensable to a full understanding of these instruments. You will see how a foundation in option pricing theory can help us understand ordinary corporate securities such as stocks and bonds in Chapter 5. In Chapter 6 we will examine warrants and rights, call options on common stocks used by firms to raise capital. We will then learn how to price bonds and preferred stocks with embedded options in Chapters 7 and 8. Embedded options include call features, conversion rights and more.

Over the years option contracts have grown more complex as we've discovered more sophisticated uses, and recently we have begun to appreciate how options analysis may be used in making capital investment decisions such as whether to renovate a plant, build a warehouse or replace a computer system. These decisions involve *real* assets rather than financial ones, hence the name *real options*. We will see how options analysis in the capital investment setting is employed in Chapters 9, 10, and 11.

We will end our excursion with a survey of applications of options in risk management in Chapter 12.

QUESTIONS AND PROBLEMS

1. What are call and put options, and how do they compare with forward contracts?

2. Match the following:

    A. Exercise price   (1) exercise anytime
    B. American-style   (2) exercise only at expiration
    C. Warrant   (3) right to sell
    D. European-style   (4) strike price
    E. Futures contract   (5) call option
    F. Put option   (6) obligation to buy or sell

3. What is an index option?

4. In general, what does the holder of a futures call option receive upon exercise?

5. What is a conversion ratio? What is meant by conversion value?

6. How do warrants differ from exchange-traded call options?

7. Suppose a call option on IBM stock is priced at $4, the exercise price is $55, and IBM stock is trading at $57. Is the call out-of-the-money? What would be the rate of return on the call if you bought it now (at $4) and the stock price remained at $57 until expiration?

8. A put option contract for 62,500 Euros has an exercise price of $0.94, and the Euro is currently trading at $0.91. Suppose you had bought one put contract originally at $0.03 per Euro and expiration is imminent. Will you exercise? What will be your rate of return?

9. A convertible preferred stock has a conversion ratio of 1.250, and the firm's common stock is priced at $44 per share. What is the conversion value of the preferred?

10. Suppose the convertible preferred in Question 9 above is callable at $50 per share. If the firm calls at this time (when the common stock price is $44), will the preferred holders convert? Or will they surrender their preferred shares for redemption?

Chapter 2

Option Strategies

In this chapter we will see how options may be employed on a stand-alone basis and in portfolios to accomplish various investment goals. We will begin by getting acquainted with one of the most important features of options — nonlinear payoffs. This feature is what makes options such powerful devices for executing investment strategies. Then we will introduce the four basic option positions — buy a call, write a call, buy a put, and write a put. Next we'll see how option positions may be combined with other options in order to fashion profits and losses to suit the expectations of the investor. For instance, suppose you believe a stock will either move up or down in value, but you don't know which way. We'll see that you can create an option position that will exploit the price movement. Finally, we will see how options may be combined with underlying assets such as stocks and currencies in order to manage risk.

NONLINEAR FEATURES OF OPTION PAYOFFS

The first feature we will highlight about options is the *nonlinear* nature of their payoffs. What this means can best be seen with an example of a *linear* payoff. Suppose you buy an asset such as a common stock today for $50 per share. If the value of the stock (with dividends) increases to, say $55 per share, then your profit is $5. If the stock price declines to $45 you lose $5. In other words, your profits and losses vary dollar for dollar with the value of the underlying asset, in this case a common stock. If you plot the dollar profits against the future stock price you will get a straight line with slope of 1. In this case the payoffs or profits are said to be linear in the asset's value.

The opposite relation holds if you sell the stock short for $50. If the price increases to $55 you lose $5, and if it drops to $45 your profit is $5. If you plot profits against future asset value you again get a straight line only this time the slope is −1. And, the profits are still linear in asset value.

Buying a Call

To see the nonlinear nature of option profits consider an ordinary call option on a stock with current price of $50. Remember that a call is the right to *buy* the asset at the specified price. Suppose the exercise price is $50 and the cost of the call option is $6. If the stock price remains at $50 the option will expire unexercised and you lose $6. If the stock declines in value to $45, $40, $35, or any price below $50, the option will expire worthless and you will lose $6. On the other hand, if the stock advances to, say $55, you will exercise the option (pay $50 for an asset worth $55). What is your profit? You make $5 but paid $6 originally, so you lose $1.

In the language of options markets calls and puts are said to be *in the money or out of the money*. This is determined by the answer to the question: If the option were expiring right now, would it be exercised? If Yes, the option is in the money. Thus a call with $50 exercise price on a stock priced at $55 is in the money, because if expiration were immediate the call would be exercised. If the stock price was only $45 the call would be out of the money — exercise would mean buying a $45 stock for the exercise price of $50, something that you would not do. A put works just the opposite. If we have a put with $50 exercise price on a stock worth $45, it would be exercised if it were about to expire, and it is deemed in the money. What if we had that rare occasion where the underlying price and the exercise price were exactly equal? You guessed it, *at the money*.

This illustrates a key point. The amount you initially paid for the option is relevant in determining profits and losses, but it is irrelevant in deciding whether to exercise. The only determinant regarding exercise is the relationship between the asset's price and the option's exercise price. This is reminiscent of our discussion of whether options are in the money. In fact, we can just as easily say that expiring options that are in the money should be exercised; expiring options that are at or out of the money should not be. In the case of a call, we exercise if the asset's price exceeds the exercise price, otherwise we allow it to expire. The price initially paid for the option is a sunk cost and should not enter into our decision. In our example, had we failed to exercise the option we would have lost $6 rather than only $1.

We can now see that the profit on the option increases linearly on a dollar for dollar basis once the stock price hits $50. But for any price below $50 the option investment loses $6. If we plot profits against stock price we no longer get a linear relationship. The relationship is nonlinear, or in this case, piecewise linear. The profits are graphed in Exhibit 2.1.

Exhibit 2.1: Profits and losses from buying a call option with exercise price of $50 when the stock is currently priced at $50. The cost of the option is $6.

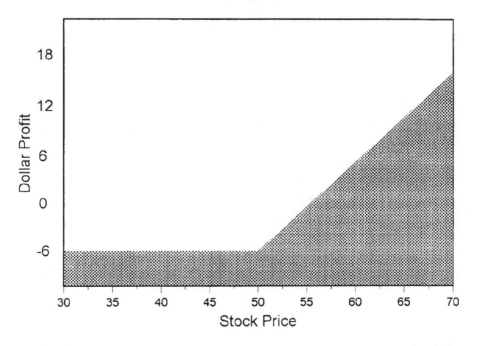

Exhibit 2.2: Profits and losses from selling a call option with $50 exercise price. The stock is presently priced at $50 and the option costs $6.

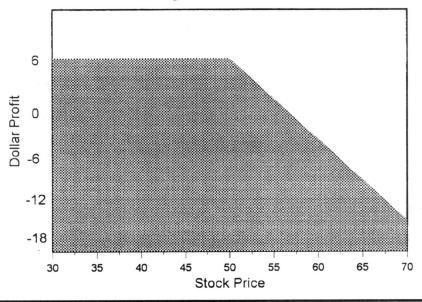

Writing a Call

In the previous case, since we bought the option, we are said to have a *long* call position. If we had written (sold) the option we would have a *short* call position and the profit graph would be turned upside down. In other words, if the stock remained at $50 or fell below, the call would expire worthless to the buyer and we (the seller) would pocket the price of the call ($6). If the stock price increased to, say $60, we would lose $4. This is so because the holder of the call would then exercise the option against us. In essence we must furnish this investor with a stock worth $60 and will receive only $50 for it, so we lose $10 at the end of the transaction. But we sold it for $6 in the first place, so our loss is only $4. This sounds like it has much in common with a short position in the stock itself, and it does.

The profits and losses from the short call position are graphed in Exhibit 2.2. As we saw earlier, the graph is like the long call only upside down. Also note that if the stock price shoots up we begin to lose dollar for dollar. If the price goes to $100 we lose $44.

Theoretically there is no limit to the amount of our loss. In this case of high risk exposure we are said to have a *naked* position.

A naked call is so risky that many financial institutions have policies against employing this strategy. This may make one wonder why anyone would ever sell a call option! And if no one would ever write a call, then how could there be a market for these instruments? The answer is that, while many investors sell calls, very few enter naked call positions. This means that calls are sold predominantly by investors who have portfolios containing other assets. When a call is sold in a portfolio, its effect on portfolio profits may be quite different from what we have seen in the naked position. We will see this illustrated shortly.

Buying a Put

Let's say a put option on a stock has an exercise price of $50 and the price of the put is $4.50. If we buy this put we have the right to sell the stock, now priced at say $50, for the exercise price $50. If the stock remains at $50 or moves higher, we will not exercise and will lose $4.50. If the stock declines to $40, we will exercise the put — that is, sell the stock at the exercise prices ($50) — and deliver the stock for $40. Our $10 gain is reduced by the $4.50 cost of the put, but we still clear $5.50.

You can imagine what happens to our profit as the stock price falls. At $50 and below our profit rises dollar for dollar as the stock price sinks. Pop quiz: What will the profit graph look like? Hint: You know it will have a flat region for stock prices of $50 and higher. What's the most you can make? If the stock price falls to zero (the bear's dream come true), you will exercise for a gross profit of $50 and a net profit of $45.50. The profits are plotted in Exhibit 2.3.

A short put means we have an obligation to buy the underlying for the exercise price, e.g., $50. The long put holder has the option to sell. If the price of the underlying exceeds the exercise price, the long put investor will not exercise. The short put then makes a profit that is the same no matter how far above $50 the underlying goes. Of course, if the underlying declines in value the put will be exercised and the short position will lose. By now you can probably imagine what the profit graph for a short put will look like — just invert Exhibit 2.3

Exhibit 2.3: Profits and losses from buying a put option with $50 exercise price. The price of the put is $4.50.

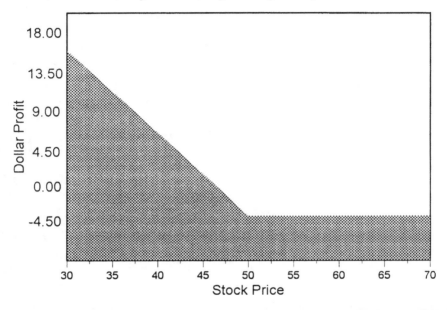

Summary of Basic Positions

Now we know the profit-loss profiles for the four basic option positions: (1) buy a call, (2) write a call, (3) buy a put, and (4) write a put. Note that the four positions apply to any underlying asset (e.g., a stock, a bond, a futures contract or a foreign currency). If the exercise prices or the option prices change, the shapes of the graphs remain the same — only their locations change.

Let's summarize what we have seen so far. A long call position gives us a fixed loss for low stock values, and our profits increase dollar for dollar for higher stock prices. A short call gives us dollar for dollar *losses* for higher stock prices, and a fixed profit for lower values. A long put features a fixed loss for high stock values, and dollar for dollar profits for lower stock prices. And a short put gives a fixed profit for higher stock prices, and dollar for dollar losses for lower stock prices. Thus, each elementary position is unique; that is, selling a call is not the same as buying a put and buying a call is not the same as selling a put.

SOME OPTION COMBINATIONS

In this section we begin to appreciate the level of flexibility afforded by options in fashioning profit diagrams to match a wide variety of expectations. For instance, by combining calls and puts creatively, we can arrange to make profits even when the price of the underlying asset doesn't budge — and by combining options a little differently, we can arrange to profit in just the opposite circumstances.

Spreads

Suppose you buy a call option and sell a call option on the same stock, with the same expiration date, but with different exercise prices. What does this suggest about your expectations regarding the future price of the stock? It depends on which call has the higher exercise price. Such a position is known generally as a *spread* and if the call that is written (sold) has the higher exercise price, this is a *bull spread*. On the other hand, if the long call has the higher exercise price, you have a *bear spread*.

A bull spread is depicted in Exhibit 2.4. The long call has a $100 exercise price and costs $4, while the short call has a $105 exercise price and costs $2. If the stock price is $105, the long call is exercised ($1 profit) and the short call is not ($2 profit) for a portfolio profit of $3. At a stock price of $100, the long call is worthless ($4 loss) and the short call gives a $2 profit for a net loss of $2. The bull spread looks like a long call position, only the upper region of profits has been flattened — if the price goes high the short call will be exercised, so our cash flow in that region is the exercise price.

Similarly, the bear spread shown in Exhibit 2.5 looks like a short call except the losses have been flattened. The reason is the same. If the stock advances substantially, the call that you have written will be exercised and you will exercise the long call. The two positions will cancel one another dealing you a net loss.

Straddles and Strangles

Now consider some more involved option strategies — *combinations* of puts and calls. Suppose you expect the price of a stock to deviate from its present level as a result of an upcoming development. For instance, in March 1994, Martin Marietta and Grumman announced an agreement to recommend merger to their respective shareholders, whereby Martin would acquire Grumman stock for $55 per share. Just before the announcement Grumman stock was priced at about $39.50, and immediately upon the announcement the price climbed to just below $55.

If the merger had fallen through and no merger with another firm had materialized, then Grumman stock would have been expected to retreat toward $39.50. On the other hand, suppose that investors had expected Martin's bid to be outdone by another firm. Indeed, later in March 1994, Northrop entered the contest with a tender offer of $60 per share for Grumman. If you had owned Grumman stock at the time of the Martin offer you would have been faced with a (happy) dilemma — hold or sell?

Exhibit 2.4: Profits and losses from buying a call option with $100 exercise price for $4, and selling a call with $105 exercise price for $2.

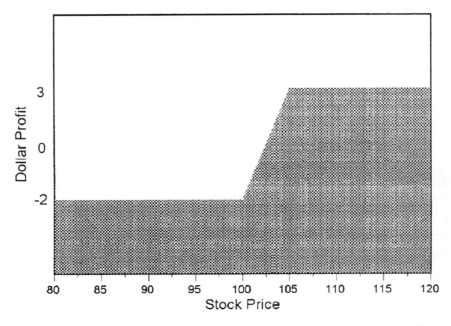

Exhibit 2.5: Profits and losses from buying a call option with exercise price of $105 for $2, and selling a call option with exercise price $100 for $4.

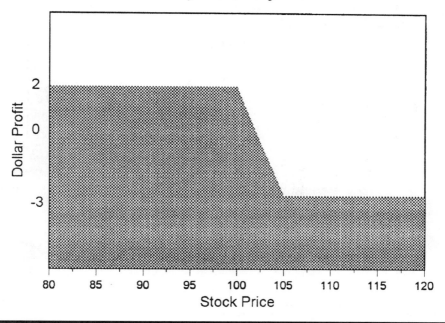

Options give yet another alternative, and this one is available to an investor who does not even own Grumman stock! Suppose you bought $55 calls on Grumman and bought $55 puts on Grumman at the time of the Martin offer, and the calls were priced at $2 and the puts at $1. If the stock remained at $55 you would have lost $3, the value of both options since neither would have been exercised. If the stock had climbed to $62 (which it finally did), you would have exercised the call and made $5, and the put would have expired worthless for a loss of $1. Your portfolio would have earned a profit of $4. If the stock had retreated to, say $40, you would have exercised the put and made $14, and the call would have expired worthless for a loss of $2. Your portfolio would have earned $12.

By buying puts and calls you can *straddle* the current stock price, profiting if the price increases or decreases, and losing if it remains about the same. Indeed, this is called a *long straddle* position and the profit graph is shown in Exhibit 2.6.

Exhibit 2.6: Profits and losses from buying a call option with $55 exercise price and buying a put option with the same exercise price.

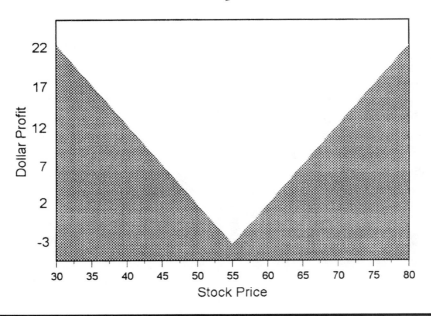

You can see that a long straddle is well suited to a volatile stock price. On the other hand, suppose that you anticipate a stable price for the stock. As you might expect, you could then sell (write) a call and a put and capture a profit if this expectation is realized. Of course, you can lose a lot if the stock turns volatile as Exhibit 2.7 shows. This is a *short (naked) straddle* position.

You may be troubled by the apparent right-angle (orthogonal) nature of the profit graphs we have seen. Are all option strategies constrained to orthogonal payoffs? For instance, is a long straddle necessarily a V-shaped profit graph where the legs of the V are perpendicular? In order for the position to be a true straddle, the answer is yes. But you can arrange profits so that their graphs do not join at right angles. For instance, suppose you would like to have a steeper angle on the upside. You could double up on the number of calls and buy one put, all with the same exercise price. This is called a *strap*. On the other hand, suppose you would like a steeper angle on the downside — if the stock price drops some you would like to profit most. Perhaps you are more confident of a decline than you are in an advance. In this case (you guessed it), you can double up on puts and buy one call. This is a *strip*.

Note that for each of the straddle positions the exercise prices for the put and the call were the same. This is important because equal exercise price defines the straddle. A valuable extension of the straddle is called the *strangle*, and in a moment we will see how it compares with the straddle. A *long strangle* involves buying a call and buying a put with unequal exercise prices. For instance, suppose the stock is priced at $50. A $55 exercise call option costs $2 and a $45 exercise put costs $1. Both are out of the money. If the stock remains at $50 both options expire worthless and your loss is $3. If the stock advances to $55, both options continue to expire worthless and your loss is $3. Similarly, if the stock declines to $45 both options are worthless and the loss is $3. Only if the stock breaks out of the range from $45 to $55 will the portfolio begin to do better than a $3 loss.

Exhibit 2.7: Profits and losses from selling a call option with exercise price of $55 and selling a put with the same exercise price.

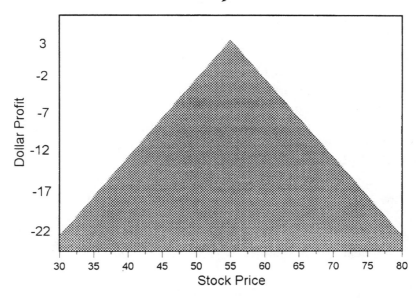

Exhibit 2.8: Profits and losses from buying a call option with $55 exercise price and buying a put option with $45 exercise price.

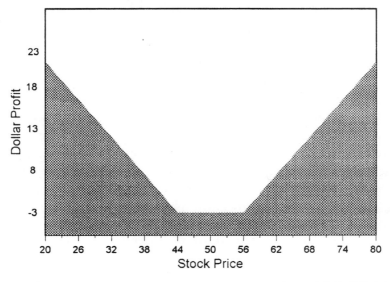

This long strangle is graphed in Exhibit 2.8. Notice that it looks like a long straddle that has been flattened at the bottom. But there is another feature that can best be seen if we add a numerical example using at-the-money puts and calls on the same stock.

Suppose a $50 exercise call is priced at $4 and a $50 exercise put is priced at $2.5. In Exhibits 2.7 and 2.8, it is clear that the strangle requires more extreme price movements to generate profits as compared with the straddle. But notice that the maximum loss is larger for the straddle ($6.50) than for the strangle ($3). Why? Recall that the options for our straddle were both at the money, and those for the strangle were both out of the money. Naturally, at-the-money options are more valuable than out-of-the-money options, all else the same, and this is why the maximum loss is less for a strangle. Thus the strangle is superior to the straddle in that the maximum loss is less, but inferior in that more extreme stock price movements are needed to produce a profit.

You can easily imagine what a *short strangle* looks like — just turn the long strangle upside down. In this case you sell (write) an out-of-the-money call and an out-of-the-money put. If you were to do this for a realistic example, then compare it with a realistically priced portfolio of at-the-money calls and puts, you would see that the resulting short straddle offers higher maximum profits, but the short strangle presents a broader region of stock prices in which profits are made.

Butterflies

The short straddle and short strangle both have the appealing feature that an investor can capture profits even when an asset's price remains about the same. But they share the disadvantage that sharp movements of the stock will inflict substantial losses; that is, the put and call positions are naked. Wouldn't it be neat if we could flatten out the graphs on the extreme ends and limit losses?

We can. This gets us to the *butterfly spread*. Suppose the stock is presently at $50. We buy one out-of-the-money call (exercise price = $55) for $1, buy one in-the-money call (exercise price = $45) for $8, and sell *two* at-the-money calls (exercise price = $50) for $3 each. Here are the profits and losses on the portfolio.

	40	45	50	55	60
long call (X=45)	−8	−8	−3	2	7
short calls (X=50)	6	6	6	−4	−14
long call (X=55)	−1	−1	−1	−1	4
portfolio	−3	−3	2	−3	−3

The profit graph looks like a witch's hat and is shown in Exhibit 2.9. Notice that we now capture a profit if the stock remains at or close to $50, as with a straddle. But in the event the stock breaks out of its current trading range, our losses are limited to $3 for the portfolio. Of course, you can reverse the buy and sell positions and the graph will be an upside down witch's hat. And you can accomplish butterflies using puts as well.

COMBINING OPTIONS AND UNDERLYING ASSETS

Now we consider strategic use of options in conjunction with their respective underlying assets. For instance, suppose we own a stock or an equity portfolio and wish to limit our possible losses. This is possible easily and conveniently with options.

Exhibit 2.9: Profits and losses from buying a call option with $45 exercise price, buying a call option with $55 exercise price, and selling two call options with $50 exercise price.

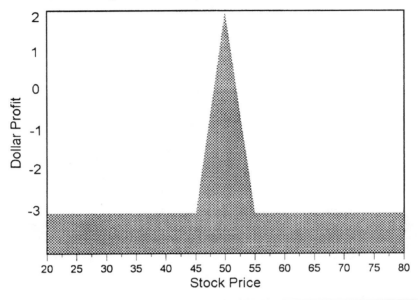

Covered Calls

As we mentioned in the beginning, option strategies can be used to control risk, and in the limit, eliminate it entirely. Suppose we own a stock presently worth $50 per share, and we write a call on this stock for $6 with exercise price of $50. This is a *covered* call position. If the stock's price rises our investment value increases due to the long stock position, but our short call position works against us. For stock prices above $50 the call will be exercised against us — the buyer will purchase the stock from us at $50 (the exercise price).

This flattens our upside profit potential. As the stock declines in value, we lose due to the long stock position, but our losses are offset by having sold a call. For stock prices of $40, $50, and $60 our profits and losses are as follows.

	40	50	60
long	−10	0	+10
short call	+6	+6	−4
portfolio	+1.5	+1.5	+1.5

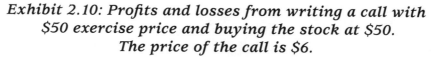

Exhibit 2.10: Profits and losses from writing a call with $50 exercise price and buying the stock at $50. The price of the call is $6.

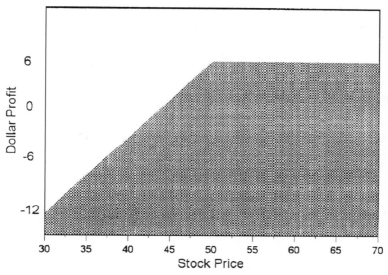

Profits and losses are plotted in Exhibit 2.10. The covered call features a fixed profit for high stock values and declining profits for low stock values.

There are a couple of very important aspects of this position. First, does it look familiar? The profits and losses from writing a put have the same shape as those depicted in Exhibit 2.10. One can thus duplicate the profit pattern of a put by holding a long position in the underlying asset and writing a call.

The second aspect, one that begs explanation, is why? Why would an investor undertake a covered call? See this by penciling in a line in Exhibit 2.10 representing profits and losses from the long stock position only. Your (straight) line passes through $50 on the horizontal axis.

Compare the two positions. The long stock position delivers a loss for any price below $50, and the covered call's profit graph is $6 higher than the stock position everywhere in this region. Thus the losses from the covered call are less severe than from the long stock position.

If the stock price rises substantially, the profile from the long stock position overtake those from the covered call. Over the full range of possible stock values, the covered call loses less and gains less than the long stock alone, hence risk is reduced in the covered call position.

Riskless Hedge

Now add to the covered call position a long put with exercise price of $50; that is, we form a portfolio containing a long stock position, sell a call, and buy a put on the stock. It may not be obvious yet but you will find that the profits will be the same regardless of the future stock price! Here is what happens. The covered call profits are positive and flat for higher stock prices, and they decline dollar for dollar for lower prices. By adding a put option, you cancel out the negative profits over the low price region, and essentially bend the left leg of the profit graph up to a horizontal position.

For example, suppose the stock is priced at $50. A call option with $50 exercise price sells for $6, and a put with the same exercise sells for $4.50. You buy the stock, sell the call, and buy the put. Here are the profits.

	40	50	60
long stock	−10	0	10
long put	+5.5	−4.5	−4.5
short call	+6	+6	−4
portfolio	+1.5	+1.5	+1.5

This position is termed a *riskless hedge*, and it is one among many ways of creating a risk-free profit. Some clarification is in order. This strategy does not represent a free lunch. Yes it is riskless and yes it is profitable, but it would be a free lunch only if the profitability were such that it exceeded competitive investments in, say Treasury bills.

This news may lead to another puzzle — if firms and investors can do just as well in Treasuries, then why would anyone undertake a riskless hedge, particularly if we take into account the brokerage fees for establishing this position? To see the answer, suppose that you own a particular stock and would like to continue to hold the shares for one of several possible reasons. Perhaps you wish to maintain voting rights in the firm. But suppose the stock is undergoing some tumultuous events and you would like to reduce the risk of ownership. You can eliminate all risk and still maintain your stock position by undertaking a riskless hedge — hold the stock, sell calls, and buy puts.

Protective Puts

Another, slightly less involved strategy is simply to add puts to your stock portfolio; forget selling calls. Consider the previous example where the stock is at $50 and puts with $50 exercise price sell for $4.50. Buy one put option for every share of stock held and the profits are as follows.

	40	50	60
stock	−10	0	10
put	+5.5	−4.5	−4.5
portfolio	−4.5	−4.5	+5.5

The profits and losses from this position are plotted in Exhibit 2.11.

Exhibit 2.11: Profits and losses from buying stock priced at $50 and buying a put option with $50 exercise price for $4.50.

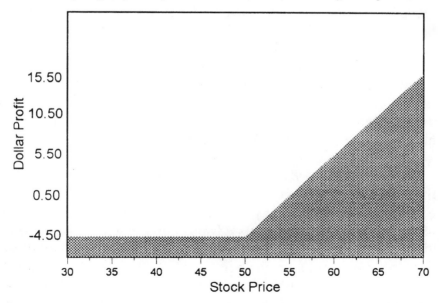

This is the central idea behind *portfolio insurance* and the position is termed a *protective put*. Suppose the underlying asset was an automobile instead of a common stock, and suppose we insure the car. Insurance is a put option. The exercise price of the auto insurance contract is the amount of coverage, say $15,000. We know that a put option is the right to sell an asset at a specified price; in this case "sell" the car to the insurance firm. You would do this only if the value of the car falls below the amount of coverage. When you view your insured automobile as an asset plus a put option you see that you have downside protection due to insurance, and the value of the total investment is reduced by the amount paid for the insurance regardless of the value of the car. In the financial markets, large stock portfolios can be insured by taking long positions in stock index put options, bond portfolios can be insured with bond index puts, and currency risk can be reduced with currency puts.

PLAYING WITH SHARP KNIVES

Let's discuss a prominent example that demonstrates how *not* to use options. You may recall the bankruptcy of a large, well established investment bank in England, Barings PLC. In late 1994, one of its traders, Nick Leeson, trading in Singapore, sold call options on the Nikkei 225 Index, analogous to the S&P 500 in the United States. He also sold puts on the same index, thus he had either a short straddle or short strangle. He was evidently straddling (or strangling) the then-current Nikkei level of about 19000 points. Thus, had the Nikkei remained at roughly 19000, Barings would have profited handsomely with virtually no capital invested and Leeson would have been a hero.

Then came the Kobe earthquake. Of course, this had a devastating effect — 5,000 lives lost, hundreds of thousands homeless, the worst disaster to strike that major city since U.S. firebombing raids in 1945. The Nikkei dropped substantially and by the time the options were to expire it had recovered only slightly to about 13000 points. At this point Leeson (hence Barings) was okay on the call side, but the puts were to be exercised and that would mean Barings paying over a billion U.S. dollars to cover the losses.

This would have been bad enough. Evidently Leeson thought that by entering Barings into futures contracts on the Nikkei 225 that would signal to other investors that the Japanese market was undervalued — then the market would turn around and the short put options would then be out of the money, or at least not as deep in the money.

Of course, futures contracts were cheap at that time and, as the Nikkei continued to fall, they became even cheaper. Leeson bought more of them. This compounded the problem. Recall that futures contracts are "marked to market" daily at the end of trading. Thus, each day the position grew still more desperate as the Nikkei index continued to perform weakly. Ultimately Barings went bankrupt and was acquired, Leeson was arrested for allegedly forging order forms, and he went to prison.

It is easy to sit in judgment after the fact. We know that the only sensible way to evaluate a risky investment strategy is to take into account the information available to the decision maker at the time of the investment, then to consider plausible outcomes to see how things logically might have turned out. But in this case, you can make some valid criticism. For starters, a short straddle is never a sound strategy on a volatile asset for a long maturity. The Japanese stock market had lost almost half of its value in five years *before* the Kobe earthquake. Why did Leeson not use butterfly spreads instead of short straddles? This would have given downside protection and would still have turned a modest profit if the expectations had been realized.

A FINAL NOTE ON OPTION STRATEGIES

As you have just seen, the number of possible strategies using options appears limitless. Thus it may appear that such a wide array of different possibilities cannot easily be summarized with a few key principles. Take heart...it is precisely the case that a few principles underlie all the strategies we have examined and more.

1. Options allow us to slice up probability distributions. If you buy a stock or any asset such as a bond or portfolio of securities, you have in essence a claim on the entire probability distribution of future values. If the stock (or bond or portfolio) appreciates in value, this means the future value is drawn from the upper end of the distribution, and you make a profit. If the stock price declines, the future price is drawn from the lower end of the distribution. The point is that your long position represents a claim on the full distribution.

A call option, on the other hand, represents a claim only on that part of the stock price distribution above the exercise price (X). A put option is a claim on the lower end of the distribution, below the exercise price. In a long call position, we exercise our right to buy when the asset's price has risen above X. In a long put position, we compel another party to exercise a claim on the asset when it has done poorly, below X. In other words, puts and calls allow us to establish claims on different slices of the asset's distribution, thus freeing us from having to accept claims on the entire distribution.

When you think of options in this way, perhaps the exotic-sounding strategies such as covered calls, protective puts, straddles, and butterflies appear less exotic. For instance, if you have a long position in a stock, that establishes a claim on the entire distribution, for good or bad. Now add a put option (protective put). This means you can push off claims on the low end of the distribution (below X) on somebody else. Thus, as the stock price declines below X, your losses on the stock are offset exactly by gains on the put. Hence the portfolio's profits will be flat in the lower range of stock values, but increasing in the upper range of values.

Now add to the protective put a short call — sell a claim on the upper end of the distribution (above X) to someone else. As the price advances, you profit from the long stock investment, but profits above X will be claimed by the call buyer. Hence the portfolio's profits will be flat in the upper end of the distribution.

If we start with a claim on the full distribution of stock values, then buy the right (put option) to assign losses to someone else, and sell the right (call option) to claim profits, the result should be equivalent to riskless lending. That is, we are giving up the right hand slice of the distribution, and pushing off the lefthand side to someone else, leaving only one point on the remaining profit distribution. This is precisely what we do when we undertake a riskless hedge.

Now think about a long straddle — long put and call positions with the same exercise price. We have a claim on the slice of the distribution above X, and we can force someone else to swallow a claim on the slice below X. Our profits increase linearly above X (call is exercised) *and* below X (put is exercised). But if the price remains at X, neither option is exercised and we forfeit the values of both.

It may help to review other strategies such as strangles and butterflies with this analogy in mind. Remember, puts and calls allow us to buy and sell price distributions one slice at a time.

2. Options are redundant. In some of the cases examined in this chapter, we have seen that other strategies would produce similar patterns. For example, a covered call looked remarkably similar to a short put. This is not a coincidence. The reason has everything to do with the first principle, that options represent claims on slices of a distribution. If you sell a put option, you make a constant profit (price of the put) if the stock price is in the range above X. If the price falls below X, you lose dollar for dollar. The put buyer will force you to buy the stock if its price falls in the lower end of the distribution, below X.

Now suppose you buy the stock. You now have a claim on the entire distribution, profiting if the price is drawn from the right hand side, and losing if from the left-hand side. If you then sell a call, you assign the right to profits (above X) to someone else, hence the upper range of profits is flattened. You now have a covered call — long stock, short call. Doesn't this sound a lot like a short put?

3. You can't have it both ways. We have seen several examples where one strategy is superior to another in some ways, yet inferior in others. If option prices are determined sensibly by investors, this will always be the case. For example, we saw that a long straddle (long put, long call, same exercise price) gives greater profit potential than a long strangle (where there is a spread between the call and put exercise prices). But the straddle also carries with it greater loss potential. This is true as long as at-the-money options cost more than out-of-the-money options, and that will be the case if investors are paying attention.

As another example, consider insuring with a protective put. If you insure with an out-of-the-money put, your downside losses will be more severe than if you had bought an at-the-money put. But there is a tradeoff. If the underlying asset increases in value, net portfolio profits will be higher using the out-of-the-money (and less expensive) put.

4. Reversing positions turns the profit graph upside down. You have already seen this in several examples. It is always true that if you reverse the positions from long to short, or from short to long, the profit pattern flips. The reason also goes back to the first principle, that options represent claims on different slices of the price distribution. Thus, a long call shows a flat loss for prices below X, and increasing profits for prices above X because this position represents a claim on the upper end of the distribution. A short call features flat profits on the lower end (below X) and declining profits on the upper end (above X) because the claim on the upside has been assigned to someone else.

5. Option strategies produce profit patterns that are independent of the identity of the underlying asset. This may be obvious by now. A covered call on a stock exhibits the same profit pattern as a covered call on a bond. A protective put on a stock looks just like a protective put on a foreign currency. In other words, all put and call strategies work the same no matter whether the underlying asset is a stock, a bond, or a portfolio. And, as we will see in later chapters, options on real assets, such as factories, exhibit the same profit characteristics as options on financial assets.

QUESTIONS AND PROBLEMS

1. Describe the investments needed in calls, puts and/or the underlying to establish the following positions:
   a. covered call
   b. protective put
   c. naked call
   d. long strangle
   e. naked straddle
   f. bull spread
   g. riskless hedge

2. Suppose a call on stock XYZ expires in 6 months and has exercise price (X) of $40. The stock is priced at $40 per share, and the call is trading at $5. If you undertake a covered call position using these securities, what will be your dollar gain (or loss) per share if the stock rises to $48 by expiration? What will be your gain (or loss) if the stock retreats to $33? Compare these gains or losses with those that would have resulted in a long position in the underlying stock only.

3. A put on stock XYZ with $40 exercise price expires in 6 months and is priced at $4. Using XYZ stock, the call described in question 2, and the put, suppose you establish a riskless hedge. What is your net investment initially? What will be your profit if the stock climbs to $50 per share? What will be your profit if the stock sinks to $28? What will be your rate of return (annualized) on the investment?

4. A call on DEF common stock has $25 exercise price and is priced at $12; another call on this stock with $30 exercise price is trading at $8; still another call on DEF with $35 exercise is priced at $6. Let's say you create a butterfly spread similar to that in Exhibit 2.9 using these calls. What will be your maximum profit (on a per share basis)? Your maximum loss?

5. Now consider *puts* on DEF stock with exercise prices of $25, $30, and $35. The puts are priced respectively at $4, $7, and $11. How would you create a butterfly spread with a profit pattern similar to that in Exhibit 2.9? What would be your maximum profit? Maximum loss?

Chapter 3

Option Valuation

In this chapter we develop the Nobel prize-winning mathematical formulas for determining the prices of European-style put and call options. We'll start off with a couple of very simple examples to illustrate the intuition behind the models. Next we will sketch the formal derivations of the put and call pricing models, and if you prefer more detail you can work through the math in the Appendix. If you are interested only in the ideas behind the derivation you can easily skip the Appendix. By sketching the derivation of the models you will see not only how they work, but why they should give prices that come close to actual market prices of calls and puts.

SOME PRELIMINARIES

Before proceeding into the challenging territory of option valuation, we should be armed with a clear understanding of why we need to be able to predict option values. As you will see in this chapter, there are two principal approaches to determining what an option *should* be worth. The first, that employed by Fischer Black and Myron Scholes[1] and Robert Merton,[2] exploits the fact that a portfolio that is arranged so as to have no risk should be priced so that it earns the risk-free rate of interest. If call and put prices are in agreement with the models developed by Black and Scholes, then investors will find that risk-free option portfolios will earn the risk-free rate.

In other words, Black and Scholes develop call and put prices that bar riskless arbitrage, and to the extent the market exploits such opportunities until prices adjust and those opportunities vanish, then

---

[1] Fischer Black and Myron Scholes, "The Pricing of Options and Corporate Liabilities," *Journal of Political Economy* (May-June 1973), pp. 637-654.

[2] Robert Merton, "The Theory of Rational Option Valuation," *Bell Journal of Economics and Management Science* (Spring 1973), pp. 141-183.

prices from the Black and Scholes model should match market prices. Black and Scholes find mathematically the same set of option prices that an alert market would identify in the normal process of arbitrage profit exploitation. You will see shortly that if market prices match those predicted by the models, portfolios such as the riskless hedge (long stock, long put, short call) will earn the risk-free rate.

The second method for determining values of options employs an approach that is reminiscent of that seen in traditional courses in corporate finance; that is, determine the expected cash flow from the option investment and discount to the present. This approach was pioneered by John Cox and Stephen Ross,[3] and gives exactly the same valuation models as Black and Scholes. The Cox-Ross approach, known as the *risk-neutral* valuation method for reasons that will be made apparent in this chapter, may at first seem peculiar because in this method we must pretend that investors ignore risk in assessing option values. This may make you feel uneasy given your training in finance, but we will see why this pretense makes sense and why Cox-Ross values agree with Black-Scholes values.

Thus the Black-Scholes method, which we shall deem the *arbitrage* approach, mimics the options market in identifying prices that preclude arbitrage profits. And the risk-neutral method evidently does the same, since it will be shown to give the same prices as Black and Scholes. You may be wondering, then, why do we need a mathematical model to tell us what an option *should* be worth, when the market will discover the same price in the course of ordinary profit seeking? The main reason is that, while the correspondence between model and market prices should be close, the model enables us to forecast values *before* the options have been marketed. For instance, when CBOE option dealers initiate new contracts, the Black-Scholes model can be used to identify the equilibrium prices that will result in no supply-demand imbalances.

In later chapters, we will see that the same methods, arbitrage and risk-neutral valuation, are applied in valuing corporate securities. If model and market prices are in agreement, then the corporate financial manager can determine a fair price for a new

---

[3] J.C. Cox and S.A.Ross, "The Valuation of Options for Alternative Stochastic Processes," *Journal of Financial Economics* (January-March 1976), pp. 145-166.

issue by using a mathematical model. This beats guessing the possible market value and issuing at too high a price resulting in a failed offering, or too low a price resulting in harmful wealth effects on the firm's stockholders.

The Arbitrage Method

Let's illustrate the first approach with a numerical example. Suppose we have a call option expiring in a few months with exercise price (X) of $100 written on a stock with current price (S) of $100, thus the option is at the money. The option's current value is denoted as CALL and we wish to determine what it should be. If the stock increases 25% to $125, the call will be worth $125 − $100 = $25; if it remains at $100 (0% change) the call will be worth zero.

How much is this call worth now? The arbitrage method entails finding another investment with known value that produces exactly the same cash flows as the option. Suppose the interest rate is 8% and that we buy one share of stock and borrow the present value of the exercise price (i.e., $100/(1.08) = $92.59). If the stock increases to $125 we will have that asset (worth $125) and must repay the loan ($100), so our net value will be $125 − $100 = $25. If the stock remains at $100 we will have an asset worth $100 and must repay the loan ($100) for a net value of zero.

The payoffs due to owning the call option are identical to those from buying the stock and borrowing the present value of the exercise price. We know that these two investments should command the same value; that is, CALL = $S − \mathrm{PV}(X)$ = $100 − $92.59 = $7.41, in an efficient capital market. If the call were priced below $7.41, it would be a bargain, superior to buying the stock and using financial leverage (borrowing). This price would not persist. On the other hand, if the call were priced above $7.41, it would be too expensive relative to a levered position in the stock — nobody would buy the call so its price would have to fall. This example also helps us see that buying a call option is akin to buying the underlying stock with leverage.

Let's continue the arbitrage approach with another example. Suppose we are considering investing in a call option with exercise price (X) of $40 on a stock with current price of $32 per share. There are three months remaining until expiration and the annual risk-free rate of interest is 8%. Consider two possible future values for the stock, $16 or $64. If we buy the call option for the as yet unknown amount CALL, we will receive either zero (if the stock is at $16) or $24 (if the stock goes to $64). Alternatively, we could buy one share of stock for $32 today; it will be worth either $16 or $64 in three months. In addition, we can borrow the present value of $16 (16/1.02 = $15.69). This means that the net cost of buying the stock and borrowing today is $32 − $15.69 = $16.31. If the stock drops to $16 in three months, our cash value will be $16 (stock) minus $16 (pay back loan), or zero. If the stock goes up to $64, the total cash value will be $48 ($64 − $16).

By combining the stock and borrowing we have created a portfolio with a payoff pattern of $0 or $48, and the net cost of the portfolio is $16.31. The call option, remember, has a payoff pattern of $0 or $24. Thus, if we bought two calls, we would have identical payoffs that would arise by buying the stock and borrowing. To prevent arbitrage the price of the two calls must be equal to the price of the portfolio, $16.31. Consequently, each call option must be worth $16.31/2 = $8.16. No other price will support an equilibrium.

These examples illustrate the intuition of arbitrage valuation, although one might object that they are unrealistically simple. They are. Considering only two possible future prices of the stock is highly restrictive. However, you shall soon see that Black and Scholes appeal to precisely the same intuition in their landmark development, but within a far more believable setting with respect to possible stock prices. Thus we shall keep the models overly simple for now in order to expose the critical ideas, then we will permit stock prices to behave more realistically.

Discounted Cash Flow Approach

Remember there is another way, risk-neutral valuation, in which we forecast the expected cash flow from owning the option, then discount to the present. This is a familiar recipe for pricing an asset, and if it is applied correctly to the two examples, we should find the options to be worth $7.41 and $8.16, respectively. But what is the appropriate discount rate? And what are the probabilities that the stock price will move up or down in the two examples? This seems like a hopeless position, but a couple of very bright guys (John Cox and Stephen Ross)[4] thought about this for some time and came up with a clever way to crack the nut.

To illustrate their method we must *pretend*. Pretend that investors do not care a jot about risk. If this were true (it isn't, but remember we're just pretending) then there would be no risk premium added to the riskless rate. This solves one of the problems — we now know what discount rate to use — 8% in our examples. But what about the probabilities that the stock price will move up or down? Continue the pretense that we are indifferent to risk, and reconsider the stock in the first example. Remember that the stock moved up 25% or remained the same, thus its *expected* rate of return is $P_u(0.25) + P_d(0)$, where P_u = probability of an upward move, and P_d = probability of a downward move (or no move at all).

If we are indifferent toward risk, the expected rate of return on the stock should be the riskless rate, 8%. To find the probabilities that would represent upward and downward movements *if* we were indifferent toward risk, we simply set the riskless rate (0.08) equal to $P_u(0.25)$ + $P_d(0)$. Solve the equation algebraically and we get $P_u = 0.32$ and $P_d = 1 - P_u = 0.68$. Now go back to the call option. Remember it will be worth either $25 or $0 depending on which way the stock moves. We now know that, in our risk-neutral fantasy, these probabilities are 0.32 and 0.68, respectively. Thus the expected cash flow is $25(0.32) + $0(0.68) = $8. And since we are indifferent toward risk we should discount the expected cash flow at the riskless rate, 8%. Thus the value of the call should be CALL = $8/(1.08) = $7.41. A coincidence?

Reexamine the second example. The stock could either go up 100% from $32 to $64, or drop 50% from $32 to $16 in three months. If we are risk neutral the three-month rate on the stock would be 2%, since the annual rate is 8%. First find the implied probabilities from $P_u(1.00) + P_d(-0.50) = 0.02$. Thus $P_u = 0.3467$ and $P_d = 1 - P_u = 0.6533$. Remember that the call has exercise price of $40, thus if the stock goes up to $64 we make $24 and if it drops to $16 we make zero. The expected cash flow is then $24(0.3467) + $0(0.6533) = $8.32. If we discount this at the three-month riskless rate we get CALL = $8.32/(1.02) = $8.16, again the same price we found with the arbitrage method.

---

[4] Cox and Ross, "The Valuation of Options for Alternative Stochastic Processes."

Note that we do not truly believe that investors are indifferent to risk. We simply use this as a device to derive implied probabilities that would hold if they were indeed risk neutral. This gets us around the major problem of specifying the appropriate discount rate for an option, and we don't need to know the true probabilities that the stock will go up or down. What we found were the "risk neutral probabilities," the probabilities that would have to apply *if* investors were risk neutral.

The prices for call options are the same using both methods — find a replicating portfolio or discount expected cash flows assuming risk neutrality. And notice that in neither case did we need to know the expected rate of return on the stock or on the option.

Something Called Delta

Before we go further, consider the following "coincidence." Remember that in the first case we found that *one* call option could replicate the payoffs on *one* share of stock, given the appropriate leverage. In the second example we needed *two* options to replicate the payoffs per share of stock. Also in the first case the possible option values at expiration ranged from $0 to $25, and the stock had values that ranged from $100 to $125. In the second case the option's values at expiration ranged from $0 to $24 and the stock's price varied from $16 to $64.

Do you see a connection? Consider the range of possible option values in comparison with the stock price range. In the first example the ratio is 25/25 and in the second it is 24/48 — that is, 1/1 and 1/2. And in the first case we have *one* option replicating the profits on *one* share of levered stock; in the second case *one* option replicates *one-half* a levered share. This ratio is important. It is called *delta*. We can now say that we could either buy a call option on a stock, or we could essentially manufacture our own option by buying *delta* shares and borrowing the balance. In the second example, CALL = $8.16 and P = $32, and *delta* = 0.5. Following this recipe we can either buy one call (outlay = $8.16) or buy 0.5 shares ($16) and borrow ($16 − $8.16 = $7.84) for a net outlay of $8.16. Algebraically we can express this transaction as:

1 long call = long delta shares − borrow difference

that is,

$$\$8.16 = 0.5 \times \$32 (= \$16) - \$7.84$$

Or we can rearrange this to get:

Lend difference = long delta shares − 1 short call

that is,

$$\$7.84 = 0.5 \times \$32 (= \$16) - \$8.16$$

This tells us that a long position in stock (delta shares) and writing a call will give us the same investment as riskless lending. Let's try it out. Remember that the stock may go up to $64 or drop to $16. If we write the call ($X = \$40$), the call will be worth $24 to the call buyer, hence −$24 to us if the stock goes up to $64. If the stock drops to $16 the option will be worthless. If we hold 0.5 shares and write 1 call, then if the stock goes up to $64 our combined value will be $32 (stock) minus $24 (short call), or $8. If the stock declines to $16 the combined value will be $8 (stock) minus $0 (short call), or $8. In other words, no matter what happens to the stock price, the portfolio of delta shares and 1 short call will be worth $8.

This sounds like riskless lending and this is indeed the case as you can see by inspecting the left-hand side of the last equation. And note that if we invest $7.84 at the 2% three-month riskless rate, it will be worth exactly $8 in three months.

Thus the left-hand side has a *present* value of $7.84, as does the right-hand side ($16 − $8.16 = $7.84). And the left-hand side has a *future* value of $8.00, as does the right-hand side. This is extremely important in practical portfolio considerations. If we know delta, we can construct a riskless portfolio by buying stock (delta shares) and writing calls. Remember that we saw how to combine 1 share, 1 call, and 1 put to form a riskless hedge earlier. Now we can do away with the put.

For reasons you will see later this is called *dynamic hedging*, whereas the put-call-share riskless hedge could be called *static*. Take these two thoughts with you as we proceed into deeper waters — (1) the ratio of the change in option value to the change in stock value is delta, and (2) buying delta shares of stock and selling a call is the same as lending at the riskless rate of interest.

Reconciliation

By the way, we can now explain why the arbitrage method and the risk neutral method happen to give the same values. In the arbitrage method, we said nothing about how investors feel about risk. The only behavioral assumption in that approach is that investors will value two assets with identical cash flow equally. The puzzle arises in the risk-neutral approach. Remember that we pretended that all assets, including risky stocks, earned the risk-free rate. We know that generally applying a risk-free discount rate to a risky cash flow is conceptually wrong, but we did it anyway. Then we used the probabilities that would describe future stock prices if investors were indifferent toward risk to assess the expected cash flow on the option, clearly a risky asset. The key to understanding why we managed to get the same prices, \$7.41 and \$8.16, lies in recognizing that while the stock and the option are themselves risky, when these two risky assets are combined in portfolios as we did in each example, the combination produces a risk-free cash flow. As long as we are consistent in the manner in which we use the risk neutrality pretense, then we must get the right answer. This is a very important insight and we will rely upon it later.

THE BLACK-SCHOLES MODEL — CALL OPTIONS

In this section, we will sketch the derivation of the option pricing models of Fischer Black and Myron Scholes following the technical steps they used in their 1973 article. The same approach was used by Robert Merton in his 1973 article, and you will hear much more about him shortly. The math will appear complicated so that at times you may wonder how it could really be useful in actual markets. After all, we don't believe that most option investors are mathematicians or physicists, so it is unrealistic to think that the markets use complicated models. The fact is that it doesn't matter whether or not investors are schooled in higher math. Remember that the model finds that set of option prices that removes arbitrage profits. It does so mathematically. The market also ultimately finds the set of prices that renders arbitrage unprofitable. It may do so by nothing more than trial and error, but it will find those prices. And the prices will be the same as those we get from our model.

The greatest conceptual drawback to the model so far is that we have supposed the stock price may either move up or down, so that there are only two possible outcomes. Thus we have restricted ourselves to a *binomial* process. For instance, in the first case, we supposed that a stock priced at \$32 might either rise to \$64 or fall to \$16 in one year's time. In reality, the number of possibilities is large, although finite. Given that it takes about one minute to execute a NYSE transaction, you can imagine that our (binomial) process will have very many possible values at the end of one day for an active stock. How about three months? How about one year? The point is that our binomial distribution quickly becomes useless in reality.

In 1827, a botanist, Robert Brown, observed that particles suspended in a liquid seem to move about continuously. In 1918, Norbert Wiener gave a rigorous mathematical description of the (Brownian) motion of particles in his Ph.D. dissertation. If we interpret a stock price (S) as representative of the position of a particle, then we can describe changes in price as a Wiener (or Brownian) process:

$$\frac{dS}{S} = \mu dt + \sigma dZ$$

$$dS = \mu S dt + \sigma S dZ$$

(1)

In the equation dS is a change in S, so dS/S is the rate of return. The equation says the rate of return equals a mean rate (μ), and we scale this by dt, the amount of time that has passed. For instance, suppose $\mu = 0.12 = 12\%$ per year, on average. If $dt = 1/12 = 1$ month, then on average we expect dP/P to be 0.01, about 1% per month.

The strange looking term σdZ has two pieces; dZ is a normal random variable coming from the standard normal distribution. And σ is the standard deviation of dS/S per unit time. If $\sigma = 0$, the stock is riskless (i.e., $dS/S = \mu dt$). The larger σ, the greater the average "bounce" of dS/S around the mean μdt. When we specify as we have that dZ is a normal (Gaussian) random variable, the process is known as a Gauss-Wiener process.

Suppose a call option's value C depends on stock price S and time t. The call's price depends on other parameters as well, such as the exercise price (X), but only S and t change over time. We may now write an expression for the change in C, given that C in turn depends on S and t, which are dynamic.

Ordinarily, if we have a function f that depends on x and y, we can write the change in f as

$$df = \frac{\partial f}{\partial x}dx + \frac{\partial f}{\partial y}dy \qquad (2)$$

But if one or more of the variables x and y are random, this expression isn't quite right. It turns out that if S follows a Gauss-Wiener process (sound familiar?), we can apply an important theorem in math (from Ito[5]) to write an expression for dC when C = a function of S and t:

$$dC = \frac{\partial C}{\partial S}dS + \frac{\partial C}{\partial t}dt + \frac{1}{2}\frac{\partial^2 C}{\partial S^2}(dS)^2 \qquad (3)$$

If we substitute $dS = \mu S dt + \sigma S dZ$ into this and do some simplification, we get:

$$dC = \frac{\partial C}{\partial S}(\mu S dt + \sigma S dZ) + \frac{\partial C}{\partial t}dt + \frac{1}{2}\frac{\partial^2 C}{\partial S^2}\sigma^2 S^2 dt \qquad (4)$$

What we seek is an expression for C and what we have in (4) is an expression for dC. To recover C from this differential equation, we might integrate. But this is a very difficult equation to solve, particularly due to the presence of the random variable dZ.

Black and Scholes attack the problem by supposing we buy 1 share of stock and sell α calls to form a portfolio with value $V = S - \alpha C$. The change in portfolio value (dV) will then be

$$dV = dS - \alpha dC \qquad (5)$$

Put the expressions for dS from equation (1) and dC from equation (4) into this and simplify to get:

$$dV = \left(1 - \alpha\frac{\partial C}{\partial S}\right)\mu S dt + \left(1 - \alpha\frac{\partial C}{\partial S}\right)\sigma S dZ - \alpha\left(\frac{\partial C}{\partial t}dt + \frac{1}{2}\frac{\partial^2 C}{\partial S^2}\sigma^2 S^2 dt\right) \qquad (6)$$

---

[5] K. Ito, "On Stochastic Differential Equations," *Memoirs, American Mathematical Society* (1951), p. 1-51.

Let's shorten this by letting $\partial C/\partial S = C_1$; $\partial C/\partial t = C_2$; and $\partial^2 C/\partial S^2 = C_{11}$ Thus,

$$dV = (1 - \alpha C_1)\mu S dt + (1 - \alpha C_1)\sigma S dZ - \alpha \left(C_2 dt + \frac{1}{2} C_{11} \sigma^2 S^2 dt \right) \quad (7)$$

This expression describes mathematically the dynamics of our portfolio value (V). V changes as time passes (through dt) and as the stock price varies randomly (through dZ). At this point, dV is unpredictable due to the presence of dZ, thus our portfolio is risky.

We can render the portfolio risk-free mathematically if we can somehow remove dZ from the dynamics. How do you suppose we can get rid of it? Suppose we choose α (number of calls) so that it equals $1/C_1$. If we do this, the equation simplifies to

$$dV = -(1/C_1)[C_2 dt + \tfrac{1}{2} C_{11} \sigma^2 S^2 dt] \quad (8)$$

No dZ term! The equation is now a nonstochastic (nonrandom) partial differential equation. What this means in words is that, if we knew α, we could sell α calls for every share held and the investment would be riskless.

Black and Scholes assert that if α is chosen to get rid of the randomness in portfolio value, the portfolio must earn the riskless rate (r). Sound reasonable? This means:

$$dV = (S - \alpha C) r dt \quad (9)$$

Set the two equations (8) and (9) equal:

$$-(1/C_1)[C_2 dt + \tfrac{1}{2} C_{11} \sigma^2 S^2 dt] = (S - (1/C_1)C) r dt \quad (10)$$

Note that dt drops out of equation (10), then solve equation (10) for C_2:

$$C_2 = rC - rSC_1 - \tfrac{1}{2} C_{11} \sigma^2 S^2 \quad (11)$$

Thus $\partial C/\partial t$ (C_2) is related to $\partial C/\partial S$ (C_1) and $\partial^2 C/\partial S^2$ (C_{11}) and we would like to know the formula for C that has this property. This is a nonstochastic differential equation and may be solved when we add a boundary condition. The condition needed is $C = \max(S - X, 0)$ at expiration. This condition implies that the call price will be $S - X$ if in-the-money, or zero if at- or out-of-the-money.

The solution to equation (11) involves finding a formula for C such that its derivatives C_2, C_1, and C_{11} satisfy the equation. This is found by integrating equation (11) and if we do this directly, we get a very messy expression. Black and Scholes recognize that the expression can be rewritten using the cumulative normal density function (area under the bell curve), and after a good deal of algebra, they report the formula for call price (C) as:

$$C = SM(d_1) - Xe^{-rT}M(d_2) \tag{12}$$

where $M(\cdot)$ denotes the cumulative normal density function, and

$$d_1 = [\ln(S/X) + (r + \sigma^2/2)T]/\sigma\sqrt{T}$$

and

$$d_2 = d_1 - \sigma\sqrt{T}$$

To evaluate $M(d_1)$ and $M(d_2)$, we first calculate d_1 and d_2, then we may refer to a table of the cumulative standard normal density function. We find the left-hand area under the normal density up to point d_1 or d_2. We'll do this with numbers shortly.

You may now be wondering what became of our earlier expression for the price of a call. Remember we showed that 1 long call = long delta shares − borrowing the difference between the share investment and the value of the call:

CALL = long delta shares − borrowing

Black and Scholes give us this expression, but with some structure. In fact, we will see that delta is $M(d_1)$ and the borrowed amount is $Xe^{-rT}M(d_2)$. Thus,

CALL = $SM(d_1) - Xe^{-rT}M(d_2)$

is equivalent to

CALL = long delta shares − borrowing

Note that this *must* be the value of a call option if S follows the Gauss-Wiener process, and if a hedge portfolio is priced to earn the riskless rate. This is all we need to derive the Black-Scholes model. A call that is priced above the Black-Scholes value allows a riskless portfolio to earn above the riskless rate; a call priced below the model value means a riskless portfolio's return is below the riskless rate.

Let's take the model on a test run — later we'll come back to some of the important details like where to get σ. We need five parameters: S, X, r, σ, and T.

Let

S = current stock price = 69.25
X = exercise price = 65
r = annual risk-free rate = 0.0575
σ = standard deviation of dS/S = 0.15
T = time to expiration (in years) = 0.25

The first step is to determine d_1 and d_2:

$$d_1 = [\ln(69.25/65) + (0.0575 + (0.15)^2/2)(0.25)]/0.15\sqrt{0.25} = 1.073$$

and

$$d_2 = 1.073 - 0.15\sqrt{0.25} = 0.998$$

In Exhibit 3.1, we have values for the cumulative standard normal distribution $N(d)$ for various values of d. From the normal table, you can see that $N(1.073) \approx 0.8588$, and $N(0.998) \approx 0.8413$. Next, note that

$$e^{-rT} = e^{-0.0575 \times 0.25} = 0.9857$$

Thus, from equation (12)

$$\text{CALL} = 69.25(0.8588) - 65(0.9857)(0.8413) = 5.57$$

This call is in the money. If it were exercised now, the cash flow would be $69.25 - $65 = $4.25, known as the intrinsic value. Thus the value of the option, or option premium, is the sum of the intrinsic value and the excess which is due to the remaining time to expiration and volatility of the underlying. In this case the excess amount is $5.57 - $4.25 = $1.32. You can think of the intrinsic value as the value of the option if it were expiring at once. If it were expiring immediately, the cash flow would be positive if in the money, and zero if at or out of the money.

Exhibit 3.1: Cumulative Standard Normal Density Function

d	N(d)	N(−d)	d	N(d)	N(−d)
0.0000	0.5000	0.5000	1.2500	0.8943	0.1057
0.0250	0.5100	0.4900	1.2750	0.8989	0.1012
0.0500	0.5199	0.4801	1.3000	0.9032	0.0968
0.0750	0.5299	0.4701	1.3250	0.9074	0.0926
0.1000	0.5398	0.4602	1.3500	0.9115	0.0885
0.1250	0.5497	0.4503	1.3750	0.9154	0.0846
0.1500	0.5596	0.4404	1.4000	0.9192	0.0808
0.1750	0.5695	0.4305	1.4250	0.9229	0.0771
0.2000	0.5793	0.4207	1.4500	0.9265	0.0735
0.2250	0.5890	0.4110	1.4750	0.9299	0.0701
0.2500	0.5987	0.4013	1.5000	0.9332	0.0668
0.2750	0.6083	0.3917	1.5250	0.9364	0.0636
0.3000	0.6179	0.3821	1.5500	0.9394	0.0606
0.3250	0.6274	0.3726	1.5750	0.9424	0.0576
0.3500	0.6368	0.3632	1.6000	0.9452	0.0548
0.3750	0.6462	0.3538	1.6250	0.9479	0.0521
0.4000	0.6554	0.3446	1.6500	0.9505	0.0495
0.4250	0.6646	0.3354	1.6750	0.9530	0.0470
0.4500	0.6736	0.3264	1.7000	0.9554	0.0446
0.4750	0.6826	0.3174	1.7250	0.9577	0.0423
0.5000	0.6915	0.3085	1.7500	0.9599	0.0401
0.5250	0.7002	0.2998	1.7750	0.9620	0.0379
0.5500	0.7088	0.2912	1.8000	0.9641	0.0359
0.5750	0.7173	0.2827	1.8250	0.9660	0.0340
0.6000	0.7258	0.2742	1.8500	0.9678	0.0322
0.6250	0.7340	0.2660	1.8750	0.9696	0.0304
0.6500	0.7421	0.2579	1.9000	0.9713	0.0287
0.6750	0.7502	0.2498	1.9250	0.9729	0.0271
0.7000	0.7580	0.2420	1.9500	0.9744	0.0256
0.7250	0.7658	0.2342	1.9750	0.9759	0.0241
0.7500	0.7734	0.2266	2.0000	0.9772	0.0227
0.7750	0.7808	0.2192	2.0250	0.9786	0.0214
0.8000	0.7881	0.2119	2.0500	0.9798	0.0202
0.8250	0.7953	0.2047	2.0750	0.9810	0.0190
0.8500	0.8023	0.1977	2.1000	0.9821	0.0179
0.8750	0.8092	0.1908	2.1250	0.9832	0.0168
0.9000	0.8159	0.1841	2.1500	0.9842	0.0158
0.9250	0.8225	0.1775	2.1750	0.9852	0.0148
0.9500	0.8289	0.1711	2.2000	0.9861	0.0139
0.9750	0.8352	0.1648	2.2500	0.9878	0.0122
1.0000	0.8413	0.1587	2.2500	0.9878	0.0122
1.0250	0.8473	0.1527	2.2750	0.9886	0.0114
1.0500	0.8531	0.1469	2.3000	0.9893	0.0107
1.0750	0.8588	0.1412	2.3250	0.9900	0.0100
1.1000	0.8643	0.1357	2.3500	0.9906	0.0094
1.1250	0.8697	0.1303	2.3750	0.9912	0.0088
1.1500	0.8749	0.1251	2.4000	0.9918	0.0082
1.1750	0.8800	0.1200	2.4250	0.9923	0.0077
1.2000	0.8849	0.1151	2.4500	0.9929	0.0071
1.2250	0.8897	0.1103	2.4750	0.9933	0.0067
			2.5000	0.9938	0.0062

If you would like to be convinced that equation (12) is the correct solution to the differential equation (11), see the Appendix. This confirms that equation (12) solves (11) by using ordinary calculus.

THE BLACK-SCHOLES MODEL — PUT OPTIONS

A put option's value also depends on stock price (S), time (t), and other parameters. Let PUT = P denote the value of the put, hence $P = f(S, t)$. If we form a portfolio by combining a share of stock and a long position in α puts, we can make the portfolio risk-free (remove dZ) by choosing $\alpha = 1/(\partial P/\partial S)$. Then by following the same steps as before, we can write a differential equation analogous to equation (11) describing the put's price:

$$-P_2 = rP - rSP_1 - (\tfrac{1}{2})P_{11}\sigma^2 S^2 \tag{13}$$

where $P_1 = \partial P/\partial S$; $P_{11} = \partial^2 P/\partial S^2$; and $P_2 = \partial P/\partial t$. The boundary condition becomes $P = \max(X - S, 0)$ at expiration. The solution found by Black and Scholes is

$$P = Xe^{-rT}[1 - M(d_2)] - S[1 - M(d_1)] \tag{14}$$

Again, let

S = 69.25
X = 65
r = 0.0575
σ = 0.15
T = 0.25

Then, from Exhibit 3.1, $M(d_1)$ = 0.8588, 1 − 0.8588 = 0.1412, $M(d_2)$ = 0.8413, and 1 − 0.8413 = 0.1587. Thus, from equation (14),

$$P = 65(0.9857)(0.1587) - 69.25(0.1412) = 0.39$$

The intrinsic value in this case is zero because the put is out of the money. That is, if expiration were imminent the put would expire worthless. The excess amount beyond the intrinsic value, $.39, accounts for the total value of the option. A confirmation that the Black-Scholes put value in equation (14) is the solution of the differential equation (13) is presented in the Appendix.

BUT IT WORKS

We now convince ourselves that Black-Scholes values of both call and put options rule out arbitrage profits. If α is chosen according to the model, investors can assemble portfolios with guaranteed pay-offs. In equilibrium, these portfolios must earn the risk-free rate. The Black-Scholes option values are the only prices that support the no-arbitrage condition. An important implication of this is that options in combination cannot be used to construct portfolios with arbitrage opportunities.

See this by using the call and put options we just used to demonstrate the models. The call is worth \$5.57 and the put is worth \$0.39, according to Black and Scholes. Suppose that we form a risk-less hedge — long one share of stock ($S = \$69.25$), long one put (\$0.39), and short one call (\$5.57). Our net investment outlay is \$69.25 + 0.39 − \$5.57 = \$64.07.

At expiration, our hedge will be worth \$65 no matter what the stock price happens to be — confirm this now if you're not sure. Our portfolio investment of \$64.07 will grow to \$65 in one quarter ($T = 0.25$), so what rate of return will we earn?

On a continuously compounded basis, the quarterly rate (rT) will be determined by

$$64.07 = 65 e^{-rT}$$

$$\frac{64.07}{65} = e^{-rT}$$

$$\ln\left(\frac{64.07}{65}\right) = -rT$$

$$-0.014411 = -r(0.25)$$

$$r = 0.0576$$

Recall that the risk-free rate (r) used in the calculations was 0.0575. The difference between this and 0.0576 is due to rounding.

So what does this mean? If we can buy the put at $0.39 and write the call for $5.57, our risk-free portfolio will earn the risk-free rate. This is precisely the result Black and Scholes aimed to achieve. If the put is priced differently from $0.39, or the call is priced differently from $5.57, our hedge portfolio will still be risk-free — it will grow to $65 in one quarter. But the initial investment outlay would be something other than $64.07, hence the portfolio return would not equal r.

AN IMPORTANT RELATIONSHIP

Suppose you buy a call on a stock with a current price (S) of $50 per share. The call has an exercise price (X) of $50. For now, ignore the current value of the call. Combine this investment with a short put on the same stock with an exercise price of $50. Both options expire at the same time T.

The terminal cash flow from this combined investment is determined as follows for stock prices of $50, $55, and $45.

	Stock Values		
	$50	$55	$45
long call	0	5	0
short put	0	0	−5
	0	5	−5

Compare this strategy with buying the stock at $50 and borrowing an amount today equal to the present value of $50. (Thus, when the loan matures you must repay $50.) The cash flow at T when the loan matures will be as follows for stock prices of $50, $55, or $45.

	Stock Values		
	$50	$55	$45
long stock	50	55	45
loan (PV of X)	−50	−50	−50
	0	5	−5

Both strategies have the same future cash flows, so the portfolios should have the same current value in equilibrium. This means

$$CALL - PUT = STOCK - PV(X)$$

or

$$C - P = S - PV(X) \tag{15}$$

This is called the "put-call parity" relation. If we rearrange as follows to find the value of a call:

$$C = S - PV(X) + P \tag{16}$$

We can now express the parity relation in terms of the put:

$$P = C - S + PV(X)$$
$$= C - S + Xe^{-rT} \tag{17}$$

Then if we substitute the Black-Scholes pricing model for C in equation (12) into equation (17) we get:

$$P = SN(d_1) - Xe^{-rT}N(d_2) - S + Xe^{-rT}$$
$$= Xe^{-rT}[1 - N(d_2)] - S[1 - N(d_1)] \tag{18}$$

This is the same expression found by Black and Scholes for the value of a put in equation (14), confirming that their model prices obey put-call parity.

We can synthesize calls, puts and even the stock itself by applying the put-call parity relationship in equation (15). In fact, suppose we re-arrange equation (15) so that $PV(X)$ is on the left-hand side and everything else is on the right:

$$PV(X) = S + P - C \tag{19}$$

Does this look familiar? The right-hand side is the familiar riskless hedge: long stock, long put, and short call. The parity relation tells us this is equivalent to a loan and, as we know, the loan is risk-free.

APPENDIX

CONFIRMATION OF THE BLACK-SCHOLES SOLUTION

In this fairly technical Appendix, we will confirm that the call option model given by equation (12) and the put option model given by equation (14) are correct solutions to the partial differential equations (11) and (13). We will confirm the results using ordinary differential calculus.

Partial Derivatives for the Call Model

The differential equation (11) for the call option model involves three partial derivatives: $\partial C/\partial S$, $\partial^2 C/S^2$, and $\partial C/\partial t$, which we express in shorthand as C_1, C_{11}, and C_2. Let's now evaluate these three derivatives, then we'll use them to confirm the pricing model. That is, we will evaluate these by differentiating the call option pricing model given by equation (12):

$$C = SN(d_1) - Xe^{-rT}N(d_2)$$

where

$$d_1 = (\ln(S/X) + (r + \sigma^2/2)T)/\sigma\sqrt{t}$$

and

$$d_2 = (\ln(S/X) + (r - \sigma^2/2)T)/\sigma\sqrt{t} = d_1 - \sigma\sqrt{t}$$

Before we go further, we must express $N(d_1)$ and $N(d_2)$ explicitly as values of the cumulative standard normal density function:

$$N(d_1) = (1/\sqrt{2\pi}) \int_{-\infty}^{d_i} e^{-X^2/2} dX, i = 1, 2 \tag{1A}$$

Now we wish to evaluate

$$\frac{\partial C}{\partial S} = \frac{\partial[SN(d_1) - Xe^{-rT}N(d_2)]}{\partial S} \tag{2A}$$

and applying the chain rule, this is

$$\frac{\partial C}{\partial S} = S\frac{\partial N(d_1)}{\partial S} + N(d_1) - Xe^{-rT}\frac{\partial N(d_2)}{\partial S} \tag{3A}$$

Evaluate $\partial N(d_1)/\partial S$ in equation (3A) as follows:

$$\frac{\partial N(d_1)}{\partial S} = \frac{\partial\left[(1/\sqrt{2\pi})\displaystyle\int_{-\infty}^{d_i} e^{-X^2/2}dX\right]}{\partial S} \tag{4A}$$

This gets a little tricky because S appears in d_1, and d_1 is the upper limit of an integral. Fortunately, there's a rule: the derivative of a function whose arguments appear in the upper limit of an integral is simply the function evaluated at the upper limit multiplied by the partial derivative of the argument (d_1) with respect to the variable (S). This means we replace X by d_1 in

$e^{-X^2/2}$, in which case equation (4A) becomes

$$\frac{\partial N(d_1)}{\partial S} = (1/\sqrt{2\pi})e^{-d_1^2/2}\frac{\partial d_1}{\partial S} \tag{5A}$$

Note that d_2 may be written as $d_1 - \sigma\sqrt{T}$, thus the derivative of d_2 with respect to S ($\partial d_2/\partial S$) is equal to $\partial d_1/\partial S$. Now use the same rule we used to get to equation (5A) to evaluate $\partial N(d_2)/\partial S$ as follows:

$$\frac{\partial N(d_2)}{\partial S} = \left(\frac{1}{\sqrt{2\pi}}\right)e^{-d_2^2/2}\frac{\partial d_1}{\partial P} \tag{6A}$$

Now we're ready to simplify the expression $\partial C/\partial S$ in equation (3A). Do this by substituting equation (5A) for $\partial N(d_1)/\partial S$ and equation (6A) for $\partial N(d_2)/\partial S$ in equation (3A) to get:

$$\frac{\partial C}{\partial S} = S\left[(1/\sqrt{2\pi})e^{-d_1^2/2}\right](\partial d_1/\partial S) + N(d_1) - Xe^{-rT}\left[(1/\sqrt{2\pi})e^{-d_2^2/2}\right](\partial d_2/\partial S) \tag{7A}$$

$$= (1/\sqrt{2\pi})(\partial d_1/\partial S)\left(Se^{-d_1^2/2} - Xe^{-rT}e^{-d_2^2/2}\right) + N(d_1)$$

This looks pretty messy at this point, but if you substitute d_2 = $d_1 - \sigma\sqrt{T}$ in the term in large brackets in equation (7A), then do a few lines of algebra you will discover a wonderful surprise — the term in brackets is *zero*, thus $\partial C/\partial S$ is simply

$$\frac{\partial C}{\partial S} = N(d_1) = C_1 \tag{8A}$$

This value is very important in portfolio management and is called *delta*. We'll see this again in the next chapter.

Next, we need to evaluate the second derivative of C with respect to S ($C_{11} = \partial^2 C/\partial S^2$), which goes a little faster because this is the same as differentiating the first derivative of C with respect to S ($\partial C/\partial S$) which we now know to be just $N(d_1)$. Thus, we wish to evaluate $\partial N(d_1)/\partial S$ and we have a good beginning in equation (5A):

$$\frac{\partial N(d_1)}{\partial S} = (1/\sqrt{2\pi})e^{-d_1^2/2}\frac{\partial d_1}{\partial S}$$

All we need now is an explicit expression for $\partial d_1/\partial S$, or

$$\frac{\partial d_1}{\partial S} = \frac{\partial[(\ln(S/X) + (r + \sigma^2/2)T)/\sigma\sqrt{T}]}{\partial S}$$

$$= (1/\sigma\sqrt{T})(\partial\ln(S/X)/\partial S) \tag{9A}$$

$$= 1/S\sigma\sqrt{T}$$

Insert equation (9A) for $\partial d_1/\partial S$ in (5A) to get:

$$\frac{\partial N(d_1)}{\partial S} = (1/\sqrt{2\pi})e^{-d_1^2/2}(1/S\sigma\sqrt{T})$$

$$= (1/S\sigma\sqrt{2\pi T})e^{-d_1^2/2} \tag{10A}$$

$$= C_{11}$$

The expression for C_{11} in equation (10A) is also important in portfolio management. It is called *gamma* and we'll see it again soon.

We must work through one more derivative before we can confirm the Black-Scholes result. For this, we need to evaluate the derivative of the call price C with respect to time t. Note that T denotes the amount of time until the expiration date (call it t^*), thus

$T = t^* - t$, where t is the current time. Rewrite the call option model given by equation (12) using this adjustment in notation:

$$C = SN(d_1) - Xe^{-r(t^*-t)}N(d_2) \tag{11A}$$

where

$$d_1 = \frac{\ln(S/X) + (r + \sigma^2/2)(t^* - t)}{\sigma\sqrt{t^* - t}}$$

and,

$$d_2 = d_1 - \sigma\sqrt{t^* - t}$$

Now apply the chain rule to equation (11A) to evaluate $\partial C/\partial t$:

$$\frac{\partial C}{\partial t} = S\frac{\partial N(d_1)}{\partial t} - Xe^{-r(t^*-t)}\frac{\partial N(d_2)}{\partial t} - rXe^{-r(t^*-t)}N(d_2) \tag{12A}$$

Then we use the chain rule to evaluate $\partial N(d_2)/\partial t$ in equation (12A):

$$\frac{\partial C}{\partial t} = S(1/\sqrt{2\pi})e^{-d_1^2/2}(\partial d_1/\partial t) \tag{13A}$$

$$- Xe^{-r(t^*-t)}(1/\sqrt{2\pi})e^{-d_2^2/2}(\partial d_2/\partial t) - rXe^{-r(t^*-t)}N(d_2)$$

To simplify equation (13A), note that $d_2 = d_1 - \sigma\sqrt{t^* - t}$, thus $d_1 = d_2 + \sigma\sqrt{t^* - t}$. This means that

$$\partial d_1/\partial t = \partial d_2/\partial t + \sigma\partial\sqrt{t^* - t}/\partial t \tag{14A}$$
$$= \partial d_2/\partial t - \sigma/2\sqrt{t^* - t}$$

Insert the expression for $\partial d_1/\partial t$ in equation (14A) into $\partial C/\partial t$ in equation (13A) to get:

$$\frac{\partial C}{\partial t} = S\left(1/\sqrt{2\pi}e^{-d_1^2/2}\right)(\partial d_1/\partial t) - S\left(1/\sqrt{2\pi}e^{-d_1^2/2}\right)\sigma/2\sqrt{t^* - t} \tag{15A}$$

$$- Xe^{-r(t^*-t)}\left(1/\sqrt{2\pi}e^{-d_2^2/2}\right)(\partial d_2/\partial t) - rXe^{-r(t^*-t)}N(d_2)$$

Gather terms in equation (15A) and rewrite as follows to uncover another happy surprise:

$$\frac{\partial C}{\partial t} = (1/\sqrt{2\pi})(\partial d_2/\partial t)\left[Se^{-d_1^2/2} - Xe^{-rt^*-t}e^{-d_2^2/2}\right]$$

$$- S\sigma e^{-d_1^2/2}/2\sqrt{2\pi(t^*-t)} - rXe^{-r(t^*-t)}N(d_2) \tag{16A}$$

The expression in brackets should look familiar — we saw it in equation (7A) and you may have confirmed that it is zero. Recalling that $T = t^* - t$, equation (16A) now simplifies to:

$$\frac{\partial C}{\partial t} = S\sigma e^{-d_1^2/2}/2\sqrt{2\pi T} - rXe^{-rT}N(d_2) = C_2 \tag{17A}$$

This is called *theta* and it tells how fast call option value changes as time passes.

The Black-Scholes Call Model is Right

The hard part of our confirmation is done. We now have expressions for C_1 (delta), C_{11} (gamma), and C_2 (theta). Remember the differential equation (11) in the chapter:

$$C_2 = rC - rSC_1 - \tfrac{1}{2}C_{11}\sigma^2 S^2$$

If the Black-Scholes call option model is right, then the derivatives C_1, C_{11} and C_2 given in equations (8A), (10A), and (17A) must satisfy the differential equation. Try this — rewrite equation (11) using the expressions in equations (8A), (10A), and (17A) and, after cancelling terms, you will see that equation (11) holds. Thus the call option model in equation (12) we met in the chapter satisfies the differential equation (11).

There is one more condition that the model given by equation (12) must satisfy and that is what makes it a model for *call* options. As t approaches t^*, T approaches zero and expiration occurs. At expiration we know that a call option must be worth

$$C = \begin{cases} S - X & \text{if } S > X \\ 0 & \text{if } S \le X \end{cases} \tag{18A}$$

Does the model given by equation (12) satisfy this (boundary) condition? Rewrite equation (12) with T set equal to zero:

$$C = SM(d_1) - XM(d_2)$$

and since $d_1 = d_2$ when $T = 0$, this becomes

$$C = SM(d_1) - XM(d_1) \tag{19A}$$

If the call expires in the money (i.e., $S > X$), then the limit of d_1 as $T \to 0$ is:

$$\lim_{T \to 0} d_1 = \frac{\ln(S/X) + (r + \sigma^2/2)T}{\sigma\sqrt{T}} = +\infty \tag{20A}$$

Thus, as $T \to 0$ and $d_1 \to +\infty$, $M(d_1) \to 1$. Now rewrite C in equation (19A) as

$$C = SM(d_1) - XM(d_1) = S - X$$

which satisfies equation (18A) when $S > X$.

    If the call is at the money at $T = 0$, then $S = X$ and equation (19A) is zero, consistent with the (boundary) condition given by equation (18A). And if the option is out of the money, $S < X$ then the limit of d_1 is $-\infty$; that is,

$$\lim_{T \to 0} d_1 = \frac{\ln(S/X) + (r + \sigma^2/2)T}{\sigma\sqrt{T}} = -\infty \tag{21A}$$

This means $M(d_1) = N(-\infty) = 0$, thus equation (19A) is zero, also consistent with the boundary condition given by equation (18A).

    Now that we've struggled through what may appear to some as a calculus jungle, it may help to put the math in perspective. We know that the differential equation (11) must hold if a riskless portfolio of *delta* shares of stock and one short call is to earn the risk-free rate (r). We now know that the Black-Scholes call model given in equation (12) satisfies this equation; thus an option priced according to equation (12) and used in such a portfolio will result in a portfolio return of r. And we know that the call model given by equation (12) also satisfies the logical condition given in equation (18A) at expiration.

Partial Derivatives for the Put Model

Now that we've been through the details in finding C_1, C_{11}, and C_2, the same derivatives involving the put option model are much simpler.

Recall the put option model (equation (14) in the chapter):

$$P = Xe^{-rT}[1 - N(d_2)] - S[1 - N(d_1)]$$

and recognize that by symmetry of the normal distribution, $1 - N(d_1) = N(-d_1)$ and $1 - N(d_2) = N(-d_2)$. Thus the put option model may also be written as

$$P = Xe^{-rT}N(-d_2) - SN(-d_1) \tag{22A}$$

Now using the same steps we used to find C_1 in equation (8A) to differentiate P in equation (22A) with respect to S, we find

$$\frac{\partial P}{\partial S} = -N(-d_1) = P_1 \tag{23A}$$

This is the put's *delta* and we'll explore it in the next chapter.

Next, evaluate the second derivative of P with respect to S, which, of course, is the derivative of P_1 in equation (23A) with respect to S, using the same steps we used to find C_{11} in equation (10A). Thus we must evaluate $\partial(-N(-d_1))/\partial S$. If we note that the two sign reversals going from $N(d_1)$ to $-N(-d_1)$ cancel, we see that

$$\frac{\partial^2 P}{\partial S^2} = \frac{\partial(-N(-d_1))}{\partial S} = \frac{\partial N(d_1)}{\partial S} = (1/S\sigma\sqrt{2\pi T})e^{-d_1^2/2} \tag{24A}$$

Therefore, *gamma* for the put is the same as that for the call.

Finally, we must evaluate $\partial P/\partial t = P_2$. Applying the same steps we took to derive C_2 in equation (17A), we find that *theta* for the put differs from that of the call by only two signs:

$$\frac{\partial P}{\partial t} = rXe^{-rT}N(-d_2) - S\sigma e^{-d_1^2/2}/2\sqrt{2\pi T} = P_2 \tag{25A}$$

The Black-Scholes Put Model is Right

Confirm that the put option model satisfies the differential equation

$$P_2 = rP - rSP_1 - (\tfrac{1}{2})P_{11}\sigma^2 S^2$$

by substituting equations (23A), (24A), and (25A) for P_1, P_{11}, and P_2. Thus the Black-Scholes model for puts satisfies the differential equation; that is, a portfolio with *delta* shares per long put will earn r as long as the put is valued according to the Black-Scholes model.

Finally, we must show that at expiration $(T = 0)$, the value of the put is:

$$P = \begin{cases} X - S \text{ if } S < X \\ 0 \text{ if } S \geq X \end{cases} \tag{26A}$$

Remember that at $T = 0$, $d_1 = d_2$, thus the Black-Scholes put option model at expiration is

$$P = XN(-d_1) - SN(-d_1) \tag{27A}$$

As $T \to 0$, $-d_1 \to -\infty$ if $S > X$, and this means that the put is out of the money. The cumulative normal density $N(-d_1)$ is then $N(-\infty) = 0$, thus the put has zero value, consistent with equation (26A). If the put is at-the-money at $T = 0$, then $S = X$ and equation (27A) is zero, consistent with the boundary condition given by equation (26A). And if the put is in the money $(S < X)$ at $T = 0$, then $-d_1 \to +\infty$, and $N(-d_1) = N(\infty) = 1$. Thus, equation (27A) becomes $X - S$, also consistent with equation (26A).

QUESTIONS AND PROBLEMS

1. Give a brief interpretation of delta?

2. A call option is equivalent to a long position in delta shares and
   _____ .

3. A put option is equivalent to lending and a short position in
   _____ .

4. According to the put-call parity relationship in equation (15) of
   the Chapter, how might one synthesize a put option using a call,
   the stock and a bond?

5. Let's work through a few long-hand calculations of call and put
   prices from the Black-Scholes-Merton models. You'll need a cal-
   culator that will handle the exponential function, and you can use
   the values of the cumulative normal density in Exhibit 3.1, or
   more precise values from a spreadsheet program such as Excel.

   a. Suppose we are analyzing a call option on a stock with current
      price of $55 per share. The exercise price is $60 so the call is out
      of the money. The option expires in 8 weeks and the rate on Trea-
      suries is 5.8%. The stock's return volatility is estimated at 48%.
      Use the model (equation (12)) to determine the theoretical price
      of the call.

   b. Now consider a put option on the same stock as in part a. The
      exercise price is also $60, hence it is in the money, and it expires
      in 8 weeks. Use the model (equation (14)) to determine the theo-
      retical value of this option.

   c. Suppose you buy the put for the price you determined in part b,
      write the call for the price you found in part a, and buy the stock
      for its current price ($55). What is your net investment (on a per
      share basis)? What is the popular name of this strategy?

d. What will be your (annualized) rate of return on this investment? Compare your answer with the Treasury rate used to determine the option prices, 5.8%.

e. Show that the put and call prices you determined in parts a and b satisfy the put-call parity relationship in equation (15).

f. In your calculations you also determined the delta values for the call and put. What are they, according to your computations, and what do they mean?

Chapter 4

Extensions and Analysis of the Option Pricing Models

Now that we have seen the ideas behind the Black-Scholes call and put pricing models we will begin adapting the models to fit a broader set of options. This requires first that we extend the models to accommodate dividends. Once we've accomplished this we will see how to apply the models to the problem of pricing stock index options and we'll discover that the same structural forms of the dividend-adjusted pricing models may be applied directly to the problem of currency option valuation.

At that point we will be ready to extract from the pricing models some very useful and widely employed tools for managing risk. This will require that we examine the sensitivity of model prices to many of the parameters used to determine those prices. For instance, we will derive the explicit formula for delta, the sensitivity of an option's price to changes in the price of the underlying. Then we'll see how to use this to execute hedging strategies for individual stocks, portfolios of stocks, and foreign currency positions.

We will refer to many of these quantitative risk management tools as the "Greeks." After we've met the "Greeks" we will examine a few more recently developed tools whose popular names are drawn from concepts in quantum physics. Despite the exotic etymology of their names we will find that they have common-sense interpretations and are quite useful in managing risk.

This chapter will end with a discussion of how we measure one of the most important parameters in the models, the volatility of the underlying.

ADJUSTMENT FOR DIVIDENDS

The original pricing model of Black and Scholes is applicable to non-dividend paying stocks. For short maturity options with no cash dividends expected before expiration, ignoring dividends is not a problem. Suppose the stock does pay a dividend, that it is significant (cannot safely be ignored), and that the next dividend will be paid before option expiration. We need an adjustment because the optionholder's claim is on the stock only, not the dividend. In a sense, the stockholder owns a claim on the full return distribution, capital gains and dividends, but the optionholder has a claim only on the capital gains (or losses in the case of puts).

Robert Merton[1] developed an extension of the model in 1973 for the case of a stock paying cash dividends with annual yield d. The adjustment adds little complication to the Black-Scholes model. Let the expected rate of return on the stock, including dividends, be denoted by μ. The change in stock price may be modeled as a Gauss-Wiener process as we saw in Chapter 3, but with the dividend adjustment:

$$\frac{dS}{S} = (\mu - d)dt + \sigma dZ \tag{1}$$

The process in equation (1) implies that the stock value will grow at the expected rate $(\mu - d)dt$, where $\mu - d$ is the expected return net of the dividend yield. If we proceed as in Chapter 3 to form a risk-free portfolio involving shares and short calls, we could derive a partial differential equation analogous to equation (11) in Chapter 3. The pricing function for the call option that satisfies the differential equation is

$$C = Se^{-dT}N(d_1) - Xe^{-rT}N(d_2) \tag{2}$$

where $d_1 = (\ln(Se^{-dT}/X) + (r + \sigma^2/2)T)/\sigma\sqrt{T}$, and $d_2 = d_1 - \sigma\sqrt{T}$

You can interpret Se^{-dT} as the current stock price net of dividends that will be received during period T. As such, the presence of dividends serves to reduce the value of call options. The value of a put option on a dividend-paying stock may be found as the solution

---

[1] R.C. Merton, "Theory of Rational Option Pricing," *Bell Journal of Economics and Management Science* (Spring 1973), pp. 141-183.

to a partial differential equation analogous to equation (13) in Chapter 3. The resulting model is:

$$P = Xe^{-rT}N(-d_2) - Se^{-dT}N(-d_1) \tag{3}$$

where d_1 and d_2 are as defined for the call given by equation (2).

Let's adjust the numerical example we used in Chapter 3 for dividends. Recall that we had assumed $S = 69.25$, $X = 65$, $r = 0.0575$, $T = 0.25$, and $\sigma = 0.15$. Now suppose the stock pays dividends at the annual rate of 2%, hence $d = 0.02$. To price a call option in this example, we first must calculate d_1 and d_2:

$$d_1 = \frac{\ln(69.25e^{-0.02 \times 0.25}/65) + (0.0575 + (0.15)^2/2)(0.25)}{0.15\sqrt{0.25}} = 1.0070$$

and

$$d_2 = 1.0070 - 0.15\sqrt{0.25} = 0.9320$$

Referring to Exhibit 3.1 we find

$$N(d_1) = N(1.0070) \cong 0.8413, \text{ and } N(d_2) = N(0.9320) \cong 0.8225$$

Recall that $e^{-rT} = e^{-0.0575 \times 0.25} = 0.9857$. Similarly, $e^{-dT} = e^{-0.02 \times 0.25} = 0.9950$. Thus the value of the call option given by equation (2) is:

$$C = 69.25(0.9950)(0.8413) - 65(0.9857)(0.8225) = 5.27$$

Compare this value with the $5.57 call price we determined in Chapter 3 with $d = 0$. The dividend reduces the call price by about $0.30.

If you use the same parameters to price a put option using equation (3), you will get about $0.44. Recall that when we determined the put price without dividends in Chapter 3 we got $0.39.

Index Options

Index calls and puts are useful for managing portfolio risk. The most popular stock index options are for the S&P 100 (ticker symbol OEX) and the S&P 500 (symbol SPX), listed on the CBOE. Most of the stocks included in these indices pay dividends, thus we must account for the divided yield in pricing puts and calls.

Let's begin by pricing calls and puts on the S&P 100 index (i.e., OEX options). The models in equations (2) and (3) are appropriate and may be applied once we have accounted for some important institutional features of these contracts. Suppose the S&P 100 index is 580.6 points. The CBOE defines the underlying as the index scaled by $100, thus the value of the underlying in this case is $58,060 and we let this represent the stock price (S) in the models. Now suppose the exercise price is specified as 585. This is also scaled by $100, thus $X = \$58,500$. The call option is therefore out of the money, while the put is in the money.

The dividend yield on the S&P 100 index is the weighted average yield of the 100 stocks included in the index:

$$d_{OEX} = w_1 d_1 + w_2 d_2 + \dots + w_{100} d_{100}$$

where the weights (w_i) are the proportional values of each stock's representation in the index. Thus the weight for stock i is the market value of the equity of firm i (number of outstanding shares times price per share) divided by the sum of the market values of all 100 firms. We can do some research and determine the index yield ourselves, or we can rely on the weekly publication of this value by the Federal Reserve. In our illustrations we will assume the index yield is 1.9%.

The volatility parameter is the standard deviation of the rate of return on the index and computational details will be explored later in this chapter. Suppose this is 20% ($\sigma = 0.20$). The options expire in six months and the annual yield on 6-month Treasury bills is 5.4% ($r = 0.054$).

The parameters needed to solve the call and put pricing models (equations (2) and (3)) are:

S	=	58,060	r =	0.054
X	=	58,500	T =	0.5
d	=	0.019	σ =	0.20

If you insert the parameters in the call option model given by equation (2) and use Exhibit 3.1 to determine the $N(d)$ values, you will find the call to be worth about $3,519. Since S and X are already scaled by $100, this price is for one contract. Applying the same parameters in the put option model given by equation (3), you should find that one put contract is worth about \$2,949. Later in this chapter we'll see how to use these options to hedge an equity portfolio.

Currency Options

Currency calls and puts are rights to buy and sell units of currencies at a fixed price (X). The underlying (currency) and the exercise price must be expressed in the same (domestic) currency for valuation to make sense. The value today of 1 unit of currency is the present value of 1, or e^{-r^*T}, where r^* is the foreign interest rate. The value today of the unit of currency expressed in the *domestic currency* is then Se^{-r^*T}, where S is the spot exchange rate.

The value of the underlying, Se^{-r^*T}, is analogous to the value of the underlying (S) in a stock option contract. We can price a currency call or put by substituting Se^{-r^*T} for S in equations (12) and (14) in Chapter 3.

The call formula given by equation (12) in Chapter 3,

$$C = SM(d_1) - Xe^{-rT}M(d_2)$$

becomes

$$C = Se^{-r^*T}M(d_1) - Xe^{-rT}M(d_2) \tag{4}$$

where

$$d_1 = \frac{\ln(Se^{-r^*T}/X) + (r + \sigma^2/2)T}{\sigma\sqrt{T}}$$

and

$$d_2 = d_1 - \sigma\sqrt{T}$$

The put formula given by equation (14) in Chapter 3,

$$P = Xe^{-rT}[1 - M(d_2)] - S[1 - M(d_1)]$$

becomes

$$P = Xe^{-rT}[1 - M(d_2)] - Se^{-r^*T}[1 - M(d_1)] \tag{5}$$

Notice that the currency option models given by equations (4) and (5) have identical structure to the dividend-adjusted models given by equations (2) and (3). Thus S plays the role of stock price and r^* plays the role of the dividend yield d.

Let's illustrate with contracts on 31,250 British pounds. Suppose the spot exchange rate (S) is $1.42 per pound, and call and put contracts have exercise price (X) of $1.40 — the calls are in the money and the puts are out. Scale S and X by 31,250 to get $44,375 and $43,750, respectively.

Suppose the contracts have three months to expiration ($T = 0.25$). The 3-month Treasury bill rate is 4.9%, and the rate on 3-month UK Government debt is 5.8% ($r^* = 0.058$).

The volatility parameter (σ) is the standard deviation of the rate of change in the spot exchange rate, say 13% ($\sigma = 0.13$). We will examine estimation of σ for currency options later in this chapter.

We now have the necessary parameter values to price the call and put option contracts on 31,250 British pounds:

$$
\begin{aligned}
S &= 44,375 & r^* (= d) &= 0.058 \\
X &= 43,750 & T &= 0.25 \\
r &= 0.049 & \sigma &= 0.13
\end{aligned}
$$

Using these values in equations (4) and (5) results in prices of $1,406 and $887 for call and put contracts, respectively.

THE GREEKS

In this section, we will develop and apply various partial derivatives of the call and put pricing models, equations (4) and (5). Several of these derivatives have acquired Greek names in practice, and all have important applications in portfolio management.

Greeks for Call Options

The Black-Scholes-Merton model adjusted for dividends is given in equation (2) for calls, repeated below:

$$C = Se^{-dT}N(d_1) - Xe^{-rT}N(d_2) \tag{2}$$

where

$$d_1 = \frac{\ln(Se^{-dT}/X) + (r + \sigma^2/2)T}{\sigma\sqrt{T}}$$

and

$$d_2 = d_1 - \sigma\sqrt{T}$$

We will differentiate equation (2) with respect to S, T, r, and σ to find the "Greeks."

Delta

You've already met delta (Δ) conceptually in Chapter 3. Delta is the first derivative of call price (C) with respect to stock price (S):

$$\frac{\partial C}{\partial S} = e^{-dT}N(d_1) = \Delta_{CALL} \tag{6}$$

and Δ_{CALL} is never negative as you can see. It tells us how sensitive the call price is to changes in the price of the underlying and it is very important in portfolio management.

Recall the example we used earlier to illustrate the call option model: $S = 69.25$, $X = 65$, $r = 0.0575$, $d = 0.02$, $T = 0.25$, and $\sigma = 0.15$. The value of the call option is \$5.27. Equation (6) evaluated with these parameters results in $\Delta_{CALL} = 0.8388$. This means that the call price should change by 0.8388 per unit change in S. By taking a long position in Δ_{CALL} ($= 0.8388$) shares of stock for each call written, we know we create a portfolio that is risk-free. Suppose we buy 8,388 shares of stock and write 100 call contracts (100 shares each). Our net investment at that point is

$$
\begin{array}{rcl}
8{,}388 \times 69.25 &=& \$580{,}869 \\
-\ 10{,}000 \times\ 5.27 &=& -52{,}700 \\
\hline
&& \$528{,}169
\end{array}
$$

Now suppose the stock price changes to \$69.75, an increase of \$0.50 which we will call dS. By how much should the price of the call increase? In general, if $y = f(x)$, then $dy = (\partial y/\partial x)dx$. In this case,

$$
\begin{aligned}
dC &= (\partial C/\partial S)dS \\
&= \Delta_{CALL}dS \\
&= 0.8388(0.50) = 0.4190
\end{aligned}
$$

Hence the call price should increase from $5.27 to ($5.27 + $0.4190 =) $5.689, or about $5.69.

What will happen to the value of our portfolio (long shares, short calls)? We have 8,388 shares now worth $69.75 each, and the short calls should be worth about $5.69, so the portfolio will be worth:

$$
\begin{array}{rcl}
8{,}388 \times 69.75 &=& \$585{,}063 \\
-\ 10{,}000 \times\ \ 5.69 &=& -56{,}900 \\
\hline
&& \$528{,}163
\end{array}
$$

The portfolio's value is nearly unchanged from its initial position ($528,169), hence it is virtually immune to small changes in S.

Now suppose we employ the index calls on OEX we examined earlier in this chapter. We would naturally use such calls to hedge an equity portfolio whose value moves closely with the S&P 100 index. Such a portfolio is called a *tracking portfolio* and an obvious way to create one is to mimic the S&P 100 index; i.e., hold the same 100 stocks that are contained in the index using the same weights found in the index.

How many call contracts do we need to hedge an equity portfolio with a market value of, say, $2,875,000? Recall that we need delta shares per call to form the hedge — but what is meant by a "share" in the case of an index? There are two steps. Suppose the index is 580.60 points. Thus the value of the underlying in one call contract is $580.60 \times \$100 = \$58{,}060$. Then determine the ratio:

$$
\frac{\text{Market value of equity portfolio}}{\text{S\&P 100 Index} \times \$100} = \frac{\$2{,}875{,}000}{\$58{,}060} = 49.5
$$

Think of this as the number of units of the underlying asset (S&P 100 index) that is equivalent in value to our equity portfolio.

Next combine the equity portfolio with short call contracts according to the ratio delta (Δ_{CALL}). Using the parameters from our earlier example ($S = 58{,}060$, $X = 58{,}500$, $d = 0.019$, $r = 0.054$, $T = 0.5$, $\sigma = 0.20$), Δ_{CALL} from equation (6) is 0.5508. Thus we determine the number of call contracts needed in the second step:

$$
\frac{49.5}{0.5508} = 89.7 \approx 90 \text{ contracts}
$$

Let's see if this works. Remember that the value of one call contract from the pricing model given by equation (2) is $3,519. Suppose we write 90 contracts and the market price agrees with our assessment of $3,519. Our net investment at that point is $2,857,000 (equity portfolio) net of the short calls (90 × $3,519 = $316,710), or $2,558,290, and this portfolio should be immune to small changes in the price of the underlying.

Suppose the index declines by 1% to 574.794 points. The change in the value of the underlying for one contract is then $dS = (574.794 - 580.60) \times \$100 = -580.60$. Recall that the change in the value of one call contract should be given by $dC = (\partial C/\partial S)dS = \Delta_{CALL}dS = 0.5508(-580.6) = -319.79$, thus the value of one contract should decline to about $3,519 - 319.79 = $3,199.21.

Our equity portfolio should also decline by about 1% since it is chosen to track the OEX. This means that as the OEX drops to 574.794, our equity portfolio should decline in value to $2,846,250. Our short call position (90 contracts) is now worth 90 × $3,199.21 = $287,928.90, or about $287,929, and our hedge portfolio should be worth:

long equity portfolio	=	$2,846,250
− call contracts	=	−287,929
		$2,558,321

Initially, the hedge portfolio had a net investment of $2,558,290. The increase to $2,558,321 represents a negligible change, thus the portfolio is essentially immune to small changes in the index.

Finally, suppose we wish to use currency call contracts to hedge an account receivable in British pounds. Recall that our call contract on 31,250 pounds with three months to expiration is worth about $1,406. Using the same parameter values to calculate Δ_{CALL} in equation (6) results in $\Delta_{CALL} = 0.5771$.

Suppose we have 419,000 pounds due in three months, about when the options expire. How many contracts are needed to form a hedge portfolio? First, divide the receivable by the contract size (i.e., 419,000/31,250 = 13.41). To see why, recall our illustration of hedging with index options. Then we divided the market value of the equity portfolio by the market value of the underlying in one option contract to find the equivalent number of "shares." Dividing the value of the receivables (419,000 British pounds) by the number of British pounds in one currency contract (31,250) also gives an equivalent number of "shares." Next, combine the British pounds receivable with short calls according to $\Delta_{CALL} = 0.5771$. This means we must write $13.41/.5771 = 23.24$, or about 23 call contracts. If we do this, our net investment in dollars consists of the dollar value of the British pounds receivable ($\$1.42 \times 419,000 = \$594,980$) net of the proceeds from writing 23 calls ($23 \times \$1,406 = \$32,338$), or about $\$562,642$. You can easily confirm that this portfolio will be immune to small changes in the spot exchange rate.

In this case, we had 419,000 British pounds receivable and to remove exchange rate risk, we wrote 23 calls. If we had 419,000 British pounds *payable* we could hedge by taking a *long* position in 23 calls. Of course, we can hedge with puts as well — short puts for payables and long puts for receivables.

Gamma

From inspection of the expression for Δ_{CALL} given by equation (6), it is clear that it changes when the value of the underlying (S) changes. In other words, a hedge portfolio must be rebalanced when the underlying changes in value, hence this type of hedging is called *dynamic*. A natural question is, How much can we expect Δ_{CALL} to change in response to a given change in S? The answer will come from differentiating Δ_{CALL} given by equation (6) with respect to S:

$$\frac{\partial \Delta_{CALL}}{\partial S} = e^{(-dT - d_1^2/2)} / S\sigma\sqrt{2\pi T} = \Gamma_{CALL} \tag{7}$$

Notice that Γ_{CALL} is also the *second* derivative of the call price with respect to S, and from inspection of equation (7), we see that Γ_{CALL} is positive. From our example stock option with parameters $S = 69.25$, $X = 65$, $r = 0.0575$, $d = 0.02$, $T = 0.25$, and $\sigma = 0.15$, Γ_{CALL} from equation (7) is 0.0460. Thus if S increases to 70.25 ($dS = 1$), the change in Δ_{CALL} is $(\partial \Delta_{CALL}/\partial S)dS = \Gamma_{CALL} dS = 0.0460 \times 1 = 0.0460$. The hedge ratio ($\Delta_{CALL}$) must be increased to $0.8388 + 0.0460 = 0.8848$ — that is, we need more shares (fewer calls written) to maintain the hedge.

Had S declined in value, we would find that Δ_{CALL} would be lower — fewer shares (or more calls) would then be needed to maintain the hedge. This will always be the case — if S increases (declines), Δ_{CALL} will increase (decline), and more (fewer) shares will be needed per call to maintain the hedge. There's a reason for this. To see it, suppose S increases in our example. The call will be deeper in the money, hence the price of the call will be more sensitive to changes in S. This means we won't need as many calls per share to maintain our hedge, which implies we will need more shares per call (i.e., Δ_{CALL} will increase if S increases). It works the same way if S declines — call price will be less sensitive to changes in S, more calls will be needed, hence fewer shares per call, thus Δ_{CALL} will decline.

Vega

How sensitive is the price of the call to changes in volatility (σ)? This is answered with the help of vega^2 (v), where v_{CALL} is the derivative of the call price with respect to σ:

$$\frac{\partial C}{\partial \sigma} = S\sqrt{T}e^{(-d_1^2/2 - dT)}/\sqrt{2\pi} = v_{CALL} \tag{8}$$

From inspection of equation (8) it is apparent that v_{CALL} is positive — higher volatility means a higher call price. Continuing with our stock option example ($S = 69.25$, $X = 65$, and so on), the value of v_{CALL} from equation (8) is $8.2783. Thus, if σ increased from 0.15 to 0.17 ($d\sigma = 0.02$), then the resulting change in the call price should be $dC = (\partial C/\partial\sigma)d\sigma = v_{CALL}d\sigma = 8.2783(0.02) = \$0.176$, or about $0.18.

Theta

As time passes, the value of a call option declines, all other factors constant. The rate of decay is given by the derivative of call price with respect to time (t):

$$\frac{\partial C}{\partial t} = -S\sigma e^{(-d_1^2/2 - dT)}/2\sqrt{2\pi T} + dSN(d_1)e^{-dT} + rXe^{-rT}N(d_2) \tag{9}$$

$$= \theta_{CALL}$$

Using our stock option example, θ_{CALL} is found to be -4.3587.

---

^{2} Careful readers will note that vega is not Greek.

The change in call price expected as a result of a change in t (dt) is given by $dC = (\partial C/\partial t)dt = \theta_{CALL}dt$. With the passage of three days time, $dt = 3/365 = 0.0082$, and the value of the call should change by $dC = \theta_{CALL}dt = -4.3587(0.0082) = -\$0.036$.

Rho

If the interest rate (r) rises, what should be the effect on call price? Remember that a call may be viewed as a long stock position minus a bond. If r increases, the value of the borrowed amount declines, thus the call should be worth more. That is, a greater net investment is needed to replicate the call.

This suggests that the derivative of call price with respect to r is positive, a result confirmed as follows:

$$\frac{\partial C}{\partial r} = XTe^{-rT}N(d_2) = \rho_{CALL} \tag{10}$$

Using the parameters for our stock option example, ρ_{CALL} given by equation (10) is found to be 13.2041. Thus an increase in r from 0.0575 to 0.0585 ($dr = 0.001$) should result in an increase in call price given by $dC = (\partial C/\partial r)dr = \rho_{CALL}dr = 13.2041(0.001) = \$0.013$.

Greeks for Puts

In this section, we develop and discuss applications of delta, gamma, vega, theta, and rho for put options. Recall the dividend-adjusted model for pricing puts given by equation (3):

$$P = Xe^{-rT}N(-d_2) - Se^{-dT}N(-d_1) \tag{3}$$

where

$$d_1 = \frac{\ln(Se^{-dT}/X) + (r + \sigma^2/2)T}{\sigma\sqrt{T}}$$

and

$$d_2 = d_1 - \sigma\sqrt{T}$$

Delta

Differentiating equation (3) with respect to S gives:

$$\frac{\partial P}{\partial S} = -e^{-dT}N(-d_1) = \Delta_{put} \tag{11}$$

From our stock option example with $S = 69.25$, $X = 65.00$, $r = 0.0575$, $d = 0.02$, $T = 0.25$, and $\sigma = 0.25$, Δ_{put} is -0.1562. Thus a unit increase in S results in a $.1562 *decline* in put value.

A hedge portfolio using this put and the underlying stock requires 0.1562 shares per long put. The put is substantially out of the money, thus its price is not terribly sensitive to changes in S. This is why we need a large number of puts (1/0.1562) per share.

Gamma

If we differentiate Δ_{put} given by equation (11) with respect to S, we get what might be a surprising result:

$$\frac{\partial \Delta_{put}}{\partial S} = e^{(-dT - d_1^2/2)} / S\sigma\sqrt{2\pi T} = \Gamma_{put} \tag{12}$$

This happens to be the same as Γ_{CALL} given by equation (7), thus it is positive.

Let's see if this makes sense. Applying the parameters from our stock option example, we find $\Gamma_{put} = 0.0460$. Suppose S declines by $1.00. Since $\Gamma_{put} = 0.0460$, the effect on Δ_{put} should be negative: $d\Delta_{put} = (\partial \Delta_{put}/\partial S)dS = 0.0460(-1) = -0.0460$. Thus the new Δ_{put} should be $-0.1562 - 0.01460 = -0.2022$. The put's price will be more sensitive to changes in S; hence we will need more shares per put to maintain balance. Why? Because if S declines, the put is not as far out of the money; hence its price should be more sensitive to changes in the stock price.

Vega

Here's another surprise. If we differentiate put price P given by equation (3) with respect to σ, we get

$$\frac{\partial P}{\partial \sigma} = S\sqrt{T}e^{(-d_1^2/2 - dT)} / \sqrt{2\pi} = \nu_{put} \tag{13}$$

This is the same as ν_{CALL}, which is 8.2783 in our stock option example. A change in σ will therefore result in equal changes in prices of calls and puts (with the same exercise price).

Theta

Differentiating the put price P given by equation (3) with respect to t yields

$$\frac{\partial P}{\partial t} = -S\sigma e^{(-d_1^2/2 - dT)}/2\sqrt{2\pi T} - dSN(-d_1)e^{-dT} + rXe^{-rT}N(d_2) \quad (14)$$

$$= \theta_{put}$$

For our example, $\theta_{put} = -2.0526$, whereas θ_{CALL} was -4.3587. In this case, the call's price declines faster than the put's price as time passes.

Borrowing from Quantum Physics

Now we meet three more derivatives that have become popular in recent years. Instead of Greek names, these have taken names used to characterize sub-atomic particles.

Speed

Suppose we differentiate Γ with respect to S (remember that $\Gamma_{CALL} = \Gamma_{put}$):

$$\frac{\partial \Gamma}{\partial S} = -\left(\frac{d_1 + \sigma\sqrt{T}}{S}\right)\Gamma = \text{SPEED} \quad (15)$$

Recall that Γ is $\partial\Delta_{CALL}/\partial S = \partial\Delta_{put}/\partial S$, which is $\partial^2 C/\partial S^2 = \partial^2 P/\partial S^2$. Thus SPEED as shown by equation (15) is the *third* derivative of the option price with respect to S. You'll see shortly what use this has. In our stock option example ($S = 69.25$, $X = 65$, $d = 0.02$, $r = 0.0575$, $\sigma = 0.15$, and $T = 0.25$), SPEED is calculated as -0.0007.

Charm

Recall that Δ_{CALL} and Δ_{put} change with S. They also change with time. Differentiating Δ_{CALL} and Δ_{put} with respect to time to expiration (T), we get

$$\frac{\partial \Delta_{CALL}}{\partial T} = \frac{\partial \Delta_{put}}{\partial T} = e^{(-dT - d_1^2/2)}(2rT - d_2\sigma\sqrt{T})/2\sigma T\sqrt{2\pi T} \quad (16)$$

In our example, CHARM is determined to be -0.9250.

Color

What's left? Recall that Γ tells us how sensitive Δ is to changes in S. How does this sensitivity change with time to expiration (T)? We answer this with the derivative of Γ with respect to T:

$$\frac{\partial \Gamma}{\partial T} = -e^{-d_1^2/2}(\sigma + [\ln(X/S) + (r + \sigma^2/2)T]d_1)/2\sigma^2 T^2 S\sqrt{2\pi} \qquad (17)$$

$$= \text{COLOR}$$

For our example, COLOR = -0.4481.

How Small is "Small"?

All the "Greeks" and those terms we've borrowed from physics are partial derivatives and, as such, they are valid for very small changes in their respective denominators. For instance, in our stock option example, $\Delta_{CALL} = \partial C/\partial S = 0.8388$. This tells us how much the call price should change in response to a very small change in S. How small? Strictly speaking, small means infinitesimal. But what if the stock price increases by, say, $10? The price of the call will not rise by $8.39. Instead it will increase by $9.52 to a new price of $14.79.

This means a plain delta hedge will be successful in removing most portfolio risk only for small changes in the underlying. But we can hedge against larger price changes if we are willing to use two option contracts (with unequal exercise prices). This is called delta-gamma hedging and it requires the underlying and two option positions.

The trick is to form a portfolio that is delta-neutral and gamma-neutral.[3] Let n represent the number of shares, and let n_1 and n_2 be the number of options 1 and 2 (exercise prices are unequal, hence $X_1 \neq X_2$). Deltas are Δ_1 and Δ_2, and gammas are Γ_1 and Γ_2, respectively. Equations (18) and (19) force a portfolio $\{n, n_1, n_2\}$ to be delta-neutral and gamma-neutral.

$$n + n_1\Delta_1 + n_2\Delta_2 = 0 \qquad (18)$$

and

$$n_1\Gamma_1 + n_2\Gamma_2 = 0 \qquad (19)$$

---

[3] For those who remember Taylor Series expansions, you recall that as we include higher order partial derivatives, we get a more accurate assessment of the change in the value of a function due to larger changes in the argument of the function.

In equation (18), the "delta" for the stock, $\partial S/\partial S$, is 1; hence equation (18) is a weighted average of the deltas of the three securities. In equation (19), "gamma" for the stock is zero, thus equation (19) is a weighted average of the portfolio gammas of the securities. There are only two equations but there are three unknowns $\{n, n_1, n_2\}$. Remedy this by setting $n = 1,000$, for example, and now the equations may be solved simultaneously.

The importance of delta-gamma hedging is that the portfolio can withstand fairly large changes in S without experiencing a substantial change in total value. What if we wish to immunize our portfolio against even larger changes in S? Recall that the third derivative of option price with respect to S is SPEED. We can form a delta-gamma-SPEED hedge if we add a third option. To make the portfolio delta-neutral, gamma-neutral and SPEED-neutral, we solve the following system:

$$n + n_1\Delta_1 + n_2\Delta_2 + n_3\Delta_3 = 0 \tag{20}$$

$$n_1\Gamma_1 + n_2\Gamma_2 + n_3\Gamma_3 = 0 \tag{21}$$

$$n_1\text{SPEED}_1 + n_2\text{SPEED}_2 + n_3\text{SPEED}_3 = 0 \tag{22}$$

The system of equations (20), (21), and (22) may be solved by setting n equal to, say, 1,000. Such a portfolio will be immune to substantial changes in the price of the underlying.

VOLATILITY

Thus far we have deferred treatment of the volatility parameter (σ) largely because unlike the other parameters such as S and X, volatility is not observable and must be estimated or somehow ordained. Let's begin by defining σ as the annualized standard deviation of the continuously compounded rate of return on the underlying — a mouthful!

This is least stressfully illustrated with an example. Suppose we wish to estimate σ from a series of recent monthly prices and dividends of the underlying such as those in Exhibit 4.1. The continuously compounded rate of return (r_t) for each month is $\ln[(S_t + \text{DIV}_t)/S_{t-1}]$. For instance, the return for month 2 is $r_2 = \ln(39.75/38.50) = 0.0320$.

We now have a series of monthly rates of return and the monthly variance is estimated using:

$$\sigma_M^2 = \sum_{t=1}^{T} (r_t - \bar{r})^2 / (T - 1) \tag{23}$$

where $\bar{r}$ = sample mean return, and T = the number of return observations.

In our example in Exhibit 4.1, $T = 7$ and $\bar{r} = 0.00926$. Calculation of σ_M^2 as given by equation (23) for the example produces $\sigma_M^2 = 0.00396$, the monthly variance estimate. Next annualize the monthly estimate to form $\sigma^2 = 12 \times \sigma_M^2$, then take the square root of σ^2. This is our estimate of volatility (σ) and for the example we get 0.21799.

For pricing currency options, we need an estimate of volatility of the spot exchange rate. The parameter σ is defined as the annualized standard deviation of continuously compounded rates of change in the spot rate. There are no dividends in this case. Therefore, the rate of change during period t is $\ln(S_t/S_{t-1})$.

Choice of Frequency

Instead of annualizing monthly variance, we annualize a weekly variance (σ_w^2) based on weekly returns by scaling by 52. Or we could annualize a daily variance (σ_d^2), and so on. An advantage of using higher frequency returns (e.g., weekly as opposed to monthly) is that we identify more observations in a given calendar time span and this may be why daily rates of return are often used in practice.

Exhibit 4.1: Data for Calculating Volatility

Month	S_t	DIV_t	r_t
1	38.50	0.00	—
2	39.75	0.00	0.0320
3	36.35	0.50	−0.0758
4	41.20	0.00	0.1252
5	40.65	0.00	−0.0134
6	38.75	0.50	−0.0350
7	39.50	0.00	0.0192
8	40.00	0.00	0.0126

But how should we annualize a daily variance estimate? Every five days we encounter a weekend and most financial markets are dormant then. Hence a return measured from Friday to Monday represents one *trading* day, but three *calendar* days. If we regard this return as a single day return, then we should annualize by scaling daily variance by the number of trading days in a year, about 272. This is common in practice.

One could seek to refine the data by merely eliminating the returns measured over weekends and holidays. Then the observations would be consistently daily returns, but this method discards data. Another approach might be to divide each weekend return by 3 to fashion daily returns, then calculate daily variance using all observations including the transformed weekend returns.[4] Of course, one can argue that a weekend return divided by 3 is not really a daily return. There's plenty of room for argument, but practitioners seem to have settled on using *all* daily observations to calculate σ_d^2, then annualizing by the number of trading days.

Choice of Sample Period

Our goal in estimating σ from the past is to find a reasonable assessment of the volatility of the underlying valid for the life of an option. This argues for using recent returns, but how far back in time should we go?

The more the merrier? Not necessarily. If we go back too far, we may find ourselves sampling from an era which is not representative of the present, much less the future. For instance, the underlying may be common stock of a firm that significantly increased its leverage nine months ago. Returns measured before this period should exhibit lower volatility than those measured recently, and the latter may be more representative of the future.

A quick diagnostic device is to plot rates of return over a long period and examine it for shifts in volatility. If it appears that fluctuations are fairly stable in magnitude, it should be safe to use the full period.

---

[4] Thanks to Professor Stephen Figleweski of New York University for pointing this out.

Implied Volatility

An alternative to estimation of σ from historical returns is to determine the volatility that the market is employing as it prices options on the underlying. This means setting the observed market price equal to the Black-Scholes-Merton model, inserting all parameters except σ, and solving for this parameter value.

It is not generally possible to solve the call and put models algebraically for σ because the parameter enters the models in upper limits of integrals (in d_1 and d_2). But solving for σ on a modern computer is not a daunting task and the method is widespread in practice.

The drawback to using implied volatility is that options must be trading on the underlying asset. This may not be the case. Also, remember that the appropriate volatility measure is that which describes the price behavior of the underlying during the life of the option. So the question is whether implied volatility is a good predictor of future volatility. It has been shown to be a reasonably good predictor, but σ estimated from historical returns tends to predict future volatility about as well.

QUESTIONS AND PROBLEMS

1. From this point on we will suppose that you have acquired software that will handle the Black-Scholes-Merton models. Dividend-adjusted call and put prices are given in equations (2) and (3) in the Chapter. Recall the call and put options from Question 5 in Chapter 3, where the stock price is $55, the exercise price for each option is $60, each has 8 weeks to expiration, the Treasury rate is 5.8%, and the stock's return volatility is 48%.

   a. Let the dividend yield (d) be 2.15%. Calculate the theoretical price of the call option. How does it compare with the price you determined in Question 5, Chapter 3 when we ignored dividends? Is this what you would have expected?

   b. Now calculate the theoretical price of the put given the 2.15% dividend yield. Compare this with the put price you found earlier. Is this what you would have expected?

2. Determine the delta for the call, and suppose the stock price declines by $0.25. What should be the new price of the call option?

3. About how many calls are needed to form a delta hedge using 10,000 shares of the stock?

4. Now calculate gamma for the call. By how much should you adjust delta in response to a $0.25 increase in stock price in order to maintain a delta hedge?

5. A call option on this stock with exercise price of $55 and 8 weeks to expiration has a theoretical price of approximately $4.25. Delta for this call is 0.5475, and gamma is 0.03811. How would you construct a hedge portfolio that is delta-gamma neutral using the call with $60 exercise price and the call with exercise price of $55? Use 10,000 ($n$) shares to form the hedge.

6. Calculate vega for the first call option, the one with exercise price of $60. By how much should the call price change if the volatility had been 50% rather than 48%?

7. The price of a zero-dividend stock is observed at the end of each week as follows:

Week	Price ($)
1	92.05
2	91.35
3	88.75
4	86.50
5	87.85
6	88.65
7	84.90
8	83.85
9	85.55
10	88.95

Calculate the continuously compounded rates of return for each week, then determine the estimated weekly variance. Finally, annualize the variance and take the square root to find the volatility parameter.

Chapter 5

Options and Corporate Finance

Now that we've endured many of the intricacies of option valuation, we turn to applications. Our focus henceforth is on problems that arise in firms, hence our viewpoint will be that of a financial manager. In this chapter, we will begin to view familiar corporate securities in a more modern light. We'll see that our understanding of many aspects of firms may be enriched by employing option concepts metaphorically to corporate securities.

Next we'll see how financing with option-embedded securities can help the firm pursue strategic capital investment programs. The option features may be triggered when and only when the firm needs cash for incremental investment. Finally, we shall note how options may be used to manage risk. We will be introduced to simple option strategies that are effective in managing operating and financial risks.

EQUITY AND DEBT

An instructive way of viewing common stock of a corporation arises from the theory of options. The insights we shall meet in this connection were set forth first by Black and Scholes,[1] then developed more explicitly by Galai and Masulis.[2] Suppose that at the end of the year the value of the firm's assets (i.e., the aggregate market value of common stock and debt), is uncertain. Let's say the firm's asset value (V) is projected to be worth $5 million in one year.

Now imagine that you are one of the stockholders and the firm has bonds that mature at the end of the year with a face value (B) of $3 million. If the firm turns out to be worth $5.75 million, for example, then you should insist that management honor the debt. Since the stockholders are the residual claimants, you will share in $5.75 − $3.00 =

---

[1] F. Black and M. Scholes, "The Pricing of Options and Corporate Liabilities," *Journal of Political Economy* (May-June 1973), pp. 637-654.
[2] D. Galai and R. Masulis, "The Option Pricing Model and the Risk Factor of Stock," *Journal of Financial Economics* (January-March 1976), pp. 53-81.

$2.75 million, the residual after the debt has been paid in full. If the debt is not paid, the bondholders can (and will) claim the firm's assets. You will get nothing and they will get $2.75 million more than they are owed. Easy choice. If $V > B$, pay off the debt and collect $V - B$.

But suppose V turns out to be only $1.6 million. If the debt is paid in full, the stockholders will have to come up with the shortfall, $1.4 million. Another option is to wash their hands of the entire matter — just walk away from the firm leaving the assets for the bondholders. The bondholders will almost certainly claim it, all $1.6 million of it, and by doing so the bondholders will then bear the shortfall. Corporate stock has limited liability; that is, unless there is fraud on their part, a stockholder can legally walk away from the firm and allow default on the debt. Another easy choice. Default on the debt.

The stockholder's claims are depicted in Panel A of Exhibit 5.1 for various future values of the firm (V). If $V \leq B$ ($3 million), the firm defaults and the stockholders' claims are worth zero. As V climbs above B, however, the firm pays B and the stockholders retain $V - B$. The payoffs in Panel A of Exhibit 5.1 resemble payoffs on a call option. We can thus view the stock claims as a call option on the firm (current value V) with exercise price B.

Now consider the creditors' payoffs depicted in Panel B of Exhibit 5.1. If $V \geq B$, the creditors are paid the full amount, $B = \$3$ million (i.e., the firm does not default). But if $V < B$ the firm defaults and the creditors receive the firm's assets. From the exhibit, you can see that creditors lose more if the firm's asset value deteriorates substantially.

You can also see in the exhibit that creditors' payoffs resemble those for a short put option. Moreover, you can see that the economic interests of stockholders and creditors are terribly misaligned. If the firm does well (V well above B), the creditors don't much care — they receive a fixed payment (B) regardless. But the stockholders care very much how well the firm does because their claims increase linearly in V.

Now consider the opposite fate. If the firm does poorly ($V < B$), the stockholders don't much care how poorly. They get zero if the firm is worth $3 million and they get the same if it is worth only $1 million. But the creditors care very much how far the asset value deteriorates below $3 million. We'll see where this story leads after we define stock value (S) and debt value (D) in more precise terms.

Exhibit 5.1: Payoffs for Stockholders (Panel A) and
Creditors (Panel B) for a Firm with
Promised Debt Payment (B) of $3 Million

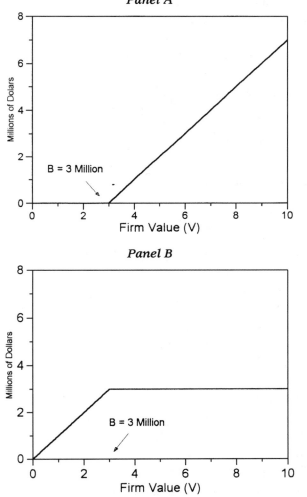

Formal Analysis

If we view the stock of a levered firm as a call option on the firm's assets with value V and exercise price equal to the bond payment (B), then we can appeal to the Black-Scholes model to add some structure to the intuition.

Let T = time to expiration of a zero-coupon bond with face value B. The riskless rate is r and the volatility of the return on the firm's assets (dV/V) is σ. The common stock, viewed as a call option, must then have value (S) given by[3]

$$S = VN(d_1) - Be^{-rT}N(d_2) \tag{1}$$

where $d_1 = (\ln(V/B) + (r + \sigma^2/2)T)/\sigma\sqrt{T}$, and $d_2 = d_1 - \sigma\sqrt{T}$.

Now recognize that the value of the firm's assets (V) must be the sum of the values of all claims; that is, $V = S + D$, and D represents the value of the debt claims. This means that debt value (D) may be expressed as $D = V - S$. Substitute the expression for S in equation (1) and doing some rearranging as follows:

$$\begin{aligned}
D &= V - S \\
&= V - [VN(d_1) - Be^{-rT}N(d_2)] \\
&= V[1 - N(d_1)] - Be^{-rT}[1 - N(d_2)] + Be^{-rT} \\
&= Be^{-rT} - [Be^{-rT}N(-d_2) - VN(-d_1)]
\end{aligned} \tag{2}$$

Be^{-rT} is the present value of B assuming the debt is riskless. What is the expression $Be^{-rT}N(-d_2) - VN(-d_1)$? It looks like a put option on V with exercise price B. In fact, D is the value of the bond if it were riskless (Be^{-rT}) less the value of a *put* option. This analogy comes from Merton.[4] Whose option? The stockholders have a put — they can (and will) push the firm's assets off on the bondholders if V falls below B.

Now that we realize that the value of a risky bond issue is the value of an otherwise identical riskless bond minus a put option retained by the stockholders, we can see how bondholders feel about σ. We know that the higher σ, the higher the value of a put; so, if σ is increased, the value of the put retained by shareholders increases. Hence D declines in value.

This reconciles easily with the payoff diagrams in Exhibit 5.1. For instance, suppose the firm undertakes a project that may

---

[3] Galai and Masulis, "The Option Pricing Model and the Risk Factor of Stock."
[4] R.C. Merton, "On the Pricing of Corporate Debt: The Risk Structure of Interest Rates," *Journal of Finance* (May 1974), pp. 449-470.

produce $V = \$8$ million or $V = \$2$ million. In the first case, the stock-holders' claim is worth $V - B = \$8$ million $- \$3$ million $= \$5$ million. In the second case, the firm defaults ($V < B$) and the stockholders receive nothing. Now consider another project which may produce $V = \$9$ million or $V = \$1$ million. If $V = \$9$ million, the stockholders receive $V - B = \$6$ million, higher than with the first project. But if $V = \$1$ million, the firm still defaults ($V < B$) and the stockholders are no worse off than if the firm had undertaken the first project.

The volatility of V with the first project ($\$8$ million versus $\$2$ million) is less than for the second project ($\$9$ million versus $\$1$ million), and the stockholders naturally prefer the second (higher σ). Of course, the creditors feel just the opposite. If the first project goes sour, they get a firm worth $\$2$ million in default, but with the second project, they get only $\$1$ million. If things go well, the creditors receive their promised payment (B) of $\$3$ million regardless of which project the firm had undertaken.

Three Problems

Let's use our expressions for S and D in equations (1) and (2) to demonstrate the problems that might arise as a result of three types of decisions often encountered by firms.

Change in Investment Policy

Suppose our firm has assets with current value (V) of $\$4$ million, and we've promised to pay our debtholders $\$3$ million (B) in five years (T). The volatility of the firm's assets (σ) is 20% and the risk-free interest rate is 6%. If you insert these values in the model for equity value given by equation (1), you should get $S = \$1,835,443$.

The value of the firm's debt (D) is given by equation (2). The first term, Be^{-rT}, is the value of the debt if it were free of default risk. This is the present value of the promised payment ($B = \$3$ million) discounted at the risk-free rate ($r = 0.06$) over five years (T), or $\$2,222,455$.

Because σ is not zero, the debt has some default risk and this is accounted for by the short put option in equation (2). If you insert the parameters ($V = \$4$ million, $B = \$3$ million, and so on) into this part of the expression, you will get $\$57,898$. Thus the debt ($D$) is worth $2,222,455 − $57,898 = $2,164,557. We can check this by adding S ($1,835,443) and D ($2,164,557) to confirm that they sum to V ($4 million).

If the firm's debt consists only of 3,000 bonds with face value $1,000 each, then each is worth $2,164,557/3,000 = $721.52. The risk-free component (Be^{-rT}) is worth $2,222,455/3000 = $740.82 for each bond, while the short put is worth $57,898/3000 = $19.30 each.

Now suppose the firm shifts its investment policy so that σ increases to 30%. To keep things simple, we'll suppose that total value (V) remains $4 million. We know the stockholders will gain and the debtholders will lose, but how much? Recalculate the value of S in equation (1), but allow σ to be 0.30. You will find S = $1,980,348, a gain of $144,905. So the stockholders are pleased with the firm's new policy.

The value of the put in the expression for D (equation (2)) increases to $202,803, exactly $144,905 more than its previous value of $57,898. Since the put is short and the risk-free value Be^{-rT} remains unchanged, D declines by $144,905 to $2,019,652. Check this by adding the new values of S and D, $1,980,348 and $2,019,652, to get V = $4 million.

With 3,000 bonds outstanding, each will now be worth $2,019,652/3,000 = $673.22 compared with $721.52 before the policy shift. The risk-free component remains at $740.82 each, while the value of the short put climbs to $67.60 for each bond (compared with $19.30 before).

The problem we've just illustrated is real and creditors naturally take steps to combat it; that is, constrain the firm so that it cannot switch to aggressive investments. We will see how the constraints are imposed later in this chapter.

Increasing Leverage

Now suppose our firm increases its debt by issuing 500 more bonds, each with $1000 face value, bringing the promised payment B to $3.5 million. Let's say the proceeds of the sale of new bonds are paid as special dividends to stockholders, thus the firm's assets remain the same and V continues to be $4 million currently. We'll also stipulate that the change leaves σ unchanged.

What will be the effect on prices of bonds that were outstanding before the increase in leverage? Recall the expression for D in equation (2), and note that the risk-free component (Be^{-rT}) is now $2,592,864 given the new value of B ($3.5 million). On a per bond basis, this amount is $2,592,864/3,500 = $740.82, the same as before.

The value of the short put given by equation (2) is now determined to be $125,170 (compared with $57,898 before). The value of the debt (D) is now $2,592,864 − $125,170 = $2,467,694, or $706.06 per bond (compare $721.52 before). The value of the short put has climbed to $35.76 per bond from $19.30.

Why? Volatility (σ) was unchanged by the leverage increase, but notice that the "exercise price" in the put option has increased from $3 million to $3.5 million. Thus the put is more valuable to stockholders and the new bond values reflect this.

This problem is also quite real and we shall see later how creditors confront it in practice.

Organizational Change

Let's return to the firm's original capital structure (i.e., B = $3 million). All the other parameters are the same as well (V = $4 million, σ = 0.20, T = 5, and r = 0.06). Let's say that our firm has two operating divisions, A and B, and the firm plans to spin off division B. To keep things simple, we'll say that each division after the spin-off will be worth $2 million (i.e., $V_A = V_B = $2 million). And we plan to split the debt burden evenly so that B_A = $1.5 million and B_B = $1.5 million.

In this case, there are no aggregate gains from the divestiture; that is, $V = V_A + V_B$, the whole equals the sum of the parts. Also, the debt-assets ratios of each new stand-alone firm are equal to the leverage ratio before the spin-off ($B_A/V_A = B_B/V_B = B/V$). So should investors be concerned with such a change in organization?

Yes! The stockholders will be delighted and we know who'll be slighted. Let's see why. The risk of a portfolio of assets is *not* in general equal to the average of the risks of the included assets. This means that the volatility (σ) of the combined firm is less than the equally weighted average of the risks of the stand-alone division $S(\sigma_A$ and $\sigma_B)$:

$$\sigma < W_A\sigma_A + W_B\sigma_B \tag{3}$$

where W_A and W_B are the proportions $V_A/V = V_B/V = \frac{1}{2}$.

The reason for this well-known result borrowed from portfolio theory is that some of the (diversifiable) risks of divisions A and B cancel out when the divisions are combined. When our two divisions were combined, we observed that operating volatility (σ) was 20%. After the spin-off, the average volatility will be greater than 20%.

For instance, suppose $\sigma_A = 0.30$ and $\sigma_B = 0.30$. You can work through equations (1) and (2) with this parameter value for each stand-alone division and you should find:

$$S_A = S_B = \$950,123 \text{ and } D_A = D_B = \$1,049,877$$

Before the spin-off S is worth \$1,835,443, whereas after the spin-off shareholders will have $S_A + S_B = \$1,900,246$. You can confirm that creditors' loss coincides with stockholders' gain.

Creditors Anticipate Problems

It would be unwise to expect creditors to ignore these potential problems as well as others we haven't examined. The problems are real. In the early 1980s, Cummins Engine Company undertook major changes in its operations and it was widely acknowledged that the firm was placing its future on the line. Bond values fell and the firm's stock rose. Recently, RJR/Nabisco announced plans to divest itself of its international tobacco operations, and eventually its domestic tobacco business. This move had been advocated by stockholders but opposed by bondholders, and considerable maneuvering was required to bring about the divestiture.

The point is that stockholders and bondholders are often enemies and bondholders anticipate this. One way to protect themselves is for creditors to place restrictions on firm's activities, hence *restrictive covenants* are included in bond contracts (indentures). As noted by Smith and Warner,[5] most indentures contain language restricting capital investment, disposition and maintenance of assets, and subsequent borrowing and liquidity, and compliance with these many restrictions appears to be quite costly.

---

[5] C.W. Smith and J.B. Warner, "On Financial Contracting: An Analysis of Bond Covenants," *Journal of Financial Economics* (June 1979), pp. 117-162.

Exhibit 5.2: Excerpt from Offering Memorandum for Hvide Marine Senior Notes, February 1998

The Indenture will contain certain covenants which, among other things, will limit the ability of Hvide and its Subsidiaries to: (i) incur additional Indebtedness and issue Preferred Stock; (ii) pay dividends or make other Restricted Payments, including certain Investments; (iii) consummate certain Asset Sales; (iv) enter into certain transactions with Affiliates; (v) enter into Sale and Lease-Back Transactions; (vi) incur liens; (vii) merge or consolidate with any other Person; (viii) sell, assign, transfer, lease, convey or otherwise dispose of all or substantially all of the assets of Hvide and its Subsidiaries, taken as a whole; or (ix) engage in lines of business other than the Related Business. Under certain circumstances, Hvide will be required to make an offer to purchase the Notes at a price equal to 100% of the principal amount thereof, plus accrued and unpaid interest (and Special Interest, if any) to the date of purchase, with the proceeds from certain Asset Sales. In addition, the Indenture imposes restrictions on the ability of the Subsidiaries to issue guarantees or to create restrictions on their ability to make distributions on their capital stock or make loans to Hvide and its Subsidiaries. These covenants are subject to important exceptions and qualifications. See "Description of Notes — Certain Covenants."

An example of such restrictions is in Exhibit 5.2. This is an excerpt from a prospectus for notes issued by Hvide Marine in the late 1990s. As you read this bear in mind how the three kinds of problems we illustrated would naturally prompt many of these restrictions.

You can imagine that extensive restrictions may still be insufficient to comfort creditors. What's left? If the firm appears so dangerous that creditors shy away, even if offered tight restrictions, they simply don't lend. Thus the firm is essentially shut out of the credit market and this may guarantee failure.

OPTIONS TO THE RESCUE

As we saw in Exhibit 5.1, the payoffs of stockholders and creditors could hardly look more different — economic interests are poorly aligned. We now see that the wedge between the two classes of investors is driven by the implicit options in their respective claims. In this section, our knowledge of options may be brought to bear on the misalignment problem.

Circumvent Limited Liability

Stockholders' payoffs in Panel A of Exhibit 5.1 are flat in the region where $V < B$, just opposite to the payoffs to creditors in that region. Suppose we could make the stockholders personally liable for the debt payment promised by their firm. Under this scheme, the payoffs would fall below zero as V sinks below B — stockholders would have to tap their personal wealth to make up the shortfall. Most important, they would then share the creditors' concerns over how low V might go, bringing about better alignment of the interests of the two groups.

Is this feasible? Yes, and for many firms it is not uncommon. Suppose you wish to form a new business and you incorporate your new firm in accordance with applicable laws. You and perhaps some family members or friends are now the stockholders. Next you visit your local bank and apply for a loan through the commercial lending department. The bank may lend you a reasonable amount — as long as you (and family and friends) are willing to sign for the loan personally. Your interests are then aligned with the bank's in the region where $V < B$. The call option has been removed.

This can and does work for small, closely held corporations but you can easily see its limitation. For larger firms with large numbers of shareholders and easily traded shares, this device quickly becomes unworkable.

Collateralize the Debt

Now let's work on the creditors' payoffs depicted in Panel B of Exhibit 5.1. Their interests clearly diverge from those of shareholders in the region where $V < B$. How can we align their payoffs with those of stockholders in this region?

This can be done by pledging collateral with value C that does not lose value as V falls below B. Thus creditors would experience default only if $V < B - C$. To see why, consider that B is the exercise price in the stockholders' long put position in the absence of collateral. In the event of default ($V < B$), stockholders forego their claim on V in exchange for forgiveness of the debt payment (B). But if stockholders must part with collateral with value C in the event of default, their net payoff is $B - C$.

This effectively reduces the exercise price in the put, diminishing its value. The greater the value of the collateral (C), the lower the value of the put in equation (2), and the less likely it is that stockholders will default. Thus the flat region in Panel B of the exhibit representing payment B would be extended to the left to a point where $V = B - C$.

Collateralized debt exists in the form of mortgage bonds and equipment trust certificates, but it is prominent only in certain industries. Collateral is effective only when underlying assets may be secured (e.g., identifiable, portable assets such as railroad cars). Assets such as the intellectual capital found in a lucrative software company make poor collateral unless they have been made transferable by patents or copyrights.

Options for Creditors

Another way to improve alignment is to modify the flat region of creditors' claims in Panel B of the exhibit. By adding claims that increase with V, we can make creditors more like stockholders.

Income bonds, though rare, allow creditors to share the riches if the firm does well. Interest payments on such bonds are tied to accounting earnings.

A more common device for improving alignment in the region where $V > B$ is the attachment of warrants or conversion features. These provisions have values that are tied directly to V, thus creditors' claims may be very similar to those of stockholders in this region. In this case, the misalignment is reduced by giving creditors call options.

The short put feature of debt is the reason the payoff diagram in Panel B of the exhibit looks as it does. Some bond contracts ("putable bonds") allow the bondholders to sell the bonds back to the firm for a specified price. Thus bondholders are given an explicit *long* put position which tends to offset the implicit short position.

Consider the excerpt in Exhibit 5.3 from a prospectus for "LYONS" issued by Jacor Communications. LYONS are "liquid yield option notes" marketed by Merrill Lynch. These notes are convertible and putable, hence they offer good alignment between creditors and stockholders. Compare the covenant protection in these with what we saw in Exhibit 5.2.

Exhibit 5.3: Excerpt from Prospectus for Jacor Communications Liquid Yield Option Notes, June 1996.

Absence of Covenant Protection

The Indenture will not limit the ability of Jacor and its subsidiaries to incur additional indebtedness, or to grant liens on its assets to secure indebtedness, to pay dividends or to repurchase shares of its capital stock. The Indenture does not contain any provisions specifically intended to protect holders of the LYONs in the event of a future highly leveraged transaction involving Jacor. Jacor could, in the future, enter into certain transactions, including certain recapitalizations of Jacor, that would not constitute a Change in Control with respect to the Change in Control purchase feature of the LYONs, but that would increase the amount of senior indebtedness outstanding at such time.

What Does it All Mean?

In this chapter, we have uncovered some important options in otherwise plain-looking corporate securities. The structure of an equity claim, given limited liability, is such that stockholders share in a long call position, where the underlying is the firm itself. Creditors have a short put position which reduces the amount they are willing to pay for the firm's debt securities. The two option positions are vastly different, thus there's plenty of room for disagreement.

Disagreement can take many forms. We examined three: change in investment policy toward more aggressive projects, increasing financial leverage, and changes in organization such as spin-offs and other divestitures. Regardless of the form it takes, the disagreement must be managed so that it imposes the least costs on the firm. The creditors themselves can manage the problem by imposing restrictions in their contracts (indentures), but these can straightjacket the firm's management. In the extreme, creditors can simply refuse to buy the firm's debt securities, thus denying the firm access to the credit markets.

The point is that when we design corporate securities, we must be sensitive to the nature of the claims so as to simultaneously raise the desired capital and minimize the costly manifestations of disagreement among classes of securities. We've seen that whereas optionality drives a wedge between security classes, options may also be used to bring them closer together — for example, put provisions, conversion features, and warrants added to debt securities.

In the chapters ahead, we will examine security design in depth. We will see how warrants are employed in corporate financing decisions, and we will see how these instruments should be valued. Then we shall explore option-embedded bonds — convertibles, putables, and callables. We will see how these are used in financing decisions and we will examine various methods to assess their values.

STRATEGIC APPLICATIONS

While options are useful in designing security contracts to improve alignment of the economic interests of investors, they are also useful in helping the firm meet its strategic objectives. In the latter chapters of this book, after we've covered warrants and option-embedded securities, we will learn to identify and evaluate *real* options. These are options on real assets (i.e., those assets used in producing goods and services). Warrants and option-embedded securities represent *financial* options (i.e., claims on financial assets, and these include stocks, bonds, notes, preferred stocks, and so on).

Financial options help the firm exploit real options. To see how, consider that real options include options to expand the scale of production; options to reduce scale, and in the limit abandon an investment entirely; and optional timing of an investment. Later we will see that the ability to expand production is analogous to a long call position, where the exercise price includes incremental investment needed to execute the expansion. And we'll see that the flexibility to cut back production or to abandon a project completely is analogous to a long put. The exercise price is the liquidation or salvage value that will be received in the event a project is curtailed.

To appreciate the interplay between financial options and real options, suppose a firm may invest today in a pioneer venture. This is a capital project of limited duration useful in deciding whether the firm should pursue production on a full commercial scale at some point in the future. Exploratory drilling for crude oil deposits is a natural example.

If the pioneer venture reveals that full scale production is merited, then the firm will have the choice of proceeding to full scale; thus, the pioneer venture may be viewed as a call option on the full-scale commercial venture. The "exercise price" in this case is the additional capital needed to commence full-scale production at the conclusion of the pioneer venture.

This setting represents a natural illustration of the usefulness of financial options such as warrants to support the firm's strategic investment plan. Suppose that the firm issues warrants and stock in order to finance the pioneer venture. As the future unfolds, suppose the results of the pioneer project are quite promising for subsequent commercial development. In this case, the firm's ability to proceed to that stage is valuable, hence its common stock should reflect that valuable opportunity. As the stock price rises the warrants may be exercised, giving the firm the needed capital (proceeds from warrant exercise) to pursue the commercial project.

Thus a financial call option, the warrants, helps the firm realize the value of its real call option. Had the pioneer venture produced results more pessimistic to the eventual success of the subsequent commercial project, the stock price may not rise to the point where the warrants will be exercised. Of course, an inflow of capital to pursue the commercial project is not needed in these circumstances. You can see that the decision to exercise the financial option is intertwined with the exercise decision on the real option.

It is clear that the firm may wish to be able to time the exercise of the warrants in the event the pioneer venture yields promising results. One way to do this is to set the expiration of the warrants to coincide approximately with the end of the pioneer venture. Still another way, even more flexible, is to include provisions in the warrants whereby they may be *called*, hence exercise is forced when and if the firm's management wishes to exploit the commercial project. This amounts to the firm using its call option on the warrants to compel exercise of the warrants (also a call option) so that it may in turn exercise its call option on the commercial project!

You can use a similar story to illustrate an important role of callable convertible securities. Suppose our firm, rather than financing the pioneer project with stock and warrants, issues convertible bonds instead. If the pioneer's results are promising, the stock price should rise and the convertible bonds should then be in the money. The firm may then call the bonds forcing their conversion. In and of itself, a bond conversion does not raise cash — convertible bondholders merely exchange their bonds for common shares and little if any cash changes hands.

So how might this help the firm exploit the full-scale commercial project, which we'll suppose demands a sizeable capital outlay? As bonds are converted, they disappear from the firm's capital structure, hence its debt load is immediately reduced as a result of a conversion-forcing call. As we will see later, conversion-forcing calls in practice cause large-scale changes in firms' balance sheets, reducing their financial leverage substantially. This translates into improved borrowing power or debt capacity. Thus a conversion-forcing call, while producing no cash inflow itself, might allow the firm to borrow the capital needed to pursue the commercial project.

Once again we could say that the firm may exploit its call option on convertibles, forcing investors to exercise their conversion (call) options on the firm's stock, so that it may exercise its call option on the commercial venture. Thus combinations of long and short call options on financial assets are valuable devices used to support strategic finance.

We can see how put options enter the picture as well. Suppose the firm disinvests in a real project and liquidates the assets. This is effectively the exercise of a (real) put option and the proceeds could then be used to retire a straight debt obligation. Thus the firm exercises its (real) put option and this facilitates exercise of its (financial) call option on the debt.

RISK MANAGEMENT

Option contracts are versatile devices for managing operating and financial risks. An example of operating risk is uncertainty about the future price of a commodity which the firm buys or sells, which implies uncertainty about costs or revenues, hence operating cash flows. Financial risk includes uncertainty about foreign exchange rates as well as interest rates. Futures and options markets have evolved largely in response to demand by firms for vehicles for managing both types of risks.

Suppose an oil company plans to sell some crude oil from its reserve to a refiner in three months, and the firm's management would like to place a floor on its revenues from the sale. Note that the company has a long position in the asset (oil), and one way to impose a floor is to employ a protective put strategy (from Chapter 2). The firm can buy a put option on crude oil futures contracts traded on the New York Mercantile Exchange. Each standard contract covers 1,000 barrels of crude. Remember from Chapter 2 that a put option on a futures contract is exercisable for a short futures position. Thus if the price of crude falls between now and the time the firm's inventory must be delivered, the firm could exercise its put and enter into a short futures position, thus offsetting to some extent the reduced revenues from the sale of crude in the event the price falls.

A textile manufacturer may see the need to protect itself from unexpected increases in the price of cotton. This may be done by taking a long position in a call option on cotton futures traded on the New York Cotton Exchange. This option is exercisable into a long futures position which would lock in a price to be paid for cotton.

We saw in Chapter 4 how firms can use currency calls and puts to hedge exchange rate risk. A firm with a receivable denominated in a foreign currency effectively has a long position. We could undertake a static hedge by buying puts on the currency in order to establish a floor. This means buying enough put contracts to cover the number of currency units receivable, thus the hedge ratio would be 1-to-1. Alternatively, as we saw in Chapter 4, we could undertake a dynamic hedge with long puts or short calls whereby the hedge ratio would be determined by the respective delta values of the options.

A payable denominated in a foreign currency may be hedged in precisely the opposite ways. This is effectively a short position, hence a static hedge using long call options on a 1-for-1 basis would establish a floor. Alternatively, a dynamic position could be achieved by long calls or short puts. In addition to options on the currencies themselves, there are also options on some currency futures contracts. The Chicago Mercantile Exchange lists such options on Japanese yen, Canadian dollars, British pounds and Swiss francs, and these options work in the same way as other futures options. Thus exercise of a call opens a long futures position in the currency, whereas exercise of a put opens a short position.

Firms may manage interest rate risk with a variety of financial options. For instance, suppose the firm has a variable rate bond issue outstanding. It would be natural to protect against rising interest rates (falling bond prices) and this may be done with long put options on Treasury Bond futures or Treasury Note futures.   Standard contracts for these futures positions are listed on the Chicago Board of Trade. As we will see in the chapters ahead, there are numerous option possibilities for managing financial risk available in the over-the-counter markets as well. For instance, the firm can purchase a cap which pays off in the event interest rates rise above a specified level. Thus, while options on bond futures have payoffs defined in terms of prices, caps' payoffs are defined in terms of rates directly.

QUESTIONS AND PROBLEMS

1. The equity of a levered corporation is metaphorically viewed as a call option. In this interpretation, what is the "underlying asset?" What is the exercise price?

2. The bondholders of a corporation have the equivalent of a risk-free bond and a put position. Is the put long, or is it short? What is the exercise price of the put?

3. Explain briefly how a change in the firm's investment policy made after debt has been issued might shift wealth away from creditors and to stockholders. Use the call and put option metaphors in Questions 1 and 2 in your discussion.

4. Some organizational changes such as spin-offs and carve-outs may help stockholders at the expense of creditors. Explain briefly.

5. What kinds of precautions might creditors take to protect themselves from problems such as those illustrated in Questions 3 and 4?

6. Our firm has assets with market value (V) of $36 million, and debt with promised payment (B) of $24 million due in 5 years. The volatility of the return on assets is about 50%, and the Treasury rate is 6%.

    a. Determine the value of the equity (S) using equation (1) in the Chapter.

    b. Determine the value of the put option component of the firm's debt, then the risk-free equivalent value of the debt, and finally the value of the debt (D) using equation (2).

    c. Now suppose that the firm redeploys assets so that the volatility increases to 60%. By how much will the value of the debt be reduced? Show that the stockholders will gain this amount.

Chapter 6

Warrants and Rights

Perhaps the most easily recognized call options used in corporate finance are *warrants*. These calls are written by firms on their own stocks and are often issued as attachments to notes, bonds or preferred stocks, or issued in conjunction with common stock offerings in the form of *units*. Often warrants issued as attachments or in units are in private placements rather than public offerings. Warrants are also used as partial compensation to underwriters for their services in placing the issues. This is a valuable device for firms who are strapped for cash and otherwise may be unable to afford underwriters' services. Another instance in which firms have little cash is bankruptcy; thus it is not uncommon for firms to give warrants to creditors as partial satisfaction of claims as they emerge from reorganization.

Subscription rights are warrants issued by firms to their current stockholders entitling them to buy (subscribe to) new security issues, often common stock. Rights holders buy new security issues by paying a subscription (exercise) price to the issuing firm. Thus, warrants and rights are useful devices for raising capital.

WARRANTS

In this section, we will examine why firms issue warrants, and we'll describe how warrants are used to raise capital. We will see how warrants may be valued by adapting the Black-Scholes-Merton call option model to account for their special features.

Why Warrants?

Financial managers report that they often issue warrants to sweeten debt or preferred stock offers.[1] Warrants may make an issue easier to sell, or their attachment may allow the firm to commit to a lower coupon rate or dividend rate. As we will see in this chapter, warrants impose costs, thus a reduction in the dividend or interest rate does not necessarily mean a lower cost of capital.

Managers also report that warrants may be useful in raising equity capital, albeit on a delayed basis.[2] Perhaps management judges that external capital is needed and the firm already has substantial debt. Thus equity financing through the sale of common stock is preferred. But suppose the market for the firm's stock, or for most stocks, is bad and management believes a better day will come. The firm can issue warrants now, perhaps attached to debt or preferred, and as the future unfolds and the equity markets improve, the warrants will be exercised. At that point, the firm receives exercise money (equity capital) and issues new shares. As a result, the firm has achieved its equity financing on a delayed basis.

Financial economists have formalized the motives for issuance of warrants in sophisticated theoretical models. For example, Schultz proposes a theory of staged equity financing involving warrants as the first stage of financing.[3] And Chemmanur and Fulghieri have developed a rigorous model of firm behavior based on uneven distribution of information between the firm and outside investors.[4] Their model reveals the conditions under which firms are likely to use warrant financing.

Another logical use of warrants which may be related to debt sweetening and delayed equity financing is in controlling conflict

---

[1] See Keith L. Broman, "The Use of Convertible Subordinated Debentures by Industrial Firms 1949–1959," *Quarterly Review of Economics and Business* (Spring 1963) and Ronald J. Hoffmeister, "Use of Convertible Debt in the Early 1970's — A Re-evaluation of Corporate Motives," *Quarterly Review of Economics and Business* (Summer 1977), pp. 23-31 for survey evidence.

[2] See Broman, "The Use of Convertible Subordinated Debentures by Industrial Firms 1949–1959" and Hoffmeister, "Use of convertible debt in the early 1970's — A re-evaluation of corporate motives."

[3] See Paul Schultz, "Calls of Warrants: Timing and Market Reaction," *Journal of Finance* (June 1993), pp. 681-696.

[4] T.J. Chemmanur and P. Fulghieri, "Why Include Warrants in New Equity Issues? A Theory of Unit IPOs," *Journal of Financial and Quantitative Analysis* (March 1997), pp. 1-24.

that arises between stockholders and creditors, as we have seen in the previous chapter. By attaching warrants to notes, bonds or preferred shares, these investors are effectively given a call option that allows them to participate in upside potential. Thus these investors should have preferences similar to those of common stockholders, and the conflict is mitigated. As we will see in later chapters, convertible securities may fulfill this role as well. And convertibles may also be used in delayed equity financing and "debt sweetening."

Warrants tend to be issued by small firms with shares listed on Nasdaq or the bulletin board markets. The firms are young and they are often riskier than other firms in the same industries. Firms which issue warrants often must rely on underwriters that are smaller and less firmly established than the major players.

Warrant Features

Most warrants that are issued as attachments to bonds, notes, and preferred stocks are almost immediately *detachable* so that they may be traded separately from the senior securities. In recent years, warrants are increasingly issued along with stock of start-up firms in their initial public offerings in the form of units. Warrants and shares issued in such units are usually tradeable separately immediately upon issuance.

A warrant has terms specified in the formal *warrant agreement* much like exchange-listed options. The *conversion ratio* is the number of shares for which one warrant may be exercised. This may be a fraction of a share, it may be 1-for-1, or it may be for several shares. Warrants are protected against *dilution* by automatic adjustment of the conversion ratio in the event of stock splits or stock dividends. For instance, a conversion ratio of 10 would change automatically to 20 in the event of a 2-for-1 stock split.

Some firms specify that warrants are exercisable for common shares *and* a second warrant issue. So-called "A warrants" are issued first and these may be exercised for common shares and "B warrants." These sequential warrant issues allow the firm to conduct staged financing.

Expiration dates are usually set so that warrants expire in a few years, unlike most exchange-listed options. Some firms have chosen to extend expiration times in cases where their common shares have not risen sufficiently to prompt the warrant holders to exercise. Increasingly, some warrants have provisions wherein their expiration dates may be *accelerated* if the underlying stock has performed well — for example, the stock is trading at or above 150% of the exercise price for a specified period of time.

Since the early 1990s, many warrants have been issued with explicit *call provisions*, akin to having expiration dates which may be accelerated in that the life of the warrants may be shortened by the firm. A call price is specified but this is usually a negligible amount. For example, $0.05 is not uncommon. If the warrant is in the money by a specified amount (e.g., 150% of exercise price), then the investor will almost surely exercise the warrant rather than surrender it for a trivial call price. This is known as *forced exercise* and the call provision allows the firm to control when the warrants will be exercised (i.e., when it will receive an inflow of equity capital).

Acceleration of the expiration date has the same effect; hence, both provisions are useful in allowing the firm to time the inflow of equity capital. Callable warrants and warrants with expiration dates which may be accelerated nearly always have some form of *call protection*. The requirement that a warrant cannot be called or accelerated unless the firm's stock has met or exceeded a certain price level is a form of *soft call protection*. Some warrants go a step further with *hard call protection*, meaning that the warrant may not be called or accelerated during a specified number of years regardless of how well the stock has performed.

In some cases where warrants are attached to notes, bonds or preferreds, the senior security itself may be used to pay the exercise price. Thus rather than spend cash to buy new common shares, the investor may surrender the senior security in lieu of cash. The face value of the senior security is the equivalent amount of cash. Such a package is essentially a convertible security.

In the event of merger or acquisition of the issuing firm, warrants may be exercisable for shares of the acquiring firm. This is usually the case in stock-for-stock acquisitions, but in the case of cash acquisitions the warrant holders of the acquiring firm may face early expiration instead. That is, the warrants may be exercised for shares of the issuing firm or not at all, and if the issuing firm's shares are set to disappear due to a cash acquisition, the warrants must be exercised (if in the money) or they will expire out of the money earlier than originally specified.

Warrants Then and Elsewhere

In the days before the establishment of the CBOE, options were traded in the over-the-counter markets and often were known as warrants. Despite their name, these were options bought and written by investors — the issuing firms were not the writers. If we go far back into history (the 1920s), we will find that warrants as we now know them were called *option warrants*. These were written by the issuing firms and they were used to raise capital much as they are now.

In some European countries, for example, Germany and France, securities called warrants are actively traded but we would view these as options. Warrants for German and French stocks are written by commercial banks in order to manage risks of stocks held in their portfolios. That is, German and French banks hold substantial positions in large, prominent firms in their respective countries, and the banks write warrants on these stocks in order to manage risk. These are covered warrant positions, much the same as covered calls in the U.S.

If you compare the number of issues and trading volume of these "warrants" with what we know in the U.S. as warrants, you will find that European countries would appear to have a much larger warrant market than the U.S. A more meaningful comparison of these warrants would be with the call options markets in the U.S., and we would find that call options in the U.S. far exceed warrants in Europe in terms of the number of issues and in trading volume.

Valuing Warrants

A warrant, by virtue that it is a call option, may be combined with shares of the underlying common stock to form a riskless portfolio (i.e., a long position in delta shares per warrant sold short). The market price of a warrant should then be such that a riskless portfolio earns the riskless rate (r), a result familiar from Chapter 3. Once the warrant is marketed we may expect investors to do the rest — trade until the market price is such that the portfolio earns r. But financial managers must know the value of the warrant before it is issued. If they overestimate and price it too high, the issue will not sell. If they underprice, the issue may sell like hotcakes — because the firm is giving away something of value for less than its cost. Either mistake is costly, so we need a method of assessing warrant value conceptually.

We desire a model and, since warrants are calls, the Black-Scholes call option pricing model seems a natural choice. Let's tell a story and see how far this model takes us. Suppose our firm seeks to raise \$3.5 million by issuing 3,500 bond-warrant units at par (\$1,000). We plan to attach 200 warrants to each bond and the conversion ratio is to be 1; thus an investor who buys one unit will be entitled to purchase 200 shares of the firm's common stock.

There are currently 2 million common shares outstanding, and if all the warrants are eventually exercised there will be 700,000 more shares (3,500 × 70,000). This will bring us to 2.7 million outstanding shares. Our investment bank helping us execute the issue advises that the straight bond value for each unit is about \$624 per \$1,000 par value if it were issued without attached warrants. If the warrants are valued so that the units sell at par (\$1,000), then the 200 warrants attached to each bond should be worth \$376 (\$1000 − \$624). Thus each warrant should be worth about \$1.88 (\$376/200).

Our firm's stock price is presently \$9.50 and the exercise price in the warrants will be set at \$10.00 per warrant. The interest rate is 6% for 3-year Treasuries and the warrants will expire in three years after issuance. Suppose that the volatility of our stock is represented by a standard deviation of about 20%.

Remember that our investment bank has advised us that the issue should sell at par, which means each warrant should be worth \$1.88. Is the bank right? Suppose we apply the call option model given by equation (12) of Chapter 3 with parameters: $S = 9.50$, $X = 10.00$, $r = 0.06$, $T = 3$, and $\sigma = 0.20$. If you work through the calculations, you should find a theoretical call price of about \$1.88, just like the bank advised! Perhaps the bank's representatives know about Black and Scholes. Or perhaps they just got lucky.

Or maybe they're just plain wrong! Remember that the Black-Scholes model is designed for call options, not warrants, and there are three crucial differences. First, when warrants are issued equity capital is received by the firm, thus warrant issuance changes the value of the underlying asset. This is not the case when ordinary call options are written by investors. The issuing firm is not a party to a call contract; that is, the price of the call option is paid to another investor, not the firm. Second, upon exercise there is another inflow of equity capital as the firm receives the exercise money, again changing the value of the underlying asset. Third, and perhaps most important, exercise of a warrant increases the number of common shares outstanding since the firm issues new shares to satisfy warrant exercise. This *dilution* effect is not the case with ordinary call options. In the case of warrants, their exercise therefore has two effects on equity value per share: (1) the equity value of the firm rises as exercise money is received and (2) more common shares are outstanding. We must take these important differences into account. Fortunately, the Black-Scholes model can be modified to accommodate these three differences.[5]

First, let's define precisely the underlying asset on which a warrant is a claim. For shorthand, define the following:

S = price per share of common stock

X = exercise price per share of stock

N = number of common shares outstanding before the warrants are exercised

n = number of new shares issued upon exercise of the warrants. This is the same as the number of warrants if the conversion ratio is 1, which we assume for now

Warrant holders have a claim on equity per share upon exercise. The firm's total equity value (E) consists of the value of the stock outstanding (NS) plus the value of the warrants themselves (nW). In symbols, $E = NS + nW$. Upon exercise, the firm's equity value increases by the inflow of exercise money (nX), and the number of outstanding shares rises to $N + n$. The value of the underlying for a warrant is then

$$\frac{E + nX}{N + n}$$

---

[5] See Dan Galai and Meir I. Schneller, "Pricing of Warrants and the Value of the Firm," *Journal of Finance* (December 1978), pp. 1333-1342.

At expiration (T), the warrant will be worth:

$$W_T = \begin{cases} (E + nX)/(N + n) - X & \text{if exercised,} \\ 0 & \text{if not exercised,} \end{cases} \tag{1}$$

This may be written as

$$W_T = \max\,[(E + nX)/(N + n),\, 0] \tag{2}$$

With some algebra, this may be expressed as:

$$\begin{aligned} W_T &= \max\left[\left(\frac{1}{1 + n/N}\right)(E/N - X, 0)\right] \\ &= \left(\frac{1}{1 + n/N}\right)\max(E/N - X, 0) \end{aligned} \tag{3}$$

The term $1/(1 + n/N)$ is the *dilution* factor and is less than 1 if n is greater than zero. The second term is recognized as the payoff on a call option with exercise price X and underlying asset value E/N. This is *not* the same as the stock price, but it will fill that role in the Black-Scholes call model. Thus the value today of a warrant is the diluted value of a call option on an underlying asset worth E/N:

$$W = \left(\frac{1}{1 + n/N}\right)[(E/N)N(d_1) - Xe^{-rT}N(d_2)] \tag{4}$$

where

$$d_1 = \frac{\ln((E/N)/X) + (r + \sigma^2/2)T}{\sigma\sqrt{T}}$$

and

$$d_2 = d_1 - \sigma\sqrt{T}$$

Note that we derived the model in equation (4) under the assumption that the conversion ratio (CR) is 1; that is, equation (4) is the value of a warrant on a per share basis. If the conversion ratio is 10, for example, we need only scale equation (4) by 10 to find the value of one warrant.

Let's try this out using the warrants which our investment bank claims are worth $1.88 each. In equation (4) we need a value for the firm's equity (E), and this is $NS + nW$. Try $W = 1.88$ for the first pass, since this is the value suggested by our underwriter. Then using $N = 2$ million shares, $S = \$9.50$, $n = 700{,}000$ new shares and $W = \$1.88$, we find $E = \$20.316$ million. The model in equation (4) requires E/N as the current price of the underlying. Thus $E/N = \$20.316$ million/$\$2$ million $= \$10.16$, which is substantially higher than $S = \$9.50$. Now use the remaining parameters ($X = \$10.00$, $T = 3$ years, etc.) in the warrant pricing model in equation (4) and you should get about $1.76.

Remember that we used $1.88 as the warrant value (W) in equation (4) on the right-hand side (in $E = NS + nW$), and the model tells us this warrant is worth $1.76. This means that our trial value of $1.76 isn't right. We must use some trial-and-error, trying different values of W on the right-hand side until the theoretical value of W on the left-hand side of equation (4) matches. If you do this accurately with the aid of a computer, you should find convergence at about $1.725; that is, $W = 1.725$ used to calculate E on the right-hand side of equation (4) gives a theoretical value of $W = \$1.725$.

Our investment bank was a little off in its assessment of the market value of the warrant issue. If we price the warrant at about $1.73 instead of the recommended $1.88, investors will find that a riskless portfolio consisting of long shares and short warrants will earn the risk-free rate of interest.

Chrysler's Warrants

Here's a neat story to illustrate the use of warrant financing and pricing warrants. In the late 1970s, Chrysler Corporation was in a dangerous predicament. Competition from Japanese automakers and other factors had brought the auto giant to its knees. CEO Lee Iacocca asked the U.S. government for help in the form of guaranteed loans that would total $1.5 billion. After much heated policy debate, the U.S. Treasury was allowed to guarantee up to $1.5 billion in Chrysler's debt. Part of the deal was that Chrysler would give the Treasury warrants to buy 14.4 million shares with an exercise price (X) of $13 and 10-year lifetime (T). At the time Chrysler stock was trading on the NYSE for about $4 per share, thus the warrants were deeply out of the money.

This is a prominent example of using warrants as a debt sweetener, and the ability of Chrysler to borrow at a low rate is widely seen as having been crucial to the firm's ultimate recovery. By 1983 Chrysler, dubbed "The New Chrysler Corporation" by Iacocca, was on the road to recovery. Its stock had risen over $28 per share, and of course the warrants were now deeply in the money.

Remember that the dilutive aspect of warrants represents an implicit cost and evidently Iacocca wished to avoid this cost. Chrysler quietly asked the Treasury to give the warrants back.

There was a huge uproar from the public and the Congress, and later Iacocca acknowledged that the request was a big mistake. Treasury officials were determined not to give the warrants back, but what should they do? The government did not fancy itself a major stockholder in Chrysler, so exercising them was not the desired course. But what should be done?

An investment banking firm (Shearson/American Express) offered to take them off the Treasury's hands for $20.10 each. In the summer of 1983, the Treasury put the warrants up for auction on a sealed-bid basis, and Chrysler was invited to participate in the auction along with several investment banks. Robert Miller, Chief Financial Officer of Chrysler, was instructed by Iacocca to get the warrants back! Mr. Miller was further warned that if his bid was one cent too low (meaning Chrysler would lose the bid), or more than one dollar too high, then he should stay in Washington and not return to Chrysler.

Let's see if Mr. Miller should have been allowed to return to Detroit. First, interpreting "more than one dollar too high" to mean a bid price that exceeds the theoretical price by at least $1, we can price the warrants using equation (3). Chrysler's stock price (S) was about $28.375 when the bids were being prepared. We know the exercise price (X) was $13. As of the summer of 1983, there were about 6.66 years (T) remaining until expiration. The Treasury rate (r) was 11.93% at the time. The warrants were exercisable for 14.4 million shares (n), and there were about 68.5 million (N) Chrysler shares outstanding.

For June-August 1983, the Friday close prices of Chrysler shares on the NYSE are given in Exhibit 6.1. Using these prices, we can calculate continuously compounded rates of return for each week, and then estimate the weekly variance. We next annualize by multiplying by 52 then take the square root to get an estimate of the volatility (σ). These calculations would give a value of about 63%.

Exhibit 6.1: Friday Close Prices of Chrysler Stock, June-August 1983

Week	Price	Week	Price
1	27.875	8	31.000
2	26.625	9	28.125
3	29.750	10	25.500
4	35.250	11	25.500
5	31.750	12	25.625
6	29.500	13	26.000
7	31.500		

The next step is to insert the parameters in the model in equation (4) and then iteratively find the value W on the right-hand side (in $E = NS + nW$) that produces the computer value of W on the left-hand side of equation (4). Doing so we get about $23.82.

Mr. Miller bid $21.602, well below our theoretical value of $23.82, thus he did not overpay for the warrants according to our calculations. First Boston bid $15.559, Morgan Stanley came in at $17.541, and Goldman Sachs/Prudential Bache bid $20.668. Chrysler won the bid and Mr. Miller was warmly received back in Detroit.

Pricing Callable Warrants

We can think of a warrant with a call provision as a portfolio of two calls, one long and one short. The long call is on the firm's common stock while the short call is an option on the warrant itself. If you calculate theoretical warrant prices from equation (4) and compare those predictions with market prices of callable warrants, you should expect to find that equation (4) overshoots the market prices on average. This is exactly what was found by Ferri, Moore, and Schirm in a study of actual market prices of callable warrants. They found that the mispricing was too great to be safely ignored.[6]

In another study, Kremer and Roenfeldt test a couple of versions of the pricing model on a large sample of warrants, several of which had call provisions.[7] They tested the Black-Scholes model

---

[6] See Michael G. Ferri, Scott B. Moore, and David C. Schirm, "Investor Expectations about Callable Warrants," *Journal of Portfolio Management* (Fall 1988), pp. 84-86.

[7] Joseph W. Kremer and Rodney L. Roenfeldt, "Warrant Pricing: Jump-Diffusion vs. Black-Scholes," *Journal of Financial and Quantitative Analysis* (1993), pp. 255-272.

adjusted according to equation (4) against an alternative that permits random jumps in the stock price. Recall the Gauss-Wiener process assumed by Black and Scholes and Merton.[8] The mechanics of this process are such that large changes in price in a short interval are of negligible probability.

This runs counter to experience; hence, economists have developed a version of the model which mixes random jumps in price with the Gauss-Wiener process (i.e., a "jump-diffusion" process). Perhaps unexpectedly, the models with this modification don't seem to fit market prices any better on average than ones based on the Gauss-Wiener process. Kremer and Roenfeldt find that both versions of the model overshoot market prices of callable warrants.

In a subsequent study, Burney and Moore develop and test a modification of equation (4) that accounts formally for callability.[9] Their model is a little beyond the scope of this book, but it may be nice to know how well such an adjustment works. For a sample of callable warrants, they find that the model *without* the adjustment for the call feature overstates market prices by an average of over 31%. But application of their call-adjusted model gives a small average pricing error of −0.24%. All of the evidence underscores the need to account for this provision when valuing callable warrants in practice.

Effects of Warrant Issuance and Exercise on Stock Values

Remember that warrants are issued most often in conjunction with other securities (e.g., as attachments to bonds or in units with common stock). What effect might the issuance of warrants have on the market value of the issuing firm's equity? Why might we expect there to be an effect?

It is plausible that *any* form of external financing, with or without warrants, could reveal negative information about the firm's cur-

---

[8] See F. Black and M. Scholes, "The Pricing of Options and Corporate Liabilities," *Journal of Political Economy* (January-March 1973), pp. 637-654 and R.C. Merton, "The Theory of Rational Option Valuation," *Bell Journal of Economics and Management Science* (Spring 1973), pp. 141-183.

[9] Robert B. Burney and William T. Moore, "Valuation of Callable Warrants: Theory and Evidence," *Review of Quantitative Finance and Accounting* (January 1997), pp. 5-18.

rent condition and future prospects. Investors might wonder: If this firm is okay then why do they need more funds? This notion is developed formally by Miller and Rock and the evidence for it is mixed.[10]

The market price of equity does experience a negative reaction to many, but not all, financing decisions. This is based on carefully controlled studies of stock price behavior around firms' announcements of financing decisions. We know from these studies that the decision to issue common stock is met by an average stock price reaction of about −3%. But the decision to issue straight debt is apparently benign — no detectable stock price reaction on average.

Why? These facts fit another formal theory that suggests that the decision to issue equity reveals to the market that the firm believes its stock to be overpriced in the market.[11] The argument formalizes some old Wall Street wisdom known as the "pecking order" of corporate finance. This holds that firms prefer financing from operating profits — retention of earnings — over external financing. If earnings retention is insufficient to meet capital needs, they turn to the debt market first. Only after they find borrowing intolerably unattractive do they go to the last resort — external equity financing, the sale of common stock.

It all comes down to information again. In general, when we seek to sell something it is not unnatural for a prospective buyer to wonder why. It is also natural to assume that the owner of the asset knows more about its quality than prospective buyers. Put these two ideas together and you can appreciate the skeptical reaction investors might display when a firm's management announces a stock issue. Why is debt better in this regard? As a rule, the value of a bond or note is less susceptible to differences in valuation among investors. This is because the terms of a debt contract are spelled out clearly in a legally enforceable document that stipulates the exact magnitude of cash payments, the precise timing of those payments, what recourse the lender has in the event of default, and so

---

[10] Merton H. Miller and Kevin Rock, "Dividend Policy under Asymmetric Information," *Journal of Finance* (September 1985), pp. 1031-1051.

[11] This theory is due to Stewart C. Myers and Nicolas S. Majluf, "Corporate Financing and Investment Decisions When Firms Have Information That Investors Do Not Have," *Journal of Financial Economics* (June 1984), pp. 187-221.

on. Consequently, while two of us may differ in our assessment of a bond's value, we won't differ much. Thus when firms issue debt, since there is little room for mispricing to start with, investors do not interpret this as a sign the issue is overvalued.

Just about the opposite is true for equity, and that includes warrants and convertibles since they are contingent equity claims. Common stocks do not come with promised dividend payments or other specifications that affect value; consequently, they are tough to value. Two investors can look at the same set of financial statements of a firm and walk away with vastly differing opinions as to what a stock is worth. This is why the choice of common stock financing, warrants, and convertibles may reveal overpricing more readily than financing via bonds.

Here's what we know about the effects of warrant issuance on stock values. When warrants are issued in units with common shares, the stock price of the issuing firm *falls* on average by nearly 2%.[12] Of course, this could be due to the stocks and not the warrants in the units. But when we examine stock price reactions to the issuance of warrants attached to *bonds*, we still find a negative effect of nearly 1.5%.[13] Remember that bonds unto themselves don't generate much of a stock price reaction, so it appears that the warrants are responsible.

What this means to financial managers is that there is a direct, upfront cost associated with warrant financing. It won't show up on the income statement or find its way onto a balance sheet, but it is a very real cost imposed directly on the owners of the firm. It is a component of the cost of capital that can be easily overlooked.

Since issuance of warrants seems to depress stock prices, what might happen when the warrants are exercised? Remember two things. First, warrant exercise is the second stage in a financing decision. It is the issuance of equity and this takes us back to the "pecking order" story. Skeptical investors might suspect the firm's stock is overpriced if management triggers the exercise of a warrant. This may be done by calling the warrant issue or by accelerat-

---

[12] This was found by Soku Byoun and William T. Moore, "Seasoned Equity Offerings: Shares versus Warrant-Share Units," working paper, University of South Carolina, 2001.

[13] See Katherine L. Phelps, William T. Moore, and Rodney L. Roenfeldt, "Equity Valuation Effects of Warrant-Debt Financing," *Journal of Financial Research* (Summer 1991), pp. 93-104.

ing the warrant's expiration date. Either way will force exercise of an in-the-money warrant issue. Second, remember that warrants are dilutive. This is particularly true in the case of forced exercise given that most warrant agreements stipulate that they cannot be called until and unless the underlying stock price exceeds the exercise price by 50% or more. Thus forced exercise causes an entire warrant issue to be exercised *en masse*, and this amounts to a substantial number of investors (the warrant holders) buying new shares at a deep discount relative to their current market price.

From careful studies of stock price behavior around exercise-forcing calls of warrants, we know that the average price reaction is major. One study reports a 3%-4% average decline, while another finds a 4%-5% average drop.[14] These price changes are registered mostly in one trading day so they represent an acute and noticeable impact on stockholders.

The adverse stock price reaction to warrant exercise represents another cost of this source of financing. The fact that warrants may be attached to bonds in order to secure a reduction in the coupon interest rates should not be interpreted as a free lunch. While the warrants may indeed allow a reduction in the *explicit* cost of debt capital, they clearly impose a cost on equity that should be taken into account.

RIGHTS

Instead of raising capital via a general cash offer to the public at large, a firm may target its offer to current stockholders in a *privileged subscription* or *rights* offering. The rights issue is a warrant; that is, it is a call option on a new security where the writer is the issuing firm. Most rights are marketable claims listed for trading on an exchange or the over-the-counter market. Since they are publicly traded, if issued in the U.S. the firm must satisfy full disclosure requirements with the Securities and Exchange Commission (SEC), just as in a general cash offer.

---

[14] See Schultz, "Calls of Warrants: Timing and Market Reaction" and L. Paige Fields and William T. Moore, "Equity Valuation Effects of Forced Warrant Exercise," *Journal of Financial Research* (Summer 1995), pp. 157-170.

Some firms have provisions in their articles of incorporations which stipulate that stockholders have a *preemptive right* to purchase (subscribe to) new securities issued by the firm. This has usually been taken to mean new issues of common stock rather than debt or preferred, and most U.S. firms have removed the preemptive rights from their corporate charters in order to allow managers the flexibility of choosing general cash offers when raising capital.

While rights issues are rare in the U.S. compared to general cash offers, they are the dominant method of external financing in the United Kingdom and in some other countries. In this section, we will examine how rights issues are executed and will explore the important question of valuation of rights. Then we will take up a long-standing puzzle in corporate finance — Why don't U.S. firms use rights issues more often?

Issuing Rights

Suppose our firm wishes to raise equity capital by issuing subscription rights to buy new common shares. The firm sets a *subscription price*, analogous to the exercise price in a call option or warrant. The firm specifies a date, usually a few weeks ahead, on which the stock goes *ex-rights*. An investor who buys the firm's stock in the secondary market on or after this date is not entitled to the subscription rights. Loss of this option is reflected in a decline in the stock price on the ex-rights day, below its previous level called the *rights-on* price.

Most rights offers are *underwritten*; that is, the firm enters into an agreement with an investment bank wherein the bank pledges to buy any unsubscribed shares at the subscription price less a *take-up* fee. You recognize from this arrangement that the issuing firm is effectively buying a put option from the bank, and the reason is the same as for buying any put — insurance in the event the stock price falls below the subscription (exercise) price before the rights expire. The price paid to the bank for the put option is called the *standby fee*.

Current stockholders who receive the rights do not have to exercise them. They can usually sell the rights on an exchange or in the over-the-counter market, or the underwriter may offer to buy them directly from the stockholders. The point is that the rights should ultimately be exercised if the stock price is above the subscription price, and if the issue is underwritten they will be exercised (by the bank) regardless. Thus in actuality the firm is issuing new shares of common stock when it uses a rights offering, and given the full disclosure requirements mandated by the SEC, a rights issue is much like a general cash offer to the public at large.

Valuing Rights

Rights are easy to value. All we need to know is the number of rights needed to subscribe to an additional share of stock, and the current (rights-on) price per share. Suppose we now own 100 shares of stock and the current price is $33 per share, thus our equity investment in this firm is $3,300. Now the firm announces a "1-for-10" rights offer such that for every 10 shares we own we may subscribe to an additional share, and the subscription price is set at $30 per share. In this case, we can purchase 10 more shares at $300, bringing our holdings to 110 shares and our total investment to $3,300 + $300 = $3,600.

Our holdings now valued at $3,600 are distributed over 110 shares. Consequently, our investment in the firm's equity after we subscribe is $3,600/110 = $32.73 per share. This should be the ex-rights price, and the difference between this and the rights-on price ($33) is the value of one right, or about $0.27. Let's see if this makes sense by supposing that another investor buys 10 rights directly at a cost of about $2.70, then exercises them for one share of stock by paying the subscription price of $30. The total cost of this purchase is about $32.70 and but for rounding is the same as the ex-rights price.

In general the value of a right is given by a simple formula. Let n be the number of rights needed to buy one share of stock. For example, in a "1-for-10" offer n is equal to 10. Now subtract the subscription price (X) from the rights-on price (S) and then divide by $n + 1$. Thus one right should be worth $(S - X)/(n + 1)$. You can predict the ex-rights price directly by the simple formula $(nS + X)/(n + 1)$. Try these out on the previous example.

The neat thing about rights offers is that the choice of the subscription price has no effect on current stockholders' wealth. For example, suppose the subscription price (X) is set at $25 in the "1-

for-10" offer, and the rights-on price is $33 as before. You'll see that the value of one right is about $0.73, and the ex-rights price should drop to about $32.27. Thus a stockholder who buys the stock rights-on obtains the right worth $0.73 which may be sold, and on the ex-rights date the stock should drop to $32.27. The value of the right plus the ex-rights price are the same ($33) as the rights-on price of the stock. The only way the stockholder can lose wealth is to allow the rights to expire without exercising them *and* without selling them. This is a self-inflicted wound for which the firm's management should not be blamed.

We are *not* saying that the choice of the subscription price doesn't matter. Remember that the firm wishes to raise new equity capital, hence a trivial subscription price is clearly wrong. On the other hand, the firm wants to make sure the issue will be subscribed, thus a very high subscription price is also wrong. Even in an underwritten rights offer a high subscription price will penalize the firm because the investment bank will charge a higher standby fee. To see this recall that the bank is writing a put, and the subscription price (net of the take-up fee) is the exercise price in the put. The higher the exercise price, the higher the price of the put and hence the greater the standby fee. If the firm chooses a subscription price that is low enough so that full subscription is likely, and high enough so that it will raise the desired amount of capital, then current stockholders — those who are alert anyway — will have no reason to complain.

A Puzzle

Rights issues that are not underwritten appear to be less expensive than general cash offers in terms of underwriter fees and other issuance expenses.[15] Even underwritten rights offers seem to be less expensive than general cash offers because the underwriters rarely earn the take-up fee — they seldom must intervene and buy unsubscribed shares.[16] Taken together, these two pieces of evidence present a puzzle. If firms

---

[15] See Clifford W. Smith, Jr., "Alternative Methods for Raising Capital: Rights versus Underwritten Offerings," *Journal of Financial Economics* (December 1977), pp. 273-307, for some detailed and persuasive evidence.

[16] See Robert S. Hansen, "The Demise of the Rights Issue," *Review of Financial Studies* (Fall 1988), pp. 289-309.

can do without the underwriters, and if rights issues that are not under-written are cheaper than general cash offers, why don't we see U.S. firms relying more on this method of raising capital, more in line with their brethren in the United Kingdom and much of Europe?

Part of the puzzle may be attributed to the observed tempo-rary stock price decline during the offering period. This imposes a cost on stockholders who would sell their shares during this period and it may make rights a little less appealing for that reason. Another possibility is that direct comparison of the issuance costs of the two methods is misleading because there are systematic differences in the types of firms which pursue one method over another. For instance, we know that the costs of issuance decline as ownership concentration increases. Therefore, a firm can issue new shares more cheaply if large holdings are concentrated in the hands of a few.[17]

But suppose rights offers really are cheaper than general cash offers, notwithstanding these possible resolutions of the puz-zle? How could it be that U.S. firms have such a pronounced prefer-ence for general cash offers? Often the investment banks have representatives on firms' boards of directors, and the banks are in a position to provide benefits to other directors. This is generally legal and it does bring up the possibility of conflict of interest. That is, if the banks are represented on boards they may be able to influ-ence firms to go with more expensive methods of raising capital, even though this is harmful to the firms' stockholders.[18]

Of course it is hard to tell, but some have suggested that the stock market's reaction to successful moves by boards to eliminate the preemptive right provision from their charters could give a clue.[19] Indeed, we know that when firms announce the removal of these provisions, thus allowing managers to avoid rights offers, their stock prices are reduced.[20]

---

[17] See Robert S. Hansen and John M. Pinkerton, "Direct Equity Financing: A Resolution of a Paradox," *Journal of Finance* (June 1982), pp. 651-665 for a full analysis.

[18] Smith discussed this possibility in "Alternative Methods for Raising Capital: Rights versus Underwritten Offerings."

[19] G. Meeks, "Rights Issues," *The New Palgrave Dictionary of Money and Finance*, edited by P. Newman, M. Milgate and J. Eatwell (New York, NY: Stockton Press), 1992, pp. 357-358.

[20] See Sanjai Bhagat, "The Effect of Pre-Emptive Right Amendments on Shareholder Wealth," *Journal of Financial Economics* (November 1983), pp. 289-310, for an excellent study.

Respected scholars in corporate finance have suggested for some time, and continue to suggest, that rights offers may be cheaper than general cash offers, and that financial managers in the U.S. should not be overly quick to eschew them in favor of general cash offers.[21]

---

[21] Richard A. Brealey and Stewart C. Myers, *Principles of Corporate Finance* (New York, NY: McGraw-Hill). 1996

QUESTIONS AND PROBLEMS

1. Firms' managers report that they add warrants to other securities when raising capital in order to accomplish two goals. What are they?

2. Many warrants have call features, or their expiration dates may be accelerated. These features prompt investors to require some forms of call protection. Distinguish between hard and soft call protection provisions.

3. How might the issuing firm's stock price respond to an announcement by management of the intention to issue warrant-debt units to raise capital? When firms call and force exercise of warrants, what effect should we expect to see on their stock prices?

4. What is a privileged subscription offer?

5. Distinguish between a take-up fee and a standby fee charged by an underwriter.

6. Suppose a firm plans to issue rights to current stockholders to purchase new shares of common stock. The firm's current stock price is $44 per share and the rights offer is "1-for-10" with a $42 subscription price. What will be the ex-rights price of the stock? Will the investor who fully subscribes to the rights offer lose wealth as a result of the ex-rights decline in stock price? Explain briefly.

7. If you have access to option pricing software this question on warrant pricing will be straightforward. Let's say our firm's current stock price is $56 per share, and we plan to issue warrants to buy 1.2 million new shares at an exercise price of $52. The warrants will expire in 3 years, their conversion ratio is 1-to-1, and they are noncallable. The firm presently has 8 million shares outstanding, and the volatility of the return on shares is about 35%. The Treasury rate is 6.2%.

   a. Determine the theoretical price per warrant using the model in equation (4) of the chapter. Remember to try different values of the warrant price (W) so that convergence is achieved.

b. How do you suppose your answer in part a would compare to the theoretical price of the warrant if 9 million shares were outstanding, instead of 8 million, and all other parameters were the same as in part a? Explain briefly, then confirm your answer.

Chapter 7

Option-Embedded Securities

Since the mid-1970s, we have had in place methods for assessing the values of option-embedded securities; e.g., callable bonds, callable, convertible preferred stocks, and securities with put features. The methods originally set forth were based on specifying a partial differential equation describing changes in the value of the firm, then establishing a hedging portfolio just as in the contributions of Black and Scholes[1] and Merton.[2] For example, a hedge may be formed by a long position in a convertible bond and a short position in Δ shares, where Δ is the sensitivity of the convertible value to changes in the stock price. We then exploit the idea that such a hedge portfolio should be priced to earn a safe rate of interest, and the value of the convertible may then be determined.[3]

For very simple securities, the resulting equation may be solved in "closed form." This means the solution may be expressed algebraically like the Black-Scholes-Merton model — insert the parameter values according to the "recipe," do some arithmetic and out pops an option value. For instance, we have algebraic solutions for prices of callable securities if they may be called immediately upon issuance, convertible securities with constant conversion terms, and callable perpetual warrants.[4] But suppose the security is a convertible bond that may be called at redemption prices that vary over time, the callability provision may not be activated until a few years after issuance, and the conversion terms may vary over time,

---

[1] F. Black and M. Scholes, "The Pricing of Options and Corporate Liabilities," *Journal of Political Economy* (May-June 1973), pp. 637-654.

[2] R.C. Merton, "The Theory of Rational Option Pricing," *Bell Journal of Economics and Management Science* (Spring 1973), pp. 141-183.

[3] See R.C. Merton, "On the Pricing of Corporate Debt: The Risk Structure of Interest Rates," *Journal of Finance* (May 1974), pp. 449-470.

[4] See Jonathan Ingersoll, "A Contingent Claims Valuation of Corporate Securities," *Journal of Financial Economics* (1977), pp. 289-321.

and so on. Such are the features of a *typical* convertible, and the solution to the differential equation is no longer so straightforward. It may be solved, but not in closed form. Instead, the analyst must program a computer to solve the equation by numerical integration and the features such as call provisions and conversion options must be specified in separate equations called boundary conditions.

In this chapter, we will examine pricing methods for option-embedded securities in general. We'll briefly review the earlier methods, then proceed to methods currently used in practice. In Chapter 8, we will devote special attention to convertibles due to their complex nature.

THE FUNDAMENTAL DIFFERENTIAL EQUATION

Robert Merton uses arbitrage arguments to derive a partial differential equation (pde) that describes the behavior of *any* corporate security.[5] Letting f denote the value of the security, and V denote the value of the firm, Merton's pde is

$$(1/2)V^2\sigma^2 f_{VV} + (rV - C) - rf + c + f_t = 0 \tag{1}$$

In equation (1), f_{VV} denotes the second derivative of f with respect to V, and f_t represents the derivative with respect to time. The risk-free rate is r, and σ^2 is the volatility of the return on firm value (dV/V). Aggregate annual cash payouts for all of the firm's securities (common dividends, preferred dividends, etc.) are represented by C, and payouts for the security of interest are denoted by c.

If equation (1) holds, then an arbitrage portfolio with the right mix of the security and the firm's common stock will earn the risk-free rate (r). The similarity between equation (1) and the pde of Black-Scholes[6] and Merton[7] is striking. Recall that we used that pde to price both calls and puts. The two were distinguished by the boundary conditions, equations specifying the payoffs at expiration (a boundary).

---

[5] Merton, "On the Pricing of Corporate Debt: The Risk Structure of Interest Rates."
[6] Black and Scholes, "The Pricing of Options and Corporate Liabilities."
[7] Merton, "The Theory of Rational Option Pricing."

To price a corporate security using equation (1), we must include boundary conditions much as we did for the option pricing models. The conditions represent equations or inequalities that specify the security's value throughout its lifetime; e.g., call provisions, conversion terms, and put provisions. The number of equations can grow large once we consider the boundary conditions in detail. For instance, it is not uncommon for a callable bond to have call prices that step down each year for several years, and an equation is needed governing each step.

In some cases, the boundary conditions are sufficiently manageable so that equation (1) may be solved analytically. For instance, Jon Ingersoll has developed analytical solutions for callable and convertible securities, but these convenient solutions arise because the boundary conditions are much simpler than those we often encounter.[8] However, in more complex cases, equation (1) may be solved numerically using finite difference approximations.[9]

The bad news is that a separate set of equations must be fashioned for each security evaluated, and the solution algorithm requires specialized computer software. The good news is, based on the few academic studies that have examined the method, it works! Ramanlal, Mann, and Moore report results of a large scale study of callable, convertible preferred stock prices.[10] They compare predicted prices from five different models with actual market prices. Four of the models they test are oversimplified for most convertible preferreds, including those in their sample. But the four models have closed form solutions, hence they may be solved without resorting to numerical solutions of equation (1). The best of these four models exhibits an average pricing error of over 3%, and the model prices systematically undershoot market prices.

[8] Jon Ingersoll, "A Contingent Claims Valuation of Convertible Securities," *Journal of Financial Economics* (May 1977), pp. 289-322.

[9] See M. J. Brennan and E. S. Schwartz, "Convertible Bonds: Valuation and Optimal Strategies for Call and Conversion," *Journal of Finance* (1977), pp. 1699-1715; M. J. Brennan and E. S. Schwartz, "Analyzing Convertible Bonds," *Journal of Financial and Quantitative Analysis* (1980), pp. 907-929; and P. Ramanlal, S. V. Mann, and W. T. Moore, "Convertible Preferred Stock Valuation: Tests of Alternative Models," *Review of Quantitative Finance and Accounting* (1998), pp. 303-319.

[10] Ramanlal, Mann, and Moore, "Convertible Preferred Stock Valuation: Tests of Alternative Models."

The fifth model they test is the numerical solution of the pde in equation (1) with full sets of boundary conditions reflecting the actual contract parameters. The average pricing error is negligible, thus the solution of equation (1) corresponds closely with market reality. The results taken together imply that using closed form solutions, though convenient, is fraught with unacceptable error. Thus the full solution is merited even though it is tough to implement.

This brings us to two approaches to pricing option-embedded securities that have been developed as a result of this conundrum — the full solution of equation (1) is tough, but shortcut (closed form) solutions aren't sufficiently accurate. One approach is to *approximate* the full solution of equation (1) by splicing together closed form components. We'll demonstrate some accurate approximations of convertible preferred stock and bond prices in Chapter 8. The other method exploits the binomial approach to option pricing[11] where we allow prices to evolve in discrete steps in which two possible prices may arise from any point on the time line. As the frequency of the binomial branching process increases, the binomial solution approaches the solution we would get from solving a differential equation. And as you are about to see, the binomial or lattice approach is easy to understand.

A BINOMIAL INTEREST RATE TREE

In the pde, equation (1), the risk-free rate is assumed to be constant over time. The binomial or lattice method allows us to escape this unrealistic restriction. In this section, we will see how to build and calibrate a binomial tree model of interest rate dynamics. To begin with, suppose the annual interest rate (R) is constant over the life of a T-year straight ("bullet") bond with annual coupon payment C. The value today of this bond is straightforward:

$$V_0 = \frac{C}{1+R} + \frac{C}{(1+R)^2} + \dots + \frac{C}{(1+R)^T} + \frac{F}{(1+R)^T} \qquad (2)$$

where F = face value in equation (2).

---

[11] The method is pioneered by J. C. Cox, S. A. Ross, and M. Robinstein, "Option Pricing: A Simplified Approach," *Journal of Financial Economics* (September 1979), pp. 229-264.

Exhibit 7.1: Binomial Interest Rate Tree for Three Time Periods

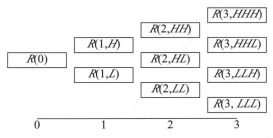

If the interest rate changes over time, the fundamental valuation approach remains the same, but we must now know something about the way rates behave over time. In practice, it is usually assumed that at each point (node) on a time line, the rate may next move to one of two possible values, $R(H)$ or $R(L)$, where $R(H) > R(L)$. Given this simple (binomial) process, if the spot (current) rate is $R(0)$, then at the end of the first period, the rate will be either $R(1,H)$ or $R(1,L)$, as shown in Exhibit 7.1.

In the next period, the rates may be R(2,HH), R(2,HL), or R(2,LL), depending on the path followed from period 1. This is also shown in Exhibit 7.1. Note that the node R(2,HL) may be realized by R moving up then down, or down then up, hence R(2,HL) or R(2,LH) represent the same rate in this representation.[12] In the third period, there are 4 possibilities as shown in Exhibit 7.1, and so on. You can see why this is called a binomial tree. This method can be used to model interest rate behavior, which then enables us to value securities when the rate varies over time.

The process we employ is backward induction; i.e., we work backward in time. We'll turn to specifics with numbers later. Recall that T = time to maturity, F = face value and C = coupon interest payment paid each period. The cash flows arranged in a tree are presented in Exhibit 7.2 for the case where $T = 3$.

If the probability of a high rate equals that for a low rate at each node,[13] then the three possible values of the bond at $t = 2$ are

---

[12] The tree is said to recombine. More general trees will permit 4, not 3, nodes arising from a given pair of nodes.

[13] This may be relaxed easily so that the probabilities are unequal and that they vary over time.

$$V(2, HH) = \left(\frac{F + C}{1 + R(2, HH)} + \frac{F + C}{1 + R(2, HH)} \right)/2 \text{ at node D} \qquad (3)$$

$$V(2, HL) = \left(\frac{F + C}{1 + R(2, HL)} + \frac{F + C}{1 + R(2, HL)} \right)/2 \text{ at node E} \qquad (4)$$

and

$$V(2, LL) = \left(\frac{F + C}{1 + R(2, LL)} + \frac{F + C}{1 + R(2, LL)} \right)/2 \text{ at node F} \qquad (5)$$

Working backward toward the left, we see that at $t = 1$, the values are:

$$V(1, H) = \left(\frac{V(2, HH) + C}{1 + R(1, H)} + \frac{V(2, HL) + C}{1 + R(1, H)} \right)/2 \text{ at node B} \qquad (6)$$

and

$$V(1, L) = \left(\frac{V(2, HL) + C}{1 + R(1, L)} + \frac{V(2, LL) + C}{1 + R(1, L)} \right)/2 \text{ at node C} \qquad (7)$$

We continue discounting (moving to the left in the tree) to find $V(0)$ at $t = 0$:

$$V(0) = \left(\frac{V(1, H) + C}{1 + R(0)} + \frac{V(1, L) + C}{1 + R(0)} \right)/2 \qquad (8)$$

By examining the tree, you may appreciate why this bond is called a "bullet." Once an investor buys the bond at $t = 0$, the interest rate path, hence the future value of the bond, is determined by nature alone — no human intervention at any node. We'll see later how this differs from an option-embedded security where cash flows may be modified at various nodes by conscious actions of decision makers.

Exhibit 7.2: Binomial Interest Rate Tree for Three Time Periods

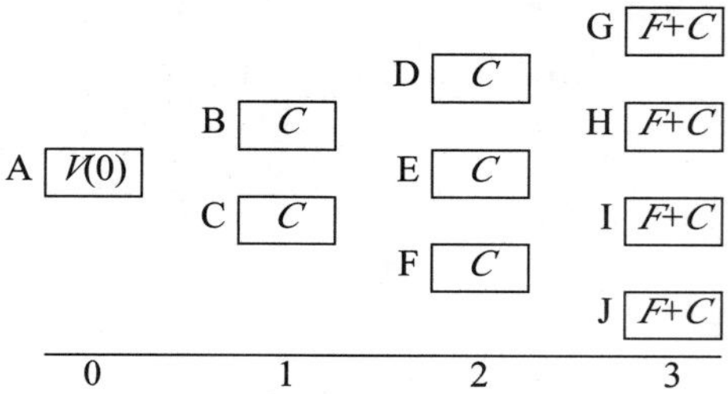

Let's now build an interest rate tree following a method that is popular among practitioners. Assume the gap between $R(1,H)$ and $R(1,L)$ is proportional to the standard deviation of the random process that generates rates. Let $\sigma^2 dt$ represent the variance of R during a period dt. Then the standard deviation is $\sigma\sqrt{dt}$. We'll work in logarithms of R and the gap between $\ln(R(1,H))$ and $\ln(R(1,L))$, divided by 2 given equal probabilities, is the expected deviation of R about its mean, or

$$\begin{aligned}\sigma\sqrt{dt} &= [\ln R(1,H) - \ln R(1,L)]/2 \\ &= \ln[R(1,H)/R(1,L)]/2\end{aligned} \tag{9}$$

The structure in equation (9) implies an important link between $R(1,L)$ and $R(1,H)$ seen by solving the equation for $R(1,H)$:

$$\begin{aligned}\ln[R(1,H)/R(1,L)]/2 &= \sigma\sqrt{dt} \\ \ln[R(1,H)/R(1,L)] &= 2\sigma\sqrt{dt} \\ R(1,H)/R(1,L) &= e^{2\sigma\sqrt{dt}} \\ R(1,H) &= R(1,L)e^{2\sigma\sqrt{dt}}\end{aligned} \tag{10}$$

If $dt = 1$ year, for instance, we have

$$R(1,H) = R(1,L)e^{2\sigma}$$

For $dt = 1$ year, suppose $\sigma\sqrt{dt} = \sigma = 0.10$ is the standard deviation of the interest rate process, and $R(1,L) = 4.755\%$. Then

$$R(1,H) = 4.755e^{2\times 0.10} = 5.81\%$$

Notice that if σ were higher than 0.10, the gap between $R(1,H)$ and $R(1,L)$ would grow, and if the gap is zero ($R(1,H) = R(1,L)$), then

$$\sigma = (1/\sqrt{dt})\ln(R(1,H)/R(1,L))/2 = (1/\sqrt{dt})\ln(1)/2 = 0$$

as expected.

Entering the second year, we have three possibilities, $R(2,HH)$, $R(2,HL)$, and $R(2,LL)$, linked according to:

$$R(2,HL) = R(2,LL)e^{2\sigma}$$

and

$$R(2,HH) = R(2,LL)e^{4\sigma}$$

Exhibit 7.3: Interest Rate Tree with Numerical Values

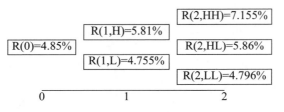

This structure allows the gap between $R(2,HH)$ and $R(2,LL)$ to expand relative to that between $R(2,HL)$ and $R(2,LL)$. For example, if $R(2,LL) = 4.796\%$, then

$$R(2,HL) = R(2,LL)e^{2\sigma} = 4.796e^{2\times0.10} = 5.86\%$$

and

$$R(2,HH) = R(2,LL)e^{4\sigma} = 4.796e^{4\times0.10} = 7.155\%$$

At this point, our interest rate tree is described in Exhibit 7.3, with a spot rate ($R(0)$) of 4.85%:

The volatility parameter (σ) is a key ingredient in the binomial process and in practice it is estimated from recent rates, or inferred from pricing models of options on bonds. In the Appendix to this chapter, we examine volatility estimation in some detail.

Calibrating a Tree

Note that $R(1,H)$, $R(2,HH)$ and $R(2,HL)$ are known once we know $R(1,L)$ and $R(2,LL)$, but where do the latter come from? Determining these is part of *calibrating* the tree and they are chosen such that they are jointly consistent with (1) the volatility ($\sigma = 0.10$); (2) the binomial process; and (3) the observed market price ($V(0)$) of the security. Unfortunately, they must be found iteratively, hence a computer is indispensable for full-fledged applications.

Let's illustrate calibration of a binomial interest rate tree for a 2-year, 4¾% Treasury bond with current market price $1005.68, or $100.568 per $100 of face value. The annual coupon interest payment is 4¾% of $1000 (face value), or $4.75 per $100 of face value. The observed 1-year spot rate on Treasury instruments with 2-year maturities is 4.44%, and the volatility of 1-year spot rates is reflected in the annualized standard deviation (σ) of 8%.[14] Hereafter, we will quote prices and coupon payments on a per face-value basis.

At maturity ($t = 2$), the bond will pay $100 in principal plus $4.75 for the final coupon. Say we begin the calibration process by trying $R(1,L) = 4.3\%$, thus $R(1,H) = R(1,L)e^{2\sigma} = 4.3e^{0.16} = 5.05\%$. Are these trial rates consistent with (1) this bond's market price ($100.568), (2) the binomial interest rate process, and (3) volatility of 8%?

We answer this by discounting the bond's cash flows at $t = 2$ back to $t = 0$ in steps as shown in Exhibit 7.4. The cells at $t = 2$, nodes D, E and F, reflect the face value ($100) and final coupon payment ($4.75). We determine the possible values of the bond at $t = 1$, $V(1,H)$ and $V(1,L)$, by discounting $104.75 at the appropriate rates, $R(1,H)$ and $R(1,L)$, respectively:

$V(1,H) = \$104.75/1.0505 = \$99.714$ at node B

and

$V(1,L) = \$104.75/1.0430 = \$100.431$ at node C

Exhibit 7.4: Trial Calibration of Binomial Tree for 2-Year, 4¾% Treasury Bond

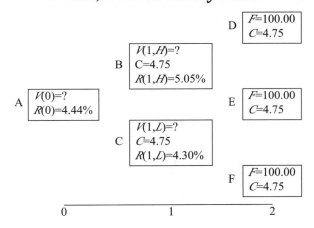

---

[14] In practice we should use as benchmarks only issues that are actively traded (i.e., "on the run" securities).

Exhibit 7.5: Calibrated Binomial Tree for 2-Year, 4¾% Treasury Bond

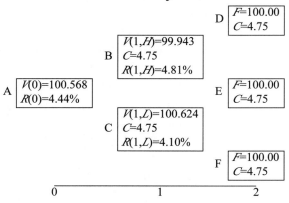

The theoretical value of the bond now ($t = 0$) is the expected value at $t = 1$, plus the coupon payment ($4.75), discounted at the current spot rate $R(0)$:

$$V(0) = \left(\frac{99.714 + 4.75}{1.044} + \frac{100.431 + 4.75}{1.044} \right)/2 = \$100.366 \text{ at node A}$$

Because the *trial* price of $100.366 is below the observed market price of $100.568, our trial rates $R(1,L)$ and $R(1,H)$ must be high. This means we must now try a rate $R(1,L)$ that is lower than 4.3%, say 4.1%. This implies $R(1,H) = R(1,L)e^{2\sigma} = 4.3e^{0.16} = 4.81\%$. Now we repeat the backward induction process by determining theoretical bond prices at period $t = 1$, nodes B and C:

$$V(1,H) = \$104.75/1.0481 = \$99.943 \text{ at node B}$$

and

$$V(1,L) = \$104.75/1.0410 = \$100.624 \text{ at node C}$$

The value today (node A) is then determined to be:

$$V(0) = \left(\frac{99.943 + 4.75}{1.0444} + \frac{100.624 + 4.75}{1.0444} \right)/2 = \$100.568$$

Thus our second trial rates, $R(1,L) = 4.10\%$ and $R(1,H) = 4.81\%$, give a theoretical price of $100.568, the same as the observed market price. Hence the 2-year tree is now calibrated and is shown in Exhibit 7.5.

Exhibit 7.6: Trial Calibration of Binomial Tree for 3-Year, 5.2% Treasury Bond

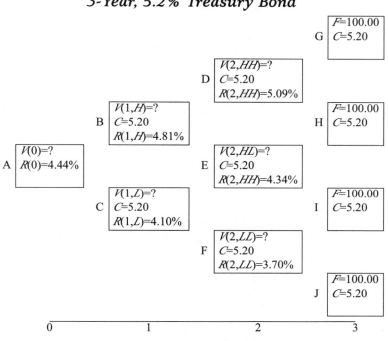

We could price any 2-year Treasury issue using the binomial interest rate structure in Exhibit 7.5. Suppose we wish to price a 3-year security. We must then grow the tree one more year by adding rats $R(2,LL)$, $R(2,HL)$, and $R(2,HH)$, then calibrating these rates. Note that we will not disturb the calibrated rate structure developed for a 2-year bond in Exhibit 7.5, thus the process of adding successive years to the life of the tree is a cumulative one.

Suppose we identify a 3-year on-the-run Treasury bond with a 5.2% coupon rate and market price of $102.146. For $R(2,LL)$, our first trial rate is 3.70%, thus $R(2,HL)$ is 4.34% $(= R(2,LL)e^{2\sigma} = 3.70e^{0.16})$, and $R(2,HH)$ is 5.09% $(= R(2,LL)e^{2\sigma} = 3.70e^{0.32})$. The trial interest rate tree is shown in Exhibit 7.6.

The three possible values at $t = 2$, $V(2,LL)$, $V(2,HL)$, and $V(2,HH)$ in nodes D, E and F are determined by discounting the payments in nodes G, H, I, and J, then averaging assuming equal probabilities, as we did before. The resulting values at $t = 2$ are

$$V(2,HH) = 105.20/1.0509 = \$100.105 \text{ at node D}$$

$$V(2,HL) = 105.20/1.0434 = \$100.824 \text{ at node E}$$

and

$$V(1,LL) = 105.20/1.0370 = \$101.446 \text{ at node F}$$

The two possible values of the 3-year bond at $t = 1$, $V(1,L)$ and $V(1,H)$, are determined using the calibrated rates $R(1,L)$ and $R(1,H)$ from Exhibit 7.5 for the 2-year bond:

$$V(1, H) = \left(\frac{100.105 + 5.20}{1.0481} + \frac{100.824 + 5.20}{1.0481}\right)/2 = \$100.815 \text{ at node B}$$

and

$$V(1, L) = \left(\frac{100.824 + 5.20}{1.0481} + \frac{101.446 + 5.20}{1.0481}\right)/2 = \$102.147 \text{ at node C}$$

Finally, we average and discount $V(1,H)$ and $V(1,L)$ at the 1-year spot rate $R(0) = 4.44\%$ to find the theoretical price of the 3-year bond:

$$V(0) = \left(\frac{100.815 + 5.20}{1.0444} + \frac{102.147 + 5.20}{1.0444}\right)/2 = \$102.146$$

It turns out that we have jumped ahead to the calibrated values of the rates $R(2,LL)$, $R(2,HL)$ and $R(2,HH)$ given that the theoretical price (\$102.146) is equal to the observed market price. Had we not been so fortunate, we would need to try a new rate $R(2,LL)$, hence $R(2,HL)$ and $R(2,HH)$, and repeat the averaging and discounting process to find the theoretical price $V(0)$, then repeat this entire process until $V(0)$ converges to the market price.

We can now price any 3-year Treasury bond using the rate structure in Exhibit 7.6. If we wish to price a 4-year bond, we must grow the tree in Exhibit 7.6 one more year by adding rates at $t = 3$; $R(3,LLL)$, $R(3,HLL)$, $R(3,HHL)$, and $R(3,HHH)$. The rates continue to be related by the volatility (σ) such that $R(3,HLL) = R(3,LLL)e^{2\sigma}$; $R(3,HHL) = R(3,LLL)e^{4\sigma}$; and $R(3,HHH) = R(3,LLL)e^{6\sigma}$. We calibrate the 4-year tree by leaving the 3-year rate structure (Exhibit 7.6) undisturbed since it is already calibrated.

The bonds we've used to illustrate binomial tree calibration feature annual coupon payments, and we recognize this is an abstraction. Treasury bonds and notes pay interest semi-annually, hence we should grow a tree which branches twice a year. For such a tree, we need a 6-month volatility measure. The 8% volatility (σ) we have used is an annualized standard deviation. To find the corresponding semi-annual volatility, we calculate half the variance (σ^2) to form a semi-annual variance, then take the square root;[15] that is,

$$\sqrt{\sigma^2/2} = \sqrt{0.0064/2} = \sqrt{0.0032} = 5.66\%$$

The possible rates for the first 6-month period are then $R(1,L)$ and $R(1,H) = R(1,L)e^{2\sigma}$, where σ is now the semi-annual volatility, 5.66%.

EMBEDDED OPTIONS

Some Treasury bonds, some municipal bonds, and many corporate bonds, notes, and preferred stocks contain options; e.g., call options where the issuer may force redemption, conversion options in which investors may exchange senior corporate securities for common shares, and put options whereby investors may sell corporate securities back to issuers under certain terms. Once we've grown and calibrated an appropriate rate tree, we may then price these securities by inserting cash flows at various nodes reflecting option payoffs. By then averaging and discounting as we've done earlier, we can price a security with all of its option features taken into account.

We may use the same tree structure to price interest rate options such as caps, as well as exchange-traded options on Treasury securities. These instruments will be presented in Chapter 12.

Callable Bonds

In Exhibit 7.7 is the calibrated tree representing the 3-year, 5.2% Treasury bond with all theoretical prices inserted. We will now suppose this bond may be called for $101 beginning at $t = 2$.

---

[15] For a quarterly tree, $\sigma = \sqrt{\sigma^2/4}$, and so on.

Exhibit 7.7: Calibrated Binomial Tree for 3-Year, 5.2% Treasury Bond

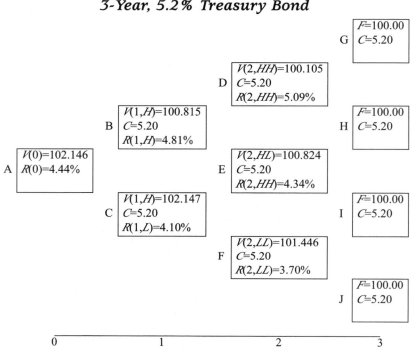

Suppose the Treasury Department has a policy of calling such instruments strictly according to the rule: execute a call if market price exceeds call price.[16] Examine the tree in Exhibit 7.7 to identify values that would trigger a call under this rule. The bond is not callable until $t = 2$, and the only node at which the rule is satisfied is node F, $V(2,LL) = \$101.446$. Assuming the issue is called at this node, the investor will receive $101 plus the coupon payment of $5.20, and subsequent nodes leading from F will vanish. This means node J at $t = 3$ will vanish, but node I will remain because it arises from node E as well as from node F. The tree with values and cash flows reflecting the call feature and the call decision rule is depicted in Exhibit 7.8.

---

[16] Call policy will be discussed at length in Chapter 8. In general, since a call feature represents the right to buy an asset (bond) at a specified price, the issuer should exercise the call when the market value of the bond exceeds the call price.

Exhibit 7.8: Calibrated Binomial Tree for 3-Year, 5.2% Treasury Bond, Callable at Year 2 for $101

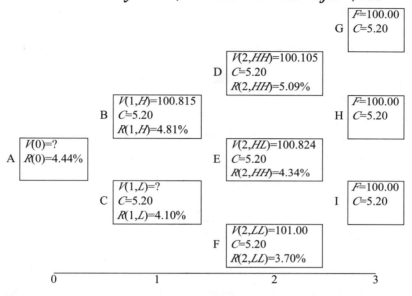

Many of the values in the tree are left undisturbed by the call provision; for example, $V(2,HH)$ and $V(2,HL)$ are unchanged, hence $V(1,H)$ remains $100.815 (node B). But $V(1,L)$ at node C must clearly change due to the revision of $V(2,LL)$ at node F. To find $V(1,L)$, we average and discount the cash flows in nodes E and F:

$$V(1, L) = \left(\frac{100.824 + 5.20}{1.041} + \frac{101.00 + 5.20}{1.041} \right)/2 = \$101.933$$

Compare this with $V(1,L)$ = $102.147 in Exhibit 7.7, the non-callable case. The theoretical price of the 3-year, 5.2%, callable Treasury bond is

$$V(0) = \left(\frac{100.815 + 5.20}{1.0444} + \frac{101.933 + 5.20}{1.0444} \right)/2 = \$102.043$$

The noncallable value was determined to be $102.146 in Exhibit 7.7, thus investors should require a discount of $0.103 for the bond with the call provision. That is, the value to the investor is the theoretical straight bond value ($102.146) *less* the value of the call feature since the call option belongs to the issuer.

In light of what we know about option value, we can speculate about the effects on the value of the call feature of various
changes in the call provision or the interest rate environment. The
call provision will be worth *more* hence the bond will be worth *less*
under any of the following circumstances:

1. The call price is less than $101. The call price is the exercise
   price in the Treasury's call option, and a lower exercise price
   implies greater value for the option, hence lower value for
   the bond.

2. The call may be executed before $t = 2$. The bond has call protection until $t = 2$, thus the value of the call option is dimin-
   ished. If the Treasury Department could call at $101 at any
   time, it is clear from Exhibit 7.7 that the call rule will lead to
   a call at node B where $V(1,L) = \$102.147$. This value would
   be replaced by $101 and nodes F and J would vanish. The
   callable bond would be worth less, hence the value of the
   call feature would exceed $0.103.

3. The volatility (σ) of the binomial interest rate process is
   greater than 8%. Vega for a call option is positive, hence
   greater volatility of the underlying increases option value.

Putable Bonds and Notes

Some corporate securities contain long put options; i.e., the investor
has a contractual right to sell the security to the issuer at a stipulated
price under specified conditions.[17] Merrill Lynch Capital Markets
has developed a popular note with a put provision as well as a conversion feature. This is known as a LYON (liquid yield option note).

In our discussion in Chapter 5, we saw that risky debt and
preferred issues have implicit put options exercised in the event of
financial distress. The underlying is the firm itself, whereas the long
puts we examine now are written on the firm's notes or bonds.
Nonetheless, the explicit (long) and implicit (short) put positions

---

[17] The put provision in some cases is triggered by a change in control of the issuing firm. Such
event risk covenants represent antitakeover devices.

offset to some degree helping to ameliorate potential conflict with equityholders described in Chapter 5.

The interest rate trees we have illustrated thus far are for Treasury securities, hence the rates do not reflect *default* risk. Clearly for nearly all corporate issuers, the rates throughout the tree will be higher to reflect the risk of default, but such a tree may be grown following the same process we used to develop trees for the Treasury issues.

This means we identify a default risk category such as BBB, then determine the 1-year spot rate; i.e., the yield to maturity on BBB bonds maturing in one year. Then we determine the volatility (σ) of spot rates on BBB bonds, and proceed to grow a tree according to $R(1,L)$ and $R(1,H) = R(1,L)e^{2\sigma}$, and so on. The tree is calibrated as before, then extended to another period, calibrated again, and so forth.

Let's pretend that the binomial tree we painstakingly calibrated in Exhibit 7.7 is for an industrial issuer with BBB rating, and that this 3-year, 5.2% bond is putable for \$101 beginning at $t = 2$. The rule would be to exercise the put if the bond value at a particular node at $t = 2$ is below \$101. In Exhibit 7.7, it is clear the rule is satisfied at nodes D and E, since $V(2,HH) = \$100.105$ and $V(2,HL) = \$100.824$. The values at these two nodes will thus be replaced by \$101, and subsequent nodes will vanish as shown in Exhibit 7.9.

By now you can anticipate the steps we must follow to price this putable bond. We have all three values for $t = 2$ based on exercise of the put in nodes D and E. The two possible values at $t = 1$ are:

$$V(1,H) = (101.00 + 5.20)/1.0481 = \$101.326 \text{ at node B}$$

and

$$V(1, L) = \left(\frac{101.00 + 5.20}{1.041} + \frac{101.446 + 5.20}{1.041}\right)/2 = \$102.232 \text{ at node C}$$

Recall that without the put (or the call feature), these values were $V(1,H) = \$100.815$ and $V(1,L) = \$102.147$, in both cases lower than with the put feature. The theoretical price of the putable bond is thus:

$$V(0) = \left(\frac{101.326 + 5.20}{1.0444} + \frac{102.232 + 5.20}{1.0444}\right)/2 = \$102.431$$

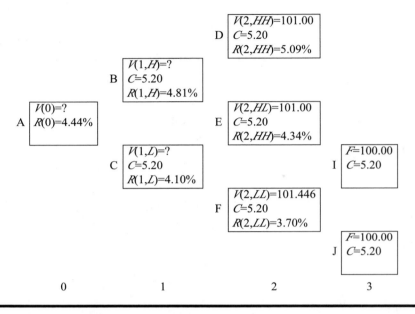

Exhibit 7.9: Binomial Tree for 3-Year,
5.2% Industrial Bond Putable for $101 at t = 2

Compare this theoretical price ($102.431) with that obtained in the option-free case ($102.146). The bond is worth $0.285 more because of the put feature. The put would be worth even more under any of the following circumstances:

1. The exercise price is increased so that it is greater than $101.

2. The deferment period is shorter; i.e., the investor could exercise the put provision before $t = 2$. In Exhibit 7.7, we see that the put would be exercised at node B when $V(1,H) = 100.815, thus the put would be worth more than $.285.

3. The volatility (σ) of the BBB spot rate is greater than 8%.

Multiple Options

In our 3-year, 5.2% bond example, the option-free price is $102.146 (using cash flows in Exhibit 7.7). With a call feature with call price of $101, the price was determined to be $102.043 (from Exhibit 7.8), thus the short call provision is worth −$0.103. The bond with the put feature, exercise price \$101, was found to be worth \$102.431 (from Exhibit 7.9), hence the long put option is worth \$0.285.

Suppose we combine the long put (at \$101) and short call (at \$101) effective at $t = 2$, then price the putable, callable bond by modifying the values in Exhibit 7.7. In this case, we would find the theoretical price ($V(0)$) to be \$102.098. If we add the price of the option-free bond and the value of the put, then subtract the value of the call, we arrive at \$102.328; that is

option-free bond price	−	value of call feature	+	value of put provision	=	value of callable, putable bond
\$102.146	−	0.103	+	0.285	=	\$102.328

In this case, the options do not interact, hence the value of the put is independent of the presence of the call feature, and vice versa. The call provision will be exercised only at node F when $V(2,LL) = \$101.446$. The put will be triggered at nodes D or E, when $V(2,HH) = \$100.105$ or $V(2,HL) = \$100.824$. You can easily imagine cases where the value of one option may not be independent of the presence of another. For instance, suppose the bond is callable at \$101 *anytime*. At node C in Exhibit 7.7, $V(1,L) = \$102.147$, and the call would be triggered. Calling the bond effectively calls the put option as well. In this case, the value of the put would be worth less than \$0.285 because of the possibility of early truncations.

If the bond contains a conversion option such that it may be converted into a specified number of common shares, then a stock price process is needed for valuation. If we value a convertible allowing for interest rate uncertainty as well, we find that the conversion feature is viewed as a *rainbow* option; that is, value is driven by more than one source of uncertainty. We will examine convertible securities in Chapter 8.

THE OPTION-ADJUSTED SPREAD

Suppose the callable 3-year bond (described in Exhibit 7.8) had a market price of \$101.532 instead of \$102.043. The bond is said to be *cheap* by \$0.511. On the other hand, if the market price is, say

$103.00, the bond is *expensive* by $0.957. Investors and issuers can compare market prices and theoretical prices to determine if they are finding bargains; i.e., investors prefer to buy *cheap* and issuers and other sellers would like to issue *expensive* bonds.

It is also useful and increasingly popular to quantify the degree to which an issue is cheap or expensive as a spread between two rate structures. One structure is the binomial tree, appropriately calibrated to give a theoretical price. The other structure is the same tree, but with a constant amount added to (subtracted from) each rate, such that the resulting value of the bond is the actual market price. The constant amount added (subtracted) is termed the *option-adjusted spread* (OAS).

If the callable 3-year bond described in Exhibit 7.8 is priced in the market at $101.532 instead of $102.043, then the OAS for this cheap bond is 0.20%, or 20 basis points. That is, if we add 20 basis points to each of the rates in the tree in Exhibit 7.8, then value the bond by the same backward induction process as before, we will find the current value ($V(0)$) to be $101.532. Assessing the bond as cheap by $0.511 is equivalent to saying that it is cheap by 20 basis points relative to the binomial tree described in Exhibit 7.8.

You may be wondering why this measure is called the option-adjusted spread. The yields on any two financial instruments may differ due to differences in (1) credit risk of the issuers, (2) liquidity risk exhibited by the markets in which the instruments are traded, (3) differential tax status of payments made on the issues, and (4) optionality. For instance, the yield on a BB-rated straight corporate bond will exceed that on a straight Treasury issue due to credit risk, whereas the yield on a straight municipal bond will be less than that on a similarly rated straight industrial bond due to tax differences. All these factors may account for a *nominal* spread between the yields on two instruments.

The yield on a callable security will exceed that on an otherwise identical noncallable issue, and the yield on a putable will be less than that on a similar issue without a put feature. The OAS removes such differences from the nominal yields of two financial instruments, hence the term, *option-adjusted.* Thus the OAS reflects differences only in (1) credit risk, (2) taxability, and (3) liquidity risk.[18]

---

[18] For a detailed discussion of the OAS, see Frank J. Fabozzi and Steven V. Mann, *Introduction to Fixed Income Analytics* (New Hope, PA: Frank J. Fabozzi Associates, 2001), pp. 136-140.

To illustrate, suppose the benchmark interest tree is for an on-the-run Treasury issue, and we calculate the theoretical price of a BB-rated, callable corporate issue using this structure. Not surprisingly, we find that the market price is substantially below the theoretical value, thus the rates that would deliver a price equal to market value would be greater than the benchmark, say by 210 basis points. Assuming we have priced the callable corporate issue taking the call feature carefully into account at each node, then the 210 basis point spread is option-adjusted. In this case, the spread represents differences in credit risk between the corporate issuer and the Treasury Department, and possibly differences in liquidity between the corporate and government bond markets.

APPENDIX

VOLATILITY ESTIMATION

The variance parameter (σ^2) for constructing an interest rate tree is defined as the annualized variance of the continuously compounded rate of change in the rate R. We may estimate σ^2 from recent rates, we may forecast σ^2 employing statistical models, and we may infer it from theoretical models of options on bonds. In this Appendix, we will demonstrate estimation from recent rates and forecasting σ^2 using one of the popular statistical methods.

Inferring σ^2 from Historical Yields

For an unbiased estimate of σ^2, we rely on the familiar model:

$$\hat{\sigma}^2 = \sum_{t=1}^{T} (X_t - \bar{X})^2 / (T-1) \tag{1A}$$

In equation (1A), X_t denotes the natural logarithm of the ratio of successive observed yields (y); $\ln(y_t/y_{t-1})$. To illustrate, suppose daily observations on the yields on 1-year Treasury securities are as given in Exhibit A1.

Exhibit A1: Estimation of Volatility from Daily Observations of the 1-Year Constant Maturity Treasury Security

t	y_t	$X_t = 100(\ln(y_t/y_{t-1}))$	t	y_t	$X_t = 100(\ln(y_t/y_{t-1}))$
0	5.20		8	4.94	−0.8065
1	5.18	−0.3854	9	5.06	2.4001
2	5.25	1.3423	10	5.03	−0.5946
3	5.19	−1.1494	11	5.10	1.3821
4	5.11	−1.5534	12	5.14	0.7813
5	5.15	0.7797	13	5.12	−0.3899
6	5.07	−1.5656	14	5.08	−0.7843
7	4.98	−1.7911	15	5.14	1.1742

The variance of X estimated from equation (1) is $\hat{\sigma}^2 = 0.000166$, and this represents the *daily* variance. To annualize this value, we must scale it by the number of days in a year. Some practitioners use trading days and some use calendar days. If we use calendar days (365), the annualized variance (σ^2) is estimated to be $365 \times 0.000166 = 0.06059$, thus the annualized standard deviation (σ) is estimated to be 24.615%.

Forecasting Volatility

The appropriate volatility needed for option valuation is that which will govern the interest rate process during the life of the option, hence historical estimates may be inadequate.[19] There are several methods for forecasting volatility that involve statistical functions of historical rate behavior. These include moving averages and other time-series techniques including generalized autoregressive conditional heteroskedasticity (GARCH) modeling.[20] A simple form of GARCH is

$$\sigma_t^2 = \omega + \alpha(X_{t-1} - \bar{X})^2 + \beta\sigma_{t-1}^2 \qquad (2A)$$

---

[19] For detailed treatment, see F. J. Fabozzi and W. Lee, "Forecasting Yield Volatility," in Frank J. Fabozzi (ed.), *Perspective on Interest Rate Risk Management for Money Managers and Traders* (New Hope, PA: Frank J. Fabozzi Associates, 1997).

[20] See T. Bolerslev, "Generalized Autoregressive Conditional Heteroscedasticity," *Journal of Econometrics* (1986), pp. 307-327. The original ARCH model was set forth by R. Engle, "Autoregressive Conditional Heteroscedasticity with Estimates of the Variance of U. K. Inflation," *Econometrica* (1982), pp. 987-1008.

In equation (2A), ω is a constant, α and β are coefficients and σ_t^2 is the variance at time t. The representation in equation (2A) is termed GARCH $(1,1)$ because the coefficient α is for a single lag

$$(X_{t-1} - \bar{X})^2$$

and β is for a single lag σ_{t-1}^2. If we included

$$(X_{t-2} - \bar{X})^2$$

we would have a GARCH $(2,1)$, and so on. The GARCH $(1,1)$ model is the most prominent.

Equation (2A) is estimated subject to the constraint that $1 - \alpha - \beta = \gamma$, where γ is a model weight for the long-term variance σ^2. Thus, if we estimate ω, α, and β in equation (2A), then divide ω by $1 - \alpha - \beta (= \gamma)$, we retrieve the estimated long-run variance (σ^2).

The details of estimating a GARCH $(1,1)$ model are beyond our scope, and specialized statistical software is needed, but let's illustrate how it is applied. Suppose we estimate a GARCH $(1,1)$ model using daily data and we find $\omega = 0.0000126$, $\alpha = 0.09$ and $\beta = 0.84$. Since $\gamma = 1 - \alpha - \beta$, we see that $\gamma = 0.07$. This implies the long-run variance (σ^2) is $\omega/\gamma = 0.0000126/0.07 = 0.00018$, thus the daily volatility is

$$\sqrt{0.00018} = 0.0134$$

or about 1.34% per day. The annualized long-run volatility is then

$$0.0134\sqrt{365} = 0.256$$

or about 25.6%.

QUESTIONS AND PROBLEMS

1. Suppose we are building a binomial interest rate tree and our first choice for the lower one-year spot rate one year from now, $R(1,L)$, is 4.891%. If the annual volatility is 14%, what should be the higher rate, $R(1,H)$, according to the exponential method demonstrated in the chapter?

2. Explain briefly how we go about calibrating an interest rate tree.

3. Suppose we have built and calibrated a binomial tree using a volatility of 14%, and now we wish to price a 10-year callable bond from this tree. We've come up with a theoretical price of $98.65 based on a call price of $100, and hard call protection until year 3. Indicate the effect on the theoretical price of this bond that should result from each of the following changes, and briefly explain each:

    a. The call price is increased to $102.

    b. Call protection is reduced so that the issue may be called beginning in year 2, at the original price, $100.

    c. We leave the call provision the same (callable at $100 beginning in year 3), but include a feature whereby the bond may be sold back to the firm for $99 beginning in year 2.

    d. Change the put feature so that it may be exercised at any time.

4. Define the option adjusted spread (OAS). What features of a bond are reflected in the OAS?

Chapter 8

Convertible Securities

C onvertibles were developed in the 1800s as occasional alternatives to straight debt and stock offerings. Now convertible bonds and preferred stocks are well recognized financing instruments issued and traded around the globe. In this chapter, we will examine why these hybrids are issued, how they are structured, and how convertible bonds and preferred stocks are valued. We shall see how these securities may be engineered to meet a variety of needs, and we will briefly survey the expansive convertible landscape to better appreciate the many innovations which characterize these instruments.

SOME BACKGROUND

In this section, we will consider why convertibles are issued, then we'll examine the costs of issuing these securities.

Why, When and Where?

One of the pioneering instances of convertible financing is attributed to J. J. Hill in 1881. Hill reportedly believed that the financial markets perceived greater risk in his railroad investment than was merited. He was unable to borrow, and he wished to avoid selling stock before the railroad's value had been accurately understood and reflected in the firm's equity value.[1]

This interesting anecdote illustrates the special and enduring role of convertibles. Financial managers consistently report that they add conversion features as "sweeteners" to make debt and preferred issues more appetizing to investors when borrowing is difficult, and they appeal to convertible financing when issuance of

---

[1] This anecdote is given by T. Anne Cox, "Convertible Structures: Evolution Continues," in *Handbook of Hybrid Instruments*, I. Nelken (ed.) (New York: John Wiley & Sons, 2000), pp. 15-60.

stock is not timely due to undervaluation.[2] Accordingly, we now have evidence that conversion features are most popular when interest rates are high, hence borrowing is difficult, and we know that convertibles are prominent when equity values are rising.[3]

As we saw in Chapter 5, these instruments can help align the interests of stockholders and creditors, and they can be particularly helpful when capital markets assess greater risk than managers believe to be merited (e.g., J. J. Hill's experience).[4] This is because the implicit short put option in risky straight securities, and the long call option representing convertibility, tend to offset one another. To appreciate what this means, suppose investors assign a high risk to an issuer. This penalizes the securities by inflating the (short) put option value, but it also increases the (long) call option value due to the conversion feature. Consequently, convertible values are relatively robust to differences in assessments of riskiness of the issuers.

Convertibles may also be useful in financing projects that require sequential or staged financing.[5] Used in conjunction strategically with call features, these instruments allow managers to match additional funding with required outlays at various stages of project development.

Corporations in the United States issue convertibles in amounts that vary dramatically over time. For instance, in the white hot equity market of 1929, over 40% of corporate bonds issued contained conversion features, whereas in the dark days of World War II, the convertible market sputtered.[6] During the twentieth century in the United

---

[2] Several surveys of financial managers have been published including J.R. Hoffmeister, "Use of Convertible Debt in the 1970s: A Reevaluation of Corporate Motives," *Quarterly Review of Economics and Business* (1977), pp. 23-32. A rigorous theoretical argument for convertible financing is by J.C. Stein, "Convertible Bonds as Backdoor Equity Financing," *Journal of Financial Economics* (August 1992), pp. 3-22.

[3] For evidence see S.V. Mann, W.T. Moore, and P. Ramanlal, "Timing of Convertible Debt Issues," *Journal of Business Research* (1999), pp. 100-105.

[4] This argument is put forth in M.J. Brennan and E.S. Schwartz, "The Case for Convertibles," *Journal of Applied Corporate Finance* (Summer 1988), pp. 55-64.

[5] See D. Mayers, "Why Firms Issue Convertible Bonds: The Matching of Financial and Real Investment Options," *Journal of Financial Economics* (January 1998), pp. 83-102.

[6] For a more complete picture of the use of conversion features from the mid-1920s through the mid-1990s, see W.T. Moore, "The Life-Cycle of Convertibles and Warrants," *Handbook of Hybrid Instruments*.

States, roughly 10% of corporate bonds have been convertibles, and roughly half of preferred stocks have had conversion features.

Interestingly, as of this writing the largest convertible bond market in the world is the Japanese market. The United States and Japan together account for about three-fourths of the world convertible market, and Japan's market is nearly 40% larger than that of the United States.[7]

Costs of Issuing Convertibles

Issuance of convertibles imposes transaction costs, some of which do not appear on income statements — but they are real nonetheless. Explicit costs, termed *flotation costs*, include fees paid to underwriters, registration fees paid to the Securities and Exchange Commission (or the appropriate regulatory agency in overseas issues), and other expenses such as special audits. Direct flotation costs of security issues vary by the amount raised, and there are economies of scale.[8] For instance, flotation costs for convertible bonds represent 2% of the amount issued on average for issues exceeding $0.5 billion, whereas they rise to 9% for small issues of under $10 million. Straight debt issues, in contrast, cost 2% for the largest issues, and about 4% for the smallest. Seasoned equity offerings are more costly than convertibles, and they also exhibit the scale economy pattern. Thus convertible issuance is a little more costly than straight debt, and less expensive than seasoned equity in terms of flotation costs.

Another important cost of security issuance is gauged by the stock market's reaction to these financing decisions. To see why, recall the Hill anecdote which highlights the problem often faced by managers when approaching the capital markets for funds. Investors know far less about the firm's true prospects than managers do, and this asymmetry of information causes problems.[9] For example, sup-

---

[7] For an in-depth survey of world convertible markets, see T.C. Noddings, S.C. Christoph, and J.G. Noddings, "International Convertible Securities," *The International Handbook of Convertible Securities* (New York: The Glendale Publishing Company, Ltd., 1998), pp. 149-172.

[8] For an excellent analysis of flotation costs of seasoned equity, initial public offerings, convertible debt and straight debt offerings, see J. Lee, S. Lochhead, J. Ritter, and Q. Zhao, "The Cost of Raising Capital," *Journal of Financial Research* (Spring 1996), pp. 59-74.

[9] This argument is presented in detail in S.C. Myers and N.S. Majluf, "Corporate Financing and Investment Decisions When Firms Have Information That Investors Do Not Have," *Journal of Financial Economics* (June 1984), pp. 187-221.

pose a firm's management knows that its stock is about to decline in price once some developing news is released. The firm may proceed with a stock issue now rather than issue at a lower price later — natural market timing. If market participants recognize the firm's motives, however, the issuance of new shares will reveal that the stock is overpriced, and the shares will be revalued downward. The problem is that the market cannot know which firms' shares are truly overvalued, thus *any* firm that offers common stock may be subject to devaluation of its existing shares. This is an information cost and it is borne by practically all firms that issue new shares.

We know from carefully conducted large-scale studies that firms' stock prices drop an average of 3% when stock issuance announcements are made, and this represents an additional cost of financing. In contrast, financing decisions involving straight bonds exhibit essentially no stock price reaction. Since convertibles have both straight and equity components, you might expect their issuance to bring about a stock price decline, perhaps between that due to equity financing and straight debt financing. This is indeed the case. On average, stock values decline by about 2% when convertible bonds are issued, and about 1.4% when convertible preferred stocks are announced.[10]

VALUING CONVERTIBLES

We now turn to the important question of pricing convertible bonds and preferred stocks. Given that the vast majority of these issues are callable, and that the call feature clearly affects convertible values, we will first examine call policy and the nature of call provisions found in convertible bond indentures and preferred stock agreements. Then we will illustrate theoretical pricing models and assess how well they work.

---

[10] For an extensive study of stock price reactions to various types of financing actions, see W.H. Mikkelson and M. Partch, "Valuation Effects of Security Offerings and the Issuance Process," *Journal of Financial Economics* (January-February 1986), pp. 31-60. Stock price reactions to preferred stock financing decisions are investigated by S.C. Linn and J.M. Pinegar, "The Effect of Issuing Preferred Stock on Common and Preferred Stockholder Wealth," *Journal of Financial Economics* (October 1988), pp. 155-184.

Call Policy

Most convertible bonds and preferred stocks are callable, and most call features are not activated until a few years after issuance. This is the *call protection period* and it is often set at 3 or 5 years. During this period a firm simply cannot call an issue — the convertible investors have *hard call protection* which we met in Chapter 6. In some cases following the hard call protection period, the firm will be able to call, but only if certain conditions are met. For instance, it may be able to call a convertible if its stock price exceeds a specified level for a certain period of time. This is *soft call protection*, familiar from our discussion of warrants in Chapter 6.

A great deal of ink has been spilled over the question of when to call a convertible security. Let's quickly examine the conceptual arguments, then we'll offer some practical advice for pricing callable convertibles. Remember that a convertible is *in the money* if its conversion value exceeds its call price; that is, the issue is worth more converted into common than it would be if it were surrendered to the firm for the stated call price. It is *out of the money* otherwise. Suppose a bond's conversion value is $700, it is priced in the market at, say $750, and its call price is quoted as 101.5, meaning 101.5% of its face value of $1,000. Assuming that the call protection period has passed, and absent soft call protection, the firm can call the issue. If it called at this point, how would the convertible bondholders feel?

Ecstatic! The moment the call is announced they will see their bonds shoot up in price to $1,015. At whose expense? The stockholders are footing the bill for what is essentially an overpayment for the bonds. Perhaps there's a good reason for the call, but the firm is still paying more for something than it is worth.

Now suppose the conversion value is $1,240, the bonds are selling at $1,265 to reflect the conversion option premium, and the firm announces a call. How do the convertible holders feel now? They're not happy, but they aren't devastated either. They will see their bonds' prices drop to the conversion value or *parity*, and they will either convert into common shares, or sell their bonds in the bond market. You can see why they would not surrender the bonds for the call price, $1,015. By calling when the bonds are priced at $1,265 the firm quashes the conversion option, bondholders suffer a small wealth loss, and the shareholders gain — their firm has essentially bought something for *less* than what it was worth. We now have the makings of a call policy, assuming our goal is to do right by the stockholders — call as soon as the issue is in the money to quash the option value.[11]

Almost. Most convertibles have a call notice period of 30-45 days; that is, the firm must give the investors time to react. What if the firm's stock price, hence conversion value, declines during this period? If conversion value dips below the call price, the firm will find itself having called an issue for cash — investors will naturally surrender for $1,015 if conversion value is below this amount. So maybe the firm should wait until conversion value exceeds call price by more than a nominal amount.[12]

Let's see how this prescription works. Consider Bristol-Myers' convertible preferred stock issued in the 1980s, convertible into 1.06 common shares, and callable at $50. The conversion value exceeded $100 for nearly a year, then climbed above $200 — no call.[13] Bristol-Myers is not unique in this regard. Alas, a beautiful hypothesis slain by an ugly fact.[14] Add to this the fact that stock prices of firms that execute conversion-forcing calls *decline* on average, so what's the benefit to stockholders?[15]

[11] Formal development of the optimal call policy is presented by J. Ingersoll, "A Contingent-Claims Valuation of Convertible Securities," *Journal of Financial Economics* (May 1977), pp. 289-321, and M.J. Brennan and E.S. Schwartz, "Convertible Bonds: Valuation and Optimal Strategies for Call and Conversion," *Journal of Finance* (December 1977), pp. 1699-1715.

[12] See D. Jaffee and A. Shleifer, "Costs of Financial Distress, Delayed Calls of Convertible Bonds, and the Role of Investment Banks," *Journal of Business* (January 1990), pp. S107-S124.

[13] This and other cases are examined by A.K. Byrd, S.V. Mann, W.T. Moore, and P. Ramanlal, "Rational Timing of Calls of Convertible Preferred Stocks," *Journal of Financial Research* (Fall 1998), pp. 293-313.

[14] J. Ingersoll finds that typically convertibles are not called until they are very deep in the money. See J. Ingersoll, "An Examination of Corporate Call Policies on Convertible Securities," *Journal of Finance* (May 1977), pp. 463-478.

[15] W. H. Mikkelson discovered that firms' stock values decline on average upon announcement of in-the-money calls of convertible bonds. See W. H. Mikkelson, "Convertible Calls and Security Returns," *Journal of Financial Economics* (September 1981), pp. 237-264. E.L. Mais, W.T. Moore, and R.C. Rogers document the same phenomenon in connection with calls of convertible preferreds in "A Re-Examination of Shareholder Wealth Effects of Calls of Convertible Preferred Stocks, *Journal of Finance* (December 1989), pp. 1401-1410.

We'll fast forward to our most recent understanding of this puzzle. Remember that the driver behind the call policy — call once the conversion safely exceeds call price — is to quash the conversion option, delivering that value to the stockholders. But suppose that, once the issue becomes callable and in the money, convertible holders begin pricing it as if it were called or that call is imminent. That is, if they do not price a conversion option in the security, there is no option value to quash. Then it doesn't matter when the firm calls.[16]

What this means is that we can price convertibles as if firms will follow the prescribed call policy — even though they don't. Since the markets price the issues as if they will be called according to the policy, we can arrive at accurate prices using theoretical models that presume the issues will be called as soon as feasible.

Some Simple Cases

In Chapter 7, we briefly mentioned a partial differential equation (pde) that describes the behavior of the price (f) of any corporate security as a function of changes in the firm's equity value (V) and the passage of time:[17]

$$(1/2)V^2\sigma^2 f_{VV} + (rV - C) - rf + c + f_t = 0 \tag{1}$$

In equation (1), f_V and f_{VV} are first and second derivatives with respect to V, f_t is the first derivative with respect to t, C = total annual cash flow including common dividends and payments to convertible security holders, and c = annual cash flow to holders of the security of interest.

The pde in equation (1) may be solved subject to boundary conditions that specify the value of the security under certain contingencies (e.g., call provisions, conversion terms, etc.). In some simple cases, the solutions to equation (1) are available in closed form; that is, we may find a mathematical formula which satisfies equation (1) to give us the value (f) of a convertible security.[18]

---

[16] Recent evidence that the option premium disappears once in-the-money preferreds become callable is reported in Byrd, Mann, Moore, and Ramanlal, "Rational Timing of Calls of Convertible Preferred Stocks."

[17] This important equation is developed in R.C. Merton, "On the Pricing of Corporate Debt: The Risk Structure of Interest Rates," *Journal of Finance* (May 1974), pp. 449-470.

[18] The solutions presented in this section are developed in Ingersoll, "A Contingent-Claims Valuation of Convertible Securities."

Let's illustrate with a callable, convertible bond. Suppose the bond is zero coupon with face value (B) of $4 million payable in 5 years. The bond's default rating is such that the appropriate discount rate is, say 7.8588%, continuously compounded. The value of the bond, if it were noncallable and nonconvertible, should be:

$$Be^{-rT} = \$4 \text{ million } X e^{-0.078588 \times 5} = \$2,700,277$$

Now suppose the bond issue is convertible into 200,000 (n) common shares, the firm has 1,000,000 (N) shares outstanding, and its equity value is $4.5 million. The conversion factor ($\alpha = n/(N + n)$) represents the proportion of equity value claimed by the convertible investors. In this case, $\alpha = 0.1667$, hence the conversion value of the bond is $\alpha V = 0.1667$ ($4.5 million) = $750,150.

The conversion option is a call option on αV with exercise price B, the amount that is forgone in the event of conversion. This means we may appeal to the call option model to value the conversion option:

$$\text{Conversion option} = \alpha V M(d_1) - Be^{-rT} M(d_2) \tag{2}$$

where $d_1 = (\ln(\alpha V/B) + (r + \sigma^2/2)T)/\sigma\sqrt{T}$ and $d_2 = d_1 - \sigma\sqrt{T}$

The volatility (σ) is the standard deviation of the rate of return on equity, r is the risk-free rate, and T is the time (in years) to expiration of the conversion option (i.e., maturation of the convertible bond). Let $\sigma = 0.45$, $r = 6\%$, and recall that $T = 5$ years. The value of the conversion feature in equation (2) is $54,316. The straight bond value is $2,700,277, thus the convertible should be worth $2,754,593 in the aggregate. If the face value per bond is $1,000, then there are 4,000 bonds outstanding ($4 million/$1,000), hence each is worth $688.65. The conversion feature is worth only $13.58 per bond. Note that the convertible is substantially out-of-the-money ($\alpha V < B$).

Suppose our bond is callable for $4,200,000 ($K$). This should *reduce* the value of the convertible because it limits the potential profits of the bondholders. The derivation of the value of the redemption feature is beyond our scope, but it turns out that its calculation is straightforward. The value of the redemption feature is developed in a technical article[19] as the difference between two call options scaled by the function:

$$(K(T)/\alpha V)^{2(r-\rho)/\sigma^2}$$

where

$K(T)$ = aggregate call price given T years to maturity;

ρ = annual rate of change in call price; if $K(T)$ is constant then $\rho = 0$

In the example, $K(T)$ = \$4,200,000 and αV = 0.1667(4,500,000) = \$750,150. Since $K(T)$ is constant over time, $\rho = 0$ and $K(T) = K$. Given $r = 0.06$ and $\sigma = 0.45$, the scaling term is:

$$(K/\alpha V)^{2(r-\rho)/\sigma^2} = 2.775$$

Remember that the value of the call feature may be calculated as the difference in values of two call options, then scaled by

$$(K/\alpha V)^{2(r-\rho)/\sigma^2}$$

The first call option ($CALL_1$) has "exercise price" $Ke^{rT}(= \$5,669,407)$ and the underlying is worth $(B/K)\alpha Ve^{-rT}(= \$529,272)$. With $\sigma = 0.45$, $r = 6\%$, and $T = 5$, $CALL_1$ is valued at \$9,839.

The second option ($CALL_2$) uses the same underlying value (\$529,272), but the "exercise price" is $Ke^{rT}/\alpha (= \$34,009,640)$. $CALL_2$ is valued at only \$47. The value of the call feature is then

$$(K/\alpha V)^{2(r-\rho)/\sigma^2} [CALL_1 - CALL_2] = 2.775[\$9,839 - 47] = \$27,172 \quad (3)$$

Thus the value of the callable convertible bond issue is:

straight bond value + conversion option − call feature

=   \$2,700,277   +   \$54,316   −   \$27,172   = \$2,727,421

Each bond is worth about \$681.86. The analytical expressions may look a little imposing, but they may be solved with ordinary call option pricing software.

---

[19] See Ingersoll, "A Contingent-Claims Valuation of Convertible Securities."

Notice that the conversion feature was valued as a European-style call, and the call provision was also priced as European-style. In practice, these features are American-style. Moreover, as we've mentioned before, most convertibles are call-protected for 3 or 5 years typically, and the model we employed does not account for this. Once these real-world features are taken into account, the *exact* solution to the pde, equation (1), must be found by numerical methods. However, some *approximations* of the solution of equation (1) are available which allow for call protection.

Call-Protected Convertible Preferred Stock

Suppose the security is perpetual, as is the case for many preferred issues, and that it is callable *anytime*. If conversion value (αV) exceeds call price (K), then we assume the issue will be called, or that the market will price it as if it will be called. This means the value in this case is $f = \alpha V =$ conversion value.

If αV is less than K, it can be shown that the solution of equation (1) is[20]

$$f = \frac{[\alpha - (c/C)(\alpha/K)F(K/\alpha)]V + (c/C - \alpha)F(V)}{[1 - (\alpha/K)F(K/\alpha)]} \tag{4}$$

where

$$F(V) = (C/r)[1 - P(a, ad) + P(a + 1, ad)/d] \tag{5}$$

$$P(a, d) = \gamma(a, ad)/\Gamma(a) = \text{incomplete gamma function ratio} \tag{6}$$

with $a = 2r/\sigma^2$ and $d = C/rV$ and

$$P(a + 1, ad) = \gamma(a + 1, ad)/\Gamma(a + 1) \tag{7}$$

The function $F(K\alpha)$ is the same as equation (5) except $d = (C/r)(K/\alpha)$. Thus the value of a convertible preferred issue callable *anytime*, which we now denote as PREF_{ANY}, is αV if $\alpha V > K$, or equation (4) if $\alpha V < K$.

Now suppose the issue is noncallable with value denoted $\text{PREF}_{\text{NEVER}}$. In this case, the value can be shown to be αV if $\alpha C > c$; that is, the common dividends received upon conversion (αC)

---

[20] See Ingersoll, "A Contingent-Claims Valuation of Convertible Securities."

exceed the preferred dividends (c). If $\alpha C < c$, then the value is $\alpha V +$ ($c/C - \alpha)F(V)$, where $F(V)$ is given in equation (5).

In general, if the issue is callable after a call protection period of length T, the exact solution does not exist in analytical form. But Ramanlal, Mann, and Moore show that the exact solution can be approximated accurately by:[21]

Call-protected convertible preferred

$$= (1 - e^{-rT})\text{PREF}_{\text{NEVER}} + e^{-rT}\text{PREF}_{\text{ANY}} \qquad (8)$$

The algorithm for $\text{PREF}_{\text{NEVER}}$ and PREF_{ANY} can be programmed in modern spreadsheet software. An example is solved in the Appendix to this chapter. The approximation in equation (8) is straightforward — it is a weighted average of two prices, one calculated under the assumption that it is noncallable, and the other found by assuming it is callable anytime. The protection period (T) forms the weights. Note that as T approaches zero — i.e., the issue is callable with no protection — equation (8) approaches PREF_{ANY}. As T grows large, the issue is protected from call for a long period, and equation (8) approaches $\text{PREF}_{\text{NEVER}}$.

But does it work? The developers of the approximation test the model against actual market prices for a healthy sample of convertible preferreds. They find that the pricing error from the approximation is very close to that from the exact solution found by the cumbersome numerical method, and that both fit market prices very closely.

Call-Protected Convertible Bond

The exact solution to equation (1) for a coupon-paying convertible bond with call protection is not available in closed form, hence an approximation is useful. Here's one developed by a highly regarded convertible fund manager.[22] First, value the bond as if it is noncallable:

$$\text{SBV} = \sum_{t=1}^{mn} (c/m)/(1 + r/m)^t + F/(1 + r/m)^{mn} \qquad (9)$$

---

[21] This is developed in P. Ramanlal, S.V. Mann, and W.T. Moore, "A Simple Approximation of the Value of Callable Convertible Preferred Stock," *Financial Management* (Summer 1996), pp. 74-85.

[22] J.P. Calamos, *Convertible Securities* (New York: McGraw-Hill, 1998), pp. 189-217.

where

c = annual interest payment

m = payment frequency per year (e.g., for semi-annual, $m = 2$)

F = face value

n = number of years to maturity

r = interest rate appropriate for the default risk and maturity of the bond

Next value the conversion option on a per share basis using

$$W = SN(d_1) - Ke^{-rT}N(d_2) \tag{10}$$

where

S = stock price

K = adjusted conversion price = stated conversion price scaled by SBV in equation (9) divided by face value (F)

r = risk-free rate

$d_1 = (\ln(0.5) + (r + (S/K)\sigma^2)T)/\sigma\sqrt{T}$

$d_2 = d_1 - \sigma\sqrt{T}$

In equation (10), T is the length of the call protection period. The value (W) from equation (10) is scaled by the conversion ratio (CR) to determine the value of the conversion option per bond, and the value of the call-protected convertible is then

$$\text{CBV} = \text{SBV} + \text{CR}(W) \tag{11}$$

As call protection (T) increases, the value of the conversion option in equation (10) grows, hence the callable convertible is worth more. To illustrate, suppose the straight value of a bond (SBV in equation (9)) is $780, and the bond is callable following a 2-year call protection period. The conversion ratio (CR) is 20 and the firm's stock (S) is presently priced at $40 per share. The face value (F) is $1,000, thus the conversion price is $50 ($F$/CR = $1,000/$20). The adjusted conversion price (K in equation (10)) is the conversion price ($50) scaled by SBV/$F$ (= 0.78), or $39. Letting $\sigma = 30\%$ and $r = 6\%$, you can confirm from equation (11) that the convertible is worth about $861.60. If you increase call protection to 3 years, you will find that the bond will be worth about $932.30.

Recall that equation (11) is only an approximation. It is easy to solve, but it should be tested on a few callable convertibles to make sure it offers sufficient accuracy for its intended use.

Back to the Trees

In many cases, the structure of call and conversion provisions is more complex than the approximations can handle. For instance, some convertibles have soft call provisions which prohibit calling unless the firm's stock price has climbed above a specified trigger point. In these cases, we must either resort to the full solution of the partial differential equation (1), or we can construct trees. In this section, we will first illustrate convertible pricing from binomial stock price trees, then we will allow for *two* binomial processes — one for stock prices and one for interest rates.

A Binomial Stock Price Tree

Suppose the risk-free rate (r) is constant at 6% and we wish to evaluate a 3-year convertible bond. The underlying stock is priced now at $75 per share and the conversion ratio for the $1,000 face value, zero-coupon bond is 12. The bond is callable at "101" or $1,010, anytime. The appropriate discount rate (r^*) for a bond of similar risk is 15%, and the stock's volatility (σ) is 20%.

The first order of business is to grow a stock price tree and we will restrict our analysis to a simple binomial process.[23] At any node in the tree, the stock may move up by amount

$$u = e^{\sigma\sqrt{dt}}$$

or down by amount

$$d = e^{-\sigma\sqrt{dt}}$$

If we build an annual tree, $dt = 1$ and $u = e^{0.20} = 1.2214$, and $d = e^{-0.20} = 0.8187$. Hence if the stock (now priced at $75) moves up, it will

---

[23] The method we illustrate is described in K. Tsiveriotis and C. Fernandes, "Valuing Convertible Bonds with Credit Risk," *Journal of Fixed Income* (September 1998), and illustrated by J.C. Hull, *Options, Futures and Other Derivatives*, 4th Ed. (Upper Saddle River, NJ: Prentice Hall, 2000), pp. 646-649.

climb to uS = 1.2214 (75) = \$91.61. If it moves down, it will drop to dS = 0.8187(75) = \$61.40. If the price increases twice in a row it will then be uuS, if it rises one year then falls the next, it will be udS = S, and so on.

In Exhibit 8.1, the stock price tree is shown for the 3-year life of the bond. The top number at each node is the stock price. What is the probability that the price will move up? Move down? Reminiscent of our analysis in Chapter 3, if we pretend we are risk-neutral, we can infer these probabilities. Define k as e^{rdt}, the growth factor for the stock if we are risk-neutral. It can be shown that the probability of an upward move is

$$p = (k - d)/(u - d)$$

thus the probability of a downward move is $1 - p$.

Using r = 6%, we see that k = 1.0618. Inserting u = 1.2214 and d = 0.8187, we find that p = 0.6037, hence $1 - p$ = 0.3963. From inspection of the expression for p, it is clear that higher r implies a higher probability of an upward move.

Beneath the stock prices at the various nodes in year 3 in Exhibit 8.1 are the conversion values. For instance, at node G, the conversion value is $12 \times \$136.66 = \$1,639.92$, thus the second number at this node is \$1,639.92. Investors will clearly convert to stock at this node. But at node J, the conversion value is only $12 \times \$41.16$ = \$493.92, and investors will hold the convertible and collect the \$1,000 face value instead.

Now we begin to discount expected values, proceeding from year 3 to year 2, and so on. The probabilities for determining expected values, p = 0.6037 and $1 - p$ = 0.3963, are already established. The troublesome part is the choice of discount rates. The risk-free rate (r = 6%) is appropriate when the bond's value is due only to the equity component; for example, at node G, we will convert for sure. In a case such as that at node J, the bond's value is due only to the debt component, hence the risk-adjusted rate (r^* = 15%) is appropriate. The third line in each node contains the equity component, then the debt component. For example, at node H, the bond is converted and the equity part is the conversion value, \$1,099.32, while the debt part is zero.

Exhibit 8.1: Binomial Tree for Callable, Convertible, Zero-Coupon Bond

```
                                                         ┌──────────────┐
                                                       G │ 136.66       │
                                                         │ 1639.92      │
                                                         │ 1639.92/0    │
                                                         │ 1939.92      │
                                         ┌──────────────┐└──────────────┘
                                       D │ 111.89       │
                                         │ 1342.68      │
                                         │ 1342.68/0    │
                                         │ 1342.68      │
                         ┌──────────────┐└──────────────┘┌──────────────┐
                       B │ 91.61        │               H│ 91.61        │
                         │ 1099.32      │                │ 1099.32      │
                         │ 996.23/116.35│                │ 1099.32/0    │
                         │ 1099.32      │                │ 1099.32      │
         ┌──────────────┐└──────────────┘┌──────────────┐└──────────────┘
       A │ 75.00        │               E│ 75.00        │
         │ 900.00       │                │ 900.00       │
         │ 757.62/221.06│                │ 624.95/341.10│
         │ 978.68       │                │ 966.05       │
         └──────────────┘┌──────────────┐└──────────────┘┌──────────────┐
                       C │ 61.40        │               I│ 61.40        │
                         │ 736.80       │                │ 736.80       │
                         │ 355.31/470.83│                │ 0/1000.00    │
                         │ 826.14       │                │ 1000.00      │
                         └──────────────┘┌──────────────┐└──────────────┘
                                       F │ 50.27        │
                                         │ 603.24       │
                                         │ 0/860.71     │
                                         │ 860.71       │
                                         └──────────────┘┌──────────────┐
                                                       J │ 41.16        │
                                                         │ 493.92       │
                                                         │ 0/1000.0     │
                                                         │ 1000.00      │
                                                         └──────────────┘
```

Note: The values in each node are

stock price
conversion value
equity component/debt component
price of convertible bond

Let's begin discounting the year 3 cash flows to year 2, beginning at node D. In this case, the only two possible moves from D involve conversion, thus the value of the equity component is

$$EC = [0.6037(\$1,639.92) + 0.3963(\$1,099.32)]e^{-0.06} = \$1,342.68$$

The debt component (DC) of the value at node D is zero because neither of the two possible moves leads to a node with a debt component. The value of the convertible bond at this node is the sum of the two components, EC + DC = $1,324.68 + 0 = $1,324.68, the fourth line in the node. Remember that this bond is callable any-time for $1,010, hence the firm could call and force conversion at node D. But the value of the bond will still be the conversion value, $1,342.68, regardless of whether the firm calls, hence this will have no effect on the price of the bond today.

The equity part at node E is found by discounting the expected equity components (from nodes H and I) at the rate $r = 6\%$:

$$EC = [0.6037(\$1,099.32) + 0.3963(0)]e^{-0.06} = \$624.95$$

The debt component at this node is found likewise by discounting at $r^* = 15\%$:

$$DC = [0.6037(0) + 0.3963(\$1,000)]e^{-0.15} = \$341.10$$

Thus the bond at node E is valued at EC + DC = $624.95 + $341.10 = $966.05. The conversion value is only $900 (12 × $75), so it makes no sense to convert, and the value ($966.05) is below the call price ($1,010), so the issuer will not call.

If you discount the debt components at nodes I and J back to node F at $r^* = 15\%$, you should get DC = $860.71. You can see in Exhibit 8.1 that EC = 0, hence the value of the convertible at this node is $860.71.

Now move back to year 1 beginning at node B. The equity component is determined as

$$EC = [0.6037(\$1,342.68) + 0.3963(\$624.95)]e^{-0.06} = \$996.23$$

The debt component is

$$DC = [0.6037(0) + 0.3963(\$341.10)]e^{-0.15} = \$116.35$$

The sum of these components is EC + DC = $996.23 + $116.35 = $1,112.58. Notice that this exceeds the call price ($1,010), and is greater than the conversion value (12 × $91.61 = $1,099.32) at this node. If the issuer calls in this case, investors will face the choice of surrendering for $1,010 or converting for $1,099.32 — easy choice. If the issuer calls, the investors will convert and the bond will be worth $1,099.32, not $1,112.58. Hence this is the value on the last row in node B.

At node C, you will find that the equity part is \$355.31 and the debt component is \$470.83. Thus the value of the bond is the sum of these, or \$826.14. You can see that it will not be converted (conversion value = \$736.80), and it will not be called. Finally, we end up where we started, at node A. The equity component is worth

$$EC = [0.6037(\$1,099.32) + 0.3963(\$355.31)]e^{-0.06} = \$757.62$$

The debt component is worth

$$DC = [0.6037(\$116.35) + 0.3963(\$470.83)]e^{-0.15} = \$221.06$$

Thus this callable, convertible bond is worth EC + DC = \$757.62 + \$221.06 = \$978.68. If the bond were straight, noncallable, it would be worth $\$1,000e^{-0.15\times3} = \$637.63$, thus the conversion feature net of the call feature contributes \$341.05 to its value.

The binomial tree structure will accommodate a host of important refinements. For example, if this bond were call protected until year 2, or if the call price declined over time, the tree in Exhibit 8.1 could easily be modified. If there were a soft call protection clause that prohibited calling unless the stock price exceeded, say \$100, the issuer would not be able to call at node B, hence the bond would be worth more.[24]

A Quadranomial Tree

In Chapter 7, we grew and calibrated a binomial interest rate tree, and we just completed our analysis of a convertible bond using a binomial stock price tree. The latter suffers from the fact that interest rate uncertainty is suppressed. Hence an important source of uncertainty is left out of convertible analysis using a binomial stock price tree.

What if we could somehow merge the two tree structures, creating a small forest so to speak? This means that there will be four branching possibilities from each node: (1) stock up, rate up; (2) stock up, rate down; (3) stock down, rate up; or (4) stock down, rate down. You can see how our small, 2-tree forest will become remarkably dense after only a few time periods. Though the compu-

---

[24] Some very useful software products have become available for valuing various option-embedded securities. One that is easy to use is *fincadXL* designed for use in Microsoft Excel. Contact http://www.fincad.com, e-mail info@fincad.com.

tational complexity is substantial, such a tree structure correctly accounts for the two chief sources of uncertainty, stock and rate volatility. In other words, convertibles should be viewed as rainbow options: options with multiple sources of volatility.

Specialized software is available that constructs quadranomial or "quadro" trees in Microsoft Excel. For instance, $ConvB^{++}$ produced by SuperComputer Consulting, Inc., is friendly to users and will value convertible bonds and preferred stocks with call and put provisions using quadranomial trees. The software will also value warrants, callable warrants, and structured convertibles.[25] The latter include mandatory convertibles; that is, conversion is automatic rather than discretionary. We turn to such specialized convertibles now.

SPECIAL CONVERTIBLES

The bonds and preferred stocks we've examined in Chapter 7 and this chapter involve traditional provisions that allow them to be converted, called or put. While these features offer much flexibility to issuers, and they have characteristics that satisfy many investors' appetites, numerous refinements are possible which allow issuers to offer a wide variety of payoff and risk profiles. Since the 1980s, investment banks have been particularly creative in engineering securities with various option packages to meet the multifaceted demands of issuers and investors alike.

Convertible Bonds with Special Features

Suppose an issuer wishes to avoid periodic cash payments and is willing to offer a conversion feature. This sounds made to order for a convertible, zero-coupon bond. But investors recognize that if interest rates rise, and the underlying stock does not do well, these bonds will lose value dramatically. Now suppose the issuer includes a put provision whereby the investor may sell the issue back to the

---

[25] Super Computer Consulting, Inc., has a web site that describes $ConvB++$ (http://www.supercc.com).

firm at a stipulated price, establishing a floor on the value of the security. Merrill Lynch developed its popular *LYONS* to meet this need. These are Liquid Yield Option Notes and they are zero-coupon. They are convertible and typically have five years of hard call protection, and they are putable usually at 5-year intervals. You can see how these could be priced using a binomial or quadranomial tree structure, but specifying and solving the partial differential equation (1) would be very challenging.

An issuer may desire a cash payment scheme that changes over time. For instance, if the firm expects to have higher cash flow in the future, it may offer a *step-up* bond — the coupon rate will be adjusted upward at a predetermined date. If the stock has done well by this date, the firm may call and force conversion, thereby avoiding the higher coupon. On the other hand, a *step-down* bond may help motivate investors to convert earlier than they might otherwise. At a predetermined date, the coupon rate declines, hence the security is less attractive as a bond.

Firms in the United States frequently issue securities abroad. This allows them to forego the demanding registration process with the Securities and Exchange Commission (SEC) that is required for domestic public issues. There is a substantial market for *Eurodollar convertible bonds*, sold outside the United States but denominated in U.S. dollars. These may be, and often are, sold to U.S. investors following a 40-day seasoning period, and dollar-denominated principal and interest payments present no currency risk to these investors.

In the mid-1990s, Japanese banks, starved for capital due to prolonged stagnancy in the economy, were persuaded toward convertible bonds. Credit was tight, hence straight borrowing was unattractive, and the equity markets were beaten down. The Bank of Tokyo issued US$2 billion in convertible bonds with a special clause which allowed it to meet bank capital requirements.[26] The issue was redeemable for cash if its stock price at maturity was less than 50% of the conversion price at issuance. As economic conditions worsened, such *mandatory reset* convertibles became fairly common financing tools of Japanese banks.

---

[26] See C. McCoole, "Mandatory Convertible Reset Structures," *Handbook of Hybrid Instruments* (New York: John Wiley & Sons, Ltd., 2000).

These important developments serve to illustrate the creative uses of options in satisfying special financing needs. With state-of-the-art pricing technology available, such as binomial and quadranomial tree-growing software, we can now predict reliable values of these complex hybrid instruments.

Convertible Preferreds with Special Features

Traditionally, investors who desired high yield investments sought straight securities such as debentures or preferred stocks. Convertibles, on the other hand, have found their strongest appeal among investors who prefer capital gains potential over current income. By structuring convertible preferred stocks to provide high yield and limited upside potential, issuers can even better satisfy investors' demands.

DECS, PRIDES, and similar products were created for this purpose. DECS, or Dividend Enhanced Convertible Stocks, were created by Salomon Brothers, and PRIDES, or Preferred Redeemable Increased Dividends Equity Securities, were developed by Merrill Lynch. DECS, PRIDES, and related securities feature high yields, mandatory conversion at maturity, and conversion ratios which are adjusted at maturity so as to limit the upside potential.

The adjustment to limit upside potential sounds complicated, so let's attack it with an example. Suppose a PRIDE has a conversion ratio (CR) of 1 for common stock prices at or below $30 per share. Then in the range $30 to $40, the conversion ratio is adjusted so that the *conversion value* is constant at $30. For instance, if the common stock price is $36 at maturity, CR is automatically set to $30/36 = 0.8333$. This means the PRIDES are converted to 0.8333 common shares, hence conversion value is $30. If the common stock price exceeds $40, then CR begins to increase automatically. Payoffs at maturity (hence mandatory conversion) are shown in Exhibit 8.2 for these PRIDES. Investors receive higher dividends than on traditional convertibles, but they must sacrifice some equity participation in exchange.

This creative engineering approach has been cloned to the point where there are many members of the alphabet jungle. PRIDE-like instruments include TRACES and ACES (Goldman Sachs), MARCS (UBS Securities), PEPS (Morgan Stanley), YEELDS and

PIES (Lehman Brothers), SAILS (CS First Boston), TAPS (Smith Barney), and TIMES (Bear Stearns). Each of these represents slight variations on a very successful theme.

Another popular type of mandatory convertible preferred also provides a higher yield than traditional convertible preferred stocks, and it features an absolute upper limit on upside potential. The conversion ratio is typically 1 up to a specified stock price level, then it is automatically reset at maturity (when conversion is automatic) so that the investor receives a fixed dollar amount of common stock. Payoffs for a preferred equity redemption cumulative stock (PERCS) are shown in Exhibit 8.3 with a cap of $70. These and their quarterly dividend cousins (PERQS) are a product of Morgan Stanley. In this example, the conversion ratio is 1 for common stock prices at or below $70 at maturity. The ratio declines thereafter so that the conversion value is capped at $70. For instance, if the stock price increases to $90, the conversion ratio will be automatically reset to $70/90 = 0.778$, hence conversion value will be $70 ($0.778 \times \$90$).

As is the case with PRIDES and DECS, the limited payoff and high yield structure of PERCS has been cloned by various investment banks — for example, CHIPS (Bear Stearns), ELKS (Salomon), EYES and MCPDPS (Merrill Lynch), TARGETS (Sun Co.), and YES (Goldman Sachs).

Exhibit 8.2: PRIDE Values at Maturity

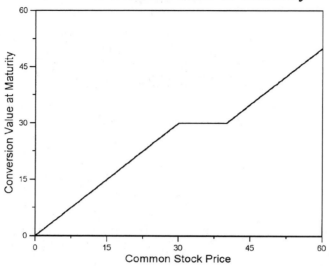

Exhibit 8.3: PERCS Values at Maturity

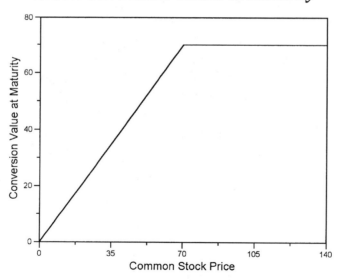

APPENDIX

APPROXIMATION OF THEORETICAL PRICE OF CALL-PROTECTED CONVERTIBLE PREFERRED STOCK

For a call-protected convertible preferred issue, we observed the following:

V = market value of firm's equity = \$2.5 billion

C = aggregate annual dividends on common stock plus dividends on the convertible preferred = \$0.0984 billion

c = aggregate annual dividends on convertible preferred issue = \$0.027 billion

   = $n/(N+n)$ = conversion factor = 0.0911

K = aggregate call price = \$0.3 billion

r = 10.4%

σ = 25.22%

First, assume the issue is callable *anytime*. Begin by calculating the functions $P(a, d)$ and $P(a+1, d)$ in equations (6) and (7) in the chapter. Determine $a = 2r/\sigma^2 = 2(0.104)/0.0636 = 3.27019$, and $d = C/rV = 0.0984/(0.104)(2.5) = 0.37846$. Thus $ad = 3.27019(0.37846) = 1.23764$.

The incomplete gamma function is:

$$\gamma(a, ad) = \gamma(3.27019, 1.23764) = \int_{0}^{1.23764} e^{-t}e^{(3.27019-1)}dt = 0.24475$$

The gamma function is then

$$\Gamma(a) = \Gamma(3.27019) = \int_{0}^{\infty} e^{-t}e^{(3.27019-1)}dt = 2.60233$$

Thus $P(a, ad) = 0.24475/2.60233 = 0.09405$. The incomplete gamma function ratio, $P(a, ad)$, may also be calculated directly in Microsoft Excel software. Next we determine $P(a+1, ad) =$

$P(4.27019, 1.23764) = 0.0256$ following the same steps as above, or by using the function in Excel.

Now we evaluate $F(V)$ in equation (5):

$$
\begin{aligned}
F(V) &= (C/r)[1 - P(a, ad) + P(a + 1, ad)/d] \\
&= (0.0984/0.104)[1 - 0.09405 + 0.0256/0.37846] \\
&= 0.92177
\end{aligned}
$$

To evaluate $F(K/\alpha)$, we replace V in equation (5) with $K/\alpha = 0.3/0.0911 = 3.29308$. Then $a = 2r/\sigma^2 = 3.27019$, and $d = C/(rk/\alpha) = 0.0984/(0.104(0.3)/0.0911) = 0.28732$. Thus $ad = 0.93959$, $P(a, ad) = 0.04742$, and $P(a + 1, ad) = 0.00996$. Thus,

$$F(K/\alpha) = (0.0984/0.104)[1 - 0.04742 + 0.00996/0.28732] = 0.93409$$

Because the issue is out-of-the-money, i.e., $\alpha V < K$, its value is given by equation (4):

$$f = \frac{[\alpha - (c/C)(\alpha/K)F(K/\alpha)]V + (c/C - \alpha)F(V)}{[1 - (\alpha/K)F(K/\alpha)]}$$

Inserting the parameters $\alpha = 0.0911$, $C = \$0.027$ billion, and so on, we determine $f = \$.282$ billion, the value of the convertible preferred issue assuming it is callable anytime. Suppose there are 7.5 million preferred shares outstanding. The theoretical price per share is then $\$37.60 = \text{PREF}_{ANY}$.

If the issue is *noncallable*, we first compare c and αC to see if it will be converted. If $c < \alpha C$, then $f = \alpha V =$ conversion value. In this case, $c > \alpha C$, hence

$$f = \alpha V + [c/C - \alpha]F(V)$$

Inserting the parameters $\alpha = 0.0911$, $V = \$2.5$ billion, and so on, we get $f = \$0.39659$ billion, or $\text{PREF}_{NEVER} = \$52.88$ per share assuming the issue is noncallable.

In fact, this issue is callable after a 5-year protection period ($T = 5$), hence we know the price should lie between $\$37.60$ (PREF_{ANY}) and $\$52.88$ (PREF_{NEVER}). To find out where, we apply the averaging procedure in equation (8):

$$\text{Call-protected convertible preferred} = (1 - e^{-rT})\text{PREF}_{NEVER} + e^{-rT}\text{PREF}_{ANY}$$
$$= (1 - e^{-0.104(5)})(52.88) + e^{-0.104(5)}(37.60) = \$43.80$$

The theoretical price is $43.80 based on the approximation of the solution to the partial differential equation (1) in the chapter. The parameters we used are for a convertible preferred issue sold by Anheuser-Busch in the early 1980s. At issuance, the issue had five years of call protection and the offer price was $44 per share. In most cases, the approximation gives a theoretical price that is within $0.25 of the actual market price.

QUESTIONS AND PROBLEMS

1. How do we determine whether a convertible security is "in the money" or "out of the money?" What should investors do when a firm calls an in-the-money convertible?

2. Suppose our firm is considering issuance of a convertible bond which may be converted in 5 years into 350,000 common shares. There are 2,500,000 shares outstanding currently, the firm's stock price is $39 per share, and the volatility of the return on equity is 40%. We will issue 17,500 convertible bonds each with face value of $1,000 due in 5 years. The risk-free rate is 6% and for simplicity we will ignore callability. If the same issue were nonconvertible, our investment bank advises that these bonds would probably sell for about $900 given the coupon rate and other provisions. Use equation (2) in the Chapter to estimate the value of the conversion feature. At what price should we expect to be able to issue the convertible bonds?

3. Now suppose the same firm is considering an alternate design of the convertible described in Question 2. The 5-year convertible will be callable at $1000 beginning in 3 years. Use the approximation in equations (10) and (11) in the Chapter to determine the theoretical value of the bond given that the conversion terms are the same as in Question 2.

4. Perhaps to help price a convertible, we wish to construct a binomial stock price tree, and the current price per common share is $48. The volatility of the stock's return is 35%, and we will build the tree with annual branching.

   a. Determine the downward move parameter (d) and the upward parameter (u) in the same manner we used to construct the tree in Exhibit 8.1.

   b. If the risk-free rate is 6%, what is the probability of an upward move? A downward move?

c. What are the two possible values of the stock price at the end of the first year?

d. Use the tree you've now constructed to answer this question. The conversion ratio for a 1-year convertible bond is 25 and the face value is $1,000. What are the two possible prices of the bond at maturity?

e. Remember that the risk-free rate is 6% and suppose the yield on bonds of similar risk to our convertible is around 12%. Estimate the value today of the bond.

5. Describe the following.

a. LYONS (liquid yield option notes).

b. DECS (dividend enhanced convertible stocks).

c. PRIDES (preferred redeemable increased dividends equity securities).

d. Step-up bond.

e. Mandatory reset convertible.

Chapter 9

Capital Investment Decisions

Most of our discussion so far in this book has concentrated on options on *financial* assets such as stocks, bonds, and futures contracts. Financial assets are themselves claims on *real* assets, those assets that are used in production of goods and services. For instance, common stock is a financial asset and is a claim on assets of a firm. An option on a common stock is a financial option because it signifies a claim on a financial asset — even though the stock itself is a claim on real assets. In some cases we have seen that the connection between financial and real assets is even less direct. For example, an option on a cotton futures contract is a claim (the option) on a claim (the futures contract) on a real asset (cotton).

In this chapter, we set the stage for analyzing and valuing options on real assets *directly*. Often these options are specified in formal contracts much as financial options are. For example, Foss Maritime, a marine transportation firm in Seattle, recently exercised an option with a shipyard for construction of a new and powerful tugboat.[1] But most often options on real assets arise due to characteristics and attributes of the assets as well as the economic setting. As we will see in Chapter 11, for example, ownership of property may afford a firm the latitude of expansion at a later date, hence the property has an embedded option.

Stewart Myers, a distinguished scholar and MIT professor, has coined the term *real options* to signify options on real assets, regardless of whether they are codified in formal contracts or they exist merely by virtue of the nature of the assets. As we will see in this chapter, the value of such options lies in the *flexibility* they offer to decision makers. We'll also see that familiar decision tools such as net present value (NPV) often do not account for real option

---

[1] The story is in the "Towing Industry" section of *Professional Mariner* (April-May 2001), pp. 44, 45.

values, at least in the way these tools are illustrated in basic textbooks. Conceptually this is easily remedied, although implementation can be challenging.

MANAGERIAL FLEXIBILITY

Suppose your firm can commence production of an electronic navigation device, a GPS (global positioning system) receiver, and the net present value of the cash flows expected from this project is $75 million. This amount is determined in the standard way, i.e., by forecasting after-tax cash flows over the expected lifetime of the investment, determining a risk-adjusted discount rate appropriate for such a venture, and discounting the cash flows to the present.

Suppose a technological improvement may develop in the next couple of years, and it promises to improve the accuracy of GPS. In anticipation you could modify the GPS now so that it could be retrofitted with the new technology when (and if) it is successful. The modification in tooling and materials results in a NPV of the decision to produce the GPS of $68 million. This amount is estimated by assuming a probability for the success of the enhancement, then multiplying by the additional cash flows generated in the event of success to form the expected marginal cash flows. These are discounted to the present and the additional installation costs are subtracted to adjust the NPV of the project, $68 million.

If your analysis begins and ends with straightforward comparison of NPVs, you will choose to produce the GPS without the features needed to retrofit the new technology ($68 million versus $75 million). It appears that utmost care is being taken in the analysis to make the important adjustments as accurately as possible. But a subtle and potentially very important oversight has been committed. If you haven't spotted it yet, consider another example. Suppose your firm could produce a solar-powered car. Investment in machinery, land, and other facilities needed for production will cost about $850 million. If sales are as forecast by the marketing staff, the resulting after-tax cash flows will have a present value of about $840 million, hence NPV is −$10 million.

These two examples have something in common. The cash flow forecasts for the GPS and the solar-powered car are conditioned on what is known at the beginning of the investment, and the NPVs calculated from these are thus conditional on what we know now. If managers were passive and could not intervene during the life of a project to alter its cash flows, then the traditional NPV rule would be fine. Sometimes we are passive. For example, suppose you buy a straight bond issued by a corporation. You forecast cash flows (coupon payments and principal), discount to the present and compare with the selling price. This is a legitimate application of traditional NPV analysis. But for many capital investment projects, opportunities may arise later that enable an active decision-maker to change course.

In the solar-powered car example, you could almost surely scrap the project after a few years, sell the land, and salvage some of the machinery. The option to *abandon* the project has been overlooked. The NPV analysis was implicitly conditioned on investing in the plant and facilities and keeping them throughout the forecast life of the project.

The GPS project has an option to *expand* in the event the technology to merit the enhancement is developed successfully. But didn't we take that into account when we assessed the probability of success?

Not quite. Suppose you are evaluating a call option on a stock currently priced at $60 per share, and the call has an exercise price of $70. You think there's a 50-50 chance of the stock rising to $90 or dropping to $40 per share, hence the expected future price of the stock is $0.5(90) + 0.5(40) = \$65$. Given the $70 exercise price, one might conclude that the expected cash flow is negative ($65 − $70 = −$5), hence the option is worthless. But you know this would be wrong because it ignores your right to decide whether to exercise. In this case, you will exercise only if the price rises to $90, in which case your cash flow would be $20. If the price declines to $40, you will not exercise. Thus the correct way to assess the expected cash flow, hence the value of the option, is to determine the probability-weighted future payoffs assuming that you will make the right decision (i.e., $0.5(20) + 0.5(0) = \$10$).

The call is worth the present value of $10 assuming we treat it correctly as an *option*. It would be worth the present value of –$5 only if we viewed it as an *obligation* — exercise no matter what the payoff. The difference between these two values can be interpreted as the "value of flexibility."

Now read the first paragraph of this section again and see where we missed the value of the option. The extra cost of modifying now represents an investment in the *right* to retrofit the GPS receivers if the technology comes through. The expected contribution to NPV may well be negative based on the probabilities we use today, but they do not take into account our option and rational exercise of it. If the technological development does not come through later, we will not incur the added costs of production associated with the modification.

IS NPV WRONG?

Short answer: No, but like any other model, the traditional version works reliably only to the extent that its underlying assumptions hold. Many capital investments are partially *reversible*, meaning if cash flows deteriorate, we can abandon or cut back and recover some capital. Thus, many projects have implicit puts. And many projects can be expanded if future cash flows are sufficient to merit incremental investment, hence an implicit call exists when the projects are undertaken. To the extent these kinds of options render an investment more valuable, their values should be incorporated in the decision analysis.

Here's a slightly more formal characterization. The cash flow series forecast used in the familiar NPV model contains forecasts *conditioned* on accepting the proposal now (at time $t = 0$) and seeing it through as planned. In essence, for a risky project you spend a given amount now (initial outlay) in exchange for a series of (probability) distributions of cash flows. The means of those distributions, i.e., the expected cash flows, are discounted to the present to determine NPV. This works fine for projects that present one decision point, or more precisely, one condition, and this is how we initially evaluated the GPS and solar-car projects. But conditions may change for many capital investments, and you as decision-maker may be able to switch to a new probability distribution given certain conditions. In such a case, use of NPV analysis as it is often presented may lead to the wrong decision.

To make things right, you should develop cash flow forecasts conditioned not only on undertaking the project initially, but also conditioned on making decisions that affect the forecasts as new developments arise. We're not saying this is easy. It takes a lot of thoughtful, careful analysis. And your estimates often will be so subjective you may think the added work is a pointless exercise. But this is decision-making under uncertainty, up close and personal. Consider the alternative of simply ignoring the options. This in effect says the options are worth zero, a value you know to be wrong.

We know that NPV is interpreted as the amount by which a project's value in present dollars exceeds its cost. Think of this as the maximum amount you would pay above and beyond the initial cost to undertake the investment. Now consider how much more you would pay for features that offer flexibility in the future as circumstances change and develop. This suggests adding the present value of options inherent in the investment to the traditional NPV measure, thus the familiar model doesn't need much modification.

Some economists have begun referring to the traditional or passive NPV of a project as the *neoclassical* NPV.[2] We'll follow suit and denote NPV* as the net present value of a project assuming complete passivity to make sure this value is option free. Thus today ($t = 0$) we will proceed as if we will commit to the project throughout its duration, accepting future cash flows, for better or worse, without intervention. By stripping NPV* of optionality we may then add the values of all options without double counting.

Thus our new measure of NPV is the sum of NPV* and the present values of all real options associated with the investment. One might call this the "postmodern" NPV. Whatever we call it, it represents a legitimate value for making capital investment decisions. Thus for a single proposal, where the decision is accept or

---

[2] See, for example, A. Dixit and R. Pindyck, *Investment Under Uncertainty* (Princeton, NJ: Princeton University Press, 1994).

reject, we compare our "postmodern" NPV (hereafter simply NPV) with zero. And for choosing among alternative proposals we select the set of projects which maximize total NPV. In other words, the NPV rule is implemented exactly as we always have, but now we take correctly into account all of the value generated by capital projects including their optionality.

REAL OPTIONS COME IN FLAVORS

Authors of some excellent books focusing exclusively on real options offer various categorizations of these options. For instance, Amram and Kulatilaka discuss waiting-to-invest, growth, flexibility, exit, and learning options.[3] Learning options apply to investing in stages contingent on the outcome of a given stage. Copeland and Antikarov arrange their presentation around deferral options, options to abandon or scale back, options to expand or extend, switching options which allow managers to switch between modes of operation, compound options which represent options on options such as staged investments, and rainbow options.[4] The latter are distinguished by more than one fundamental source of uncertainty.

The taxonomy we adopt is a little more parsimonious. We'll discuss *timing* options (waiting-to-invest or deferral options) in Chapter 10. In Chapter 11, we examine *expansion* options (includes growth and extension options), and *scale reduction* options, where *abandonment* is the pathological case (exit options). Any of these options may be compound (options on options), and they may be of the rainbow variety (multiple sources of uncertainty).

Timing Options

In introductory courses in finance we learn an important decision rule regarding acceptance or rejection of capital investment projects. Accept the project if its NPV is positive — this means the

---

[3] M. Amram and N. Kulatilaka, *Real Options* (Boston, MA: Harvard Business School Press, 1999).

[4] T. Copeland and V. Antikarov, *Real Options – A Practitioner's Guide* (New York: TEXERE, 2001).

asset is essentially worth more than it costs in present value terms. This is equivalent to the project's (internal) rate of return exceeding the cost of capital. And if you search through an introductory corporate finance textbook you may find a third decision rule based on discounted cash flows (DCF), the present value index (PVI), the present value of the project's cash flows divided by the initial outlay. Thus if the PVI exceeds one the project is acceptable.

But there are times when positive NPV, hence an internal rate of return in excess of the cost of capital, hence a PVI greater than one, does *not* indicate acceptance, at least not immediately. It may be that if we wait to invest, the project may be more valuable even in today's dollars. And even if a project has *negative* NPV today, by waiting we may find that it ultimately is acceptable.

Here's a typical example. Suppose your firm owns drilling rights to an oil reserve and the price of crude is expected to grow over the next several months. You could commence extraction now and, assuming the revenue from sale of the oil exceeds the extraction costs, we have positive NPV. But if the price of crude is expected to grow significantly, it may be that NPV in today's terms will be even higher if we wait. In the meantime we can deploy our capital elsewhere.

We'll see in the next chapter that, while deferring a positive NPV investment has a cost, it may also have benefits, and if we can somehow match the marginal costs with the marginal benefits we can maximize NPV. And we'll see that the oft-neglected PVI measure has a natural role to play in the timing decision.

Here's another example. Suppose we plan to invest in an assembly process for laptop computers, and the prices of microprocessors are highly uncertain. If we are in a position to defer the investment, we may discover that at least some of the uncertainty is resolved. Thus another source of benefits to waiting is uncertainty resolution. By waiting to invest we may find that the NPV of the venture in today's terms is higher than the project's NPV if undertaken immediately.

In the next chapter we will see that, once again, PVI has a natural role to play in the timing decision when a key benefit of waiting is uncertainty resolution. When all is said and done we will recognize that the familiar decision rules — accept if NPV is positive, if the rate of return exceeds the cost of capital, and if PVI exceeds one, often do not lead to the right investment decision when we have the luxury of waiting to execute.

Scale Expansion Options

We shall see in Chapter 11 that an option to expand or grow is logically viewed as a call option. In some industries such as pharmaceuticals and oil, the real option value of many projects will dramatically exceed the traditional measure of value, NPV*. Indeed, NPV* will often be negative hence the only reason for entertaining such projects is due to their optionality. This helps explain why many firms in such industries employ real options analysis in their capital investment decision-making.

To illustrate expansion options, suppose our firm plans to develop and test a new method for removing arsenic from drinking water. The development will require a significant cash outlay initially, then it will require additional outlays for testing for, say, three years. Clearly this is a negative NPV* proposal. At the end of year 3, if the new purification method works and seems economically viable, for an additional outlay we can commence production and sale of the apparatus needed for the method on a commercial scale.

Based on what we know today, suppose our projected sales revenues and costs in the commercial phase are such that the NPV* of that phase is close to zero based on its projected 6-year life. If we splice together the two time lines, the three years for development and testing, and the additional six years for commercial production, then discount all the *currently projected* cash flows to the present, we will end up with negative NPV*. This suggests that the full project, including testing, development and commercial production, should not be undertaken.

As we will see later in this chapter, this scenario characterizes most research and development (R&D) ventures, thus it is tough to justify these on a standard discounted cash flow (DCF) basis. But suppose we view the negative NPV* of the development and testing phase as the price of a *call option*. The call option is the flexibility of producing the apparatus on a commercial scale, and without the development and testing phase, the commercial project will be impossible. The "exercise price" in the call is the outlay required in year 3 to proceed with commercial production. The "expiration date" for the call option is about three years.

The "underlying" is the value assessed at the end of year 3 of the *then-projected* cash flows over the 6-year life of the commercial stage. Thus, at the end of year 3 we will assess the prospects for commercial production, discount projected cash flows to that year, then compare the value with the "exercise price," the outlay needed for commercial production at the end of year 3. The value *today* of the "underlying" is our best estimate based on what we project given what we know *now*. This is the value that could be used as the "stock price" in the call option model.

Remember that we had supposed that the expected NPV* of the commercial project as of year 3 would be close to zero, thus discounting the expected 6-year cash flow stream back to the current period will reduce the value of the cash flows even further below the outlay required for commercial production. Thus the call option is currently *out of the money*. However, while its *intrinsic value* is zero, the option will have value as long as there is uncertainty about the cash flows to be generated in the commercial phase. Of course, this is true of financial options and the analogy to real options is straightforward. Thus, if we are fairly confident today of our projected cash flows that would be generated in the commercial phase, we can dismiss the entire project without further analysis. But uncertainty spells opportunity, and to the extent that the cash flows from the commercial phase may substantially exceed our *current* projections, the value of the call may be sufficient to outweigh the negative NPV* of the development and testing phase. That is, even though the project has little value based on what we know *now*, the option component *may* be worth a great deal in three years' time.

Scale Reduction Options

Often capital assets come in sizes or scales which may not fit changing circumstances perfectly. We will call this the "Goldilocks" problem — some assets are too small, some are too large, and only rarely are they just right. Suppose Maritrans Corporation invests in an oceangoing oil barge, one that is very large and therefore requires a large tug with high horsepower. Based on current projections there will sufficient demand for oil transportation in the Gulf of Mexico and the Atlantic to merit the investment, but suppose the investment has marginal NPV*, possibly negative, based on current projections.

Remember that the projections used to calculate NPV* are conditioned on what we know now, and on pursuing the investment throughout its economically useful life. But suppose that in the next few years, if demand for oil transportation in the Gulf of Mexico or the Atlantic declines, that the barge can be sold perhaps to a barge company on the West Coast or elsewhere.

The flexibility to sell the barge in the event demand, hence revenue, is insufficient to merit continuation is an American-style *put option*. Thus the ability to abandon a capital project represents a put option and the added flexibility should add value to the proposal. The value (put option) should be high to the extent future demand is uncertain and the possible selling price of the barge remains high. The selling price is the "exercise price" in the put option, thus the value of the option will decline as the selling price falls over time as the barge depreciates.

The "underlying" is the value of the cash flows remaining in the life of the barge which would be generated if it continued in service. This is what is given up if the option is "exercised" (i.e., the barge is sold at some time in the future). The conditions of exercise are identical to those of a financial put — if the value of the underlying falls below the exercise price, one should exercise. To the extent the flexibility to abandon has value, this amount is added to NPV* to form the NPV measure that is useful for making such decisions.

Of course, it is not necessary to abandon an asset entirely in order to meet shrinking demand. It is often possible to scale back an investment, and this flexibility is also a put option. For instance, if demand for the output of an assembly plant falls we may reduce the number of shifts. The "underlying" in this case would be the marginal cash flows produced by operating with the third shift, and the "exercise price" would be the present value of the savings generated by operating on a reduced scale.

Why Real Options Analysis is Important

It may be easy for some to dismiss real options as merely the latest academic novelty, although serious scholars and practitioners seem convinced that real options analysis is a valuable way of thinking, and that it helps quantify strategic plans. The traditional measure of investment value, NPV*, has long been held in low esteem by many decision makers precisely because it ignores the value of flexibility. With no alternative, these decision makers have had to make do with "seat-of-the-pants" judgments and heuristic devices. Real options analysis offers a way to fix the NPV rule so that such decisions may be made with more objectivity.

Executives in the pharmaceutical industry are embracing real options analysis and it is easy to see why.[5] Only a handful of chemical compounds initially tested are found to be pharmacologically active; that is, they can induce the necessary reactions in the human body to remedy a particular ailment. Of the handful that are found to be pharmacologically active, only about one in 15 survives the development process to become a drug that is ultimately marketed and distributed. Thus the probability of eventual success that is assessed in the initial stage is very low.

The development process in the U.S. takes between 12 and 15 years typically, and outlays in the hundreds of millions of dollars are required to develop each drug. The process involves pre-clinical testing in laboratory animals, then testing on healthy humans to detect unacceptable side effects, then testing on human subjects who have the target ailment — all under the watchful eye of the U.S. Food and Drug Administration (FDA).

When NPV* (NPV without optionality) is calculated based on expected cash flows it very likely will be negative given the low probability of a drug making it through the process. But as we've seen earlier in this chapter, this implicitly assumes that a drug will be taken through all of the development process lasting from 12 to 15 years. This clearly is not the case since the firm will not continue development of a drug that fails any of the test phases along the

---

[5] Judy Lewent, Chief Financial Officer of Merck and Company, is a leading proponent of real options analysis in this industry. For an illuminating interview, see Nancy Nichols, "Scientific Management at Merck," *Harvard Business Review* (January-February 1994), pp. 89-99.

way. Thus investment in, say pre-clinical trials, for example, should be viewed as the purchase of an option to proceed to human testing and so on. We should view the development process as a series of options on options — compound options — each of which will be exercised only if the preceding phase is successful.

Any industry that conducts research and development (R&D) on a significant scale must confront the inherent limitations of NPV*. In the mid-1980s General Electric's R&D group toyed with the idea of using *antimatter* for noninvasive medical diagnosis. The idea was to inject positively charged electrons (called positrons) into the human body. A positron is the antiparticle for an ordinary electron and when a sub-atomic particle and its antiparticle counterpart come in contact with one another they annihilate. They disappear, or at least they cease to exist as matter. Where does the matter go? It turns almost immediately into energy (in the form of photons). This energy can be detected and it was thought that it could be used to cast an image of human tissue so that a technician could "see" inside the body without the need for surgery. In a sense the body could be photographed from inside out, a little like x-ray diagnosis, only better. This technology might be able to reveal metabolic functions rather than a snapshot of anatomy, hence its potential applications were very appealing.

This may sound like science fiction, and one can imagine that such a project was characterized by very large, negative NPV*. But GE's management proceeded despite the unpromising financial outlook. The project succeeded through the development stage and eventually went into commercial production as the familiar PET Scan. PET is short for positron emission tomography whereby a patient is administered a substance such as glucose containing positron emitting radioactive isotopes. PET is now used in diagnosing and monitoring cancer as well as diseases of the heart, lungs, and brain; the technology has been advanced and its availability is growing. This valuable medical diagnostic device might not have been developed if GE's management had adhered to traditional DCF analysis.[6]

---

[6] An excellent critique of traditional DCF analysis from an industry leader is by Terrence Faulkner, "Applying 'Options Thinking' to R&D Valuation," *Research and Technology Management* (May-June 1996), pp. 50-56.

A CAUTIONARY NOTE BEFORE WE GO FURTHER

Before we end this introductory chapter on real options, it may be helpful to anticipate one of the major drawbacks of this type of analysis. The parameters for analyzing, employing, and valuing *financial* options are, for the most part, unambiguous. Many of the parameters of these options such as the expiration date and exercise price are clearly defined in contracts. The nature of the underlying is unambiguous and its current value is often observable in the financial markets. We may disagree about the appropriate volatility parameter, which must be estimated, but for the most part, financial options are clearly defined and their parameters are relatively precise.

In the case of real options that are not specified in contracts, and most are not, virtually *every* parameter is the result of a forecast, an estimate, or merely a guess. For instance, to value an abandonment option accurately we must know the exercise price — the future selling price of the capital asset. Unlike a *financial* put option, there is no counterparty in this case who bears the obligation to buy the asset from us at a specified price, thus we must somehow estimate the selling price of the asset now in the event we abandon it in the future — often a daunting task.

In the next few chapters, we will illustrate a couple of devices that may be useful in dealing with the inevitable uncertainty about the parameter values in real options analysis. One device involves working backward from the decision to a particular parameter. For example, in the abandonment case, we may be able to determine the minimum selling price necessary to give sufficient value to the option, hence total NPV, so that we can decide among alternatives. Thus instead of requiring a point estimate of the possible selling price, we can pose the question as: How low must the selling price be to cause the NPV of the proposal to fall below the NPV of an alternative?

Another useful device is *sensitivity analysis*. Once we have developed the NPV of a proposal — that is, the NPV including relevant option features — we may then repeat the computations with different (and plausible) parameter values to see whether alternative values would change the decision. Notice that the question is whether they will change the *decision*, not change the *NPV*. We know that different values will alter NPV but the task is to identify those that are crucial to the decision.

For instance, we may find that for a given level of uncertainty the NPV in our barge example is positive for most plausible values of the selling price (the "exercise price") in the event we abandon. But for lower levels of uncertainty, we may discover that the sign of NPV becomes very sensitive to the selling price. On the other hand, we may find that the sign of NPV is relatively robust to the choice of the interest rate parameter. The point is that sensitivity analysis allows us to identify pivotal parameters which may then be investigated further.

As we go about the business of valuing real options, it may be helpful to be reminded of Voltaire's advice, *Le mieux est l'ennemi du bien* — the best is the enemy of the good. This dated message (1764) has been rediscovered in more modern times. In World War II, General Patton was known for sharing the same advice with his subordinate commanders, although perhaps in less moderate language. His meaning was that while a brilliant staff invests time and resources in developing a *perfect* and foolproof battle plan, the enemy may inflict defeat by relying simply on a *good* plan. In other words, real options analysis is hardly an arena for an obsession with perfection. Precision can only be pushed so far.

QUESTIONS

1. "Accept all positive NPV investments." This rule is analogous to, "Accept proposals with IRRs that exceed the cost of capital," as well as, "Undertake all projects with PVIs greater than 1.0." Evaluate these rules in light of what you've seen in this Chapter.

2. Compare the process of analyzing financial options with that for real options. Focus on the aspects of real options analysis which make it more complex than financial options analysis.

3. What is sensitivity analysis? How is it used in valuing real options?

4. Suppose a firm has the flexibility to switch modes of production from one which requires natural gas as a fuel to one which requires coal. Is this a call option, or is it a put? Explain.

5. What would be an example of a capital project which gives the firm the flexibility to invest later in another flexible investment? For instance, a call option might be exercised for another call option.

Chapter 10

Timing Options

Some financial managers and academicians evidently hold divergent views of appropriate discount rates to be used in capital investment decisions, and even the appropriate tools for reaching those decisions. For instance, managers may require a project's projected rate of return to exceed a "hurdle rate" often set above the cost of capital appropriate for project risk. We will see in this chapter that it may be that academicians have been "less correct" about the prescriptions than practitioners.[1] We will see that the best decision may not follow the familiar rules: accept a project if its internal rate of return (IRR) exceeds the cost of capital, or if its net present value (NPV) exceeds zero.

The reason is that, while a project may be economically profitable today, it may be even more profitable if undertaken later. This could be because revenues are expected to grow, or because costs are projected to decline, or perhaps because risk is expected to diminish. If the firm's circumstances permit it to defer execution of a project, such changes in the environment may make waiting worthwhile. In light of such flexibility and possible benefits of waiting, the decision rules must be amended. Practicing financial managers may have suspected this all along.

There are costs associated with waiting too. For instance, revenues may be expected to decline due to increased competition. And of course, the longer we delay a profitable investment, the lower will be its value in present terms due to the time value of money. What this means is that there may be an optimal point at which to invest. We will develop special decision rules explicitly for

---

[1] Recently, we have seen some reconciliation. Academicians are coming to realize that practitioners' rules of thumb may be closer to optimal behavior than traditional prescriptions that ignore the value of flexibility. For a superb discussion, see Robert L. McDonald, "Real Options and Rules of Thumb in Capital Budgeting," *Project Flexibility, Agency, and Competition*, Michael J. Brennan and Lenos Trigeorgis (eds.) (New York: Oxford University Press, 2000).

determining the optimal point at which investment is triggered, and we will uncover a role of a sometimes overlooked decision tool, the profitability index (or present value index (PVI)), in establishing trigger points.

BENEFITS AND COSTS OF WAITING

In this section, we will illustrate the central ideas behind the timing decision using some highly simplified examples. You will see how delaying an investment may be beneficial due to eventual resolution of uncertainty about project value. Next, you will see that the firm's opportunity cost of capital represents a cost of waiting.

We'll Know More Later

Suppose we can invest $3.2 million in a plant today that will generate a perpetuity of either $400,000 or $200,000 per year, with equal probability. The expected value today of the perpetual cash flow is 0.5(400,000) + 0.5(200,000) = $300,000 and the cost of capital is 8%. The expected NPV conditional on investing now is:

$$E(NPV \mid now) = 300,000/0.08 - 3,200,000 = \$550,000$$

This is a clear signal that we should proceed, and if we had no other choice, that's what we would do. But suppose it is feasible for us to defer for one year, then see how things are shaping up — that is, wait and resolve some uncertainty. Let's say by then we will know whether demand for our product is high ($400,000 cash flow) or low ($200,000). If it turns out that cash flow is high ($400,000), we can then jump in (at $t = 1$) and capture positive NPV even greater than $550,000. If it turns out that demand is low ($200,000 cash flow), we'll apply our capital elsewhere because, were we to invest at this point, NPV would be $200,000/0.08 - $3,200,000 = -$700,000. So we have a clear benefit of waiting, namely the resolution of uncertainty that allows us to avoid negative NPV. We also have a cost of waiting in that, if demand turns out to be high, we have jumped in a little late.

What should we do? If we plan on deferring investment, our opportunity today has expected NPV given by:

$$E(NPV \mid defer) = 0.5[(400,000/0.08 - 3,200,000)/1.08] + 0.5(0)$$
$$= \$833,333$$

Expected NPV if we invest now is \$550,000, and expected NPV assessed now, but based on waiting a year, is \$833,333, thus the decision is clear. The project is worth an additional \$283,333 (\$833,333 − 550,000) because we have the flexibility to defer. The net present value (NPV*) ignoring optionality (\$550,000) plus the value of the timing option (\$283,333) represents the NPV appropriate for decision-making.

In this case, the benefit of waiting is due to reduction in uncertainty about the level of cash flows, and you can easily imagine similar stories illustrating resolution of uncertainty about interest rates, factor costs, tax rates, and so on — anything that affects project value.

Delaying Comes with a Cost

Suppose Wal-Mart owns land near an urban area where population and demand for retail shopping are growing. Management of Wal-Mart may recognize a benefit of waiting a while longer to construct a store, long enough for population growth to merit investment. But the longer Wal-Mart defers, the more likely K-Mart will build in the same area, thus seizing the first mover advantage. Increased threat of competition is clearly a cost of waiting in this case.

Even in the absence of competitive pressures, there is a cost of waiting. The longer we defer a positive NPV investment, the lower its present value. To pinpoint the cost of waiting, let's modify our numerical example. Suppose the initial outlay is \$3.2 million and the cost of capital is 8%, the same as before. Now we'll say the investment will generate either \$500,000 or \$300,000 in perpetuity, with equal probability assessed now. In a year, we will know which level of cash flows to expect. Should we wait?

The expected NPV conditioned on commencing the investment now is

$$E(NPV \mid now) = \frac{0.5(500,000) + 0.5(300,000)}{0.08} - 3,200,000 = \$1,800,000$$

If we are in a position to defer for a year, and it turns out that perpetual cash flow then promises to be $500,000, NPV at that time (denoted by NPV_1) will be $3.05 million ($500,000/0.08 − $3,200,000). If we defer for a year and cash flow turns out to be only $300,000, NPV_1 will be $550,000 ($300,000/0.08 − $3,200,000). We will enjoy positive NPV in either outcome.

Today, the expected NPV is based on the probability of 0.5 assigned to each possibility, thus $E(NPV_1)$ = 0.5($3.05 million) + 0.5($550,000) = $1.8 million. In today's dollars, this is worth $1.8 million/1.08 = $1.667 million.

In this example, there is no benefit to waiting even though we have dramatic resolution of uncertainty. The reason is that the change in uncertainty will not alter our decision, hence it offers no value. This allows us to isolate the *cost* of waiting which is $133,333 ($1.8 million − $1.667 million). This is the amount we sacrifice by deferring the opportunity, and the cost accrues at 8%, the cost of capital ($1.8 million is 8% more than $1.667 million).

What Factors Affect Benefits and Costs of Waiting?

Let's return to our first example where the expected perpetual cash flow is $300,000 per year, the outlay is $3.2 million, and the cost of capital is 8%. But now suppose the expected $300,000 annual cash flow is based on two equally likely outcomes, $450,000 or $150,000. In the first example, the possibilities were $400,000 or $200,000, thus the current example features greater uncertainty.

If we invest now, NPV is $550,000, the same as in the first example. If we wait a year and annual cash flow promises then to be $150,000, we will reject the investment. In that case, NPV_1 would be −$1.325 million ($150,000/0.08 − $3.2 million). If the cash flow turns out to be $450,000, on the other hand, we will capture positive NPV_1 of $2.425 million ($450,000/0.08 − $3.2 million). Thus, based on what we know now, expected NPV_1 is 0.5(0) + 0.5($2.425 million) = $1,212,500, and the present value of this opportunity is $1,122,685 ($1,212,500/1.08).

The value of the option to defer is the amount by which $E(NPV \mid defer)$, or $1,122,685, exceeds $E(NPV \mid now)$ or $550,000. Thus the option is worth $572,685. Recall that in the first example, the timing option was worth only $283,333, thus the added uncertainty makes the option to defer even more valuable.

This suggests that as a rule, firms tend to defer investment during uncertain times. This hardly comes as a surprise, but now you recognize that a rational explanation for it can be couched in the language of options. Increased uncertainty increases the value of options in general and the option to delay in particular.

What might increase the *cost* of waiting relative to the benefit? In general, any change that makes expected NPV higher now will increase the opportunity cost of waiting. To illustrate, suppose the cost of the investment is only $2.8 million instead of $3.2 million. Clearly E(NPV | now) and E(NPV | defer) will be higher, but the gap will be narrower. If you work this out assuming equal probabilities of cash flows of $200,000 and $400,000, and an 8% discount rate, you'll find E(NPV | now) = $950,000 (it was $550,000). And E(NPV | defer) = $1,018,519 (it was $833,333). In the first case, with investment outlay (I) of $3.2 million, the timing option adds $833,333 − $550,000 = $283,333 to NPV. In the second case (I = $2.8 million), it adds only $68,519. It still pays to wait in this case, but the benefit of waiting is nearly offset by its cost, due to delaying the start of a profitable investment.

If this is clear so far, you should expect a reduction in expected cash flow to decrease the cost of waiting. To illustrate, let I = $3.2 million, and let cash flows be either $400,000 or $180,000 with equal probabilities. This means E(NPV | now) = $290,000/ 0.08 − $3,200,000 = $425,000, a little lower than before because expected cash flow is now only $290,000 instead of $300,000. If you work it out, you'll find that E(NPV | defer) = $833,333, thus the option to defer is even more valuable than before (i.e., $833,333 − $425,000 = $408,333). It was worth $283,333 when expected cash flow was $300,000.

This reasoning may help explain some aspects of aggregate investment as it relates to governmental policies. For instance, suppose the U.S. government reinstates an investment tax credit, effectively reducing the investment outlay (I) for capital projects. You should see now that the option to defer is then less valuable, hence more current investment should result. Thus the tax credit has a double effect — it increases profitability thereby stimulating investment, and it makes immediate investment more lucrative. Conversely, an increase in the corporate tax rate drives down expected cash flow, thus reducing the cost of waiting. The result? Lower current investment.

OPTIMAL TIMING

The examples we've seen so far in this chapter illustrate whether we should invest now or wait until a specified period of time has passed. It will be clear in this section that, under certain conditions, we can say at what point we should invest in order to maximize NPV. The result arises from classical microeconomics — choose the starting time that equates *marginal costs* and *marginal benefits* of waiting.

Negligible Uncertainty

For the moment, we shall assume that uncertainty about the value of cash flows is negligible. This will represent one of those rare cases where an option may have value even under certainty about the future. To illustrate, suppose we own land sufficient to build a department store in an area with a growing population. If we build a store with a 10-year expected life today, its value may be less than the value today of building essentially the same store a few years from now. If we can specify a reasonably accurate growth rate in the value of the 10-year cash flow stream, we can determine how long we should delay.

The growth rate (g) in the value of the cash flow stream (V_t) at period t is, say 2%, and for convenience we'll say this is a continuously compounded rate. Suppose the value today (V_0) of the 10-year cash flow stream is \$3.2 million, and if we undertake the investment now, an outlay (I) of \$2.87 million will be required. The NPV of the investment is simply $V_0 - I = \$3.2$ million $-\$2.87$ million $= \$330,000$.

If we wait to invest at some period t in the future, the value of the cash flow stream will be $V_t = V_0 e^{gt}$, and NPV at that time will be $\text{NPV}_t = V_0 e^{gt} - I$, assuming the outlay ($I$) remains the same.[2] For instance, if we wait one year ($t = 1$), the cash flows should be worth

---

[2] We could include in our analysis the case where I grows over time but the additional structure doesn't add much to our understanding at this point.

$V_t = V_0 e^{gt} = 3.2 e^{0.02} = \$3.2646$ million, hence NPV at that time will be $V_1 - I = \$3.2646 - 2.87 = \$0.3946$ million. Should we wait? If the cost of capital (r) is 14%, continuously compounded, then NPV today of the investment at period t will be given by

$$\begin{aligned} \text{NPV}_0 &= e^{-rt}\text{NPV}_t \\ &= e^{-rt}(V_0 e^{gt} - I) \end{aligned} \tag{1}$$

In this case, we begin at $t = 1$, thus $\text{NPV}_0 = e^{-0.14}(\$3.2 e^{0.02} - \$2.87)$ million $\cong \$343,000$.

Thus we are better off in today's dollars ($\text{NPV}_0 = \$343,000$) by waiting a year than we are by proceeding now ($\text{NPV}_0 = \$330,000$). Should we wait even longer? We can determine how long we should wait by finding the value of t that equates the marginal benefit (due to g) and the marginal cost (due to the opportunity cost r) of waiting.[3] This means maximizing NPV_0 with respect to t. Since NPV_0 in equation (1) is concave in t, the optimal starting time (t^*) may be found by differentiating NPV_0 with respect to t and setting the result equal to zero:

$$\begin{aligned} \frac{\partial \text{NPV}_0}{\partial t} &= \frac{\partial e^{-rt}(V_0 e^{gt} - I)}{\partial t} \\ &= e^{-rt}(V_0 e^{gt}(g - r) + rI) = 0 \end{aligned} \tag{2}$$

Eliminating e^{-rt} and solving for t yields

$$t^* = \frac{1}{g}\ln\left[\frac{rI}{(r-g)V_0}\right] \tag{3}$$

Equation (3) will have a negative sign if $rI < (r - g)V_0$, since the logarithm of a fraction is negative, so to force t^* to be non-negative, we may write it as

$$t^* = \max\left(\frac{1}{g}\ln\left[\frac{rI}{(r-g)V_0}\right], 0\right) \tag{4}$$

In our example with $V_0 = \$3.2$ million, $I = \$2.87$ million, $r = 0.14$, and $g = 0.02$, we find from equation (4) that t^* is about 2.27 years:

---

[3] The development that follows is examined in detail in A. K. Dixit and R. S. Pindyck, *Investment Under Uncertainty* (Princeton, NJ: Princeton University Press, 1994).

$$t^* = \max\left(\frac{1}{0.02}\ln\left[\frac{0.14(2.87)}{(0.14-0.02)3.2}\right], 0\right) = 2.27$$

Despite the odd-looking nature of equation (4), the intuition behind it is straightforward — investing at t^* equates marginal costs and benefits. To see this, re-arrange equation (2), the first order condition for maximum NPV_0. Equation (2) set equal to zero implies

$$gV_0e^{gt} = r(V_0e^{gt} - I) \tag{5}$$

The left-hand side of equation (5) is the *marginal benefit* of waiting, whereas the right-hand side is the *marginal cost*. At any date t, the passage of a small amount of time (dt) will increase the benefit of waiting by $gV_0e^{gt}dt$, and it will increase the cost of waiting by $r(V_0e^{gt} - I)dt$.

If we start the project before t^* (2.27 years), the marginal benefit of waiting (gV_0e^{gt} in equation (5)) will *exceed* the marginal cost ($r(V_0e^{gt} - I)$ in equation (5)), thus NPV_0 will not be maximized. If we delay beyond t^*, the marginal cost ($r(V_0e^{gt} - I)$) will exceed the marginal benefit (gV_0e^{gt}). You can confirm this by inserting a value of t less than 2.27, then a value greater than 2.27, in the marginal benefit and cost expressions in equation (5). You will see that they are unequal for any value of $t \neq 2.27$.

If we commence the project at t^* (2.27 years), then NPV_0 in equation (1) will be

$$NPV_0 = e^{-0.14 \times 2.27}(3.2e^{0.02 \times 2.27} - 2.87) \cong \$348,300 \tag{6}$$

Notice that NPV_0 in equation (6) assuming optimal timing exceeds NPV_0 assuming immediate execution, \$330,000, and NPV_0 assuming execution at $t = 1$. No value of t other than 2.27 years will produce NPV_0 as high as \$348,300.

Timing and the Profitability Index

There is another way to determine when to invest in a case such as this, and it relies on a capital budgeting tool that usually takes a backseat to NPV. The profitability index or present value index (PVI), is the present value of a project's cash flows *divided* by the outlay. Thus, if we execute the project now, $PVI_0 = V_0/I$. If we wait until period t, $PVI_t = V_t/I = V_0e^{gt}/I$. PVI is presented in many corporate finance textbooks as a tool for the accept-or-reject decision. If PVI exceeds 1.0, the decision is to accept. Of course, this implies that NPV is greater than zero, so the two rules are harmonious.

But PVI was developed not as an alternative to NPV, but as a supplemental tool. It may be seen as a benefits-cost ratio; that is, it quantifies how much "bang for the buck" is produced by the investment. If the firm's investment outlay is constrained such that it can undertake only a subset of proposed investments, management can use PVI to identify the subset that will provide maximum NPV.[4]

In our example, had we started immediately, the PVI would be $V_0/I = 3.2/2.87 = 1.115$. Since PVI exceeds 1.0, NPV must be positive, thus PVI leads to the same decision as NPV. It turns out we can use this tool to determine *when* to invest.[5]

Suppose we undertake our example project at t^* (2.27 years). At that time, the PVI will be $PVI_t = V_0e^{gt}/I = 3.2e^{0.02 \times 2.27}/2.87 = 1.167$. The project's cash flow stream will be worth 16.7% more than the required outlay if we wait 2.27 years. If you re-arrange equation (5), which equates marginal benefit and marginal cost, you will find that the equation implies:

$$\frac{V_0e^{gt}}{I} = \frac{r}{r-g} \tag{7}$$

The left-hand side of equation (7) is PVI_t, and we know equation (7) holds when marginal benefit and marginal cost are equal.

Inserting $r = 0.14$ and $g = 0.02$ in equation (7), we find that $r/(r-g) = 1.167$. Sound familiar? This is the value we got for PVI_t assuming we waited for 2.27 years, and it is no coincidence. Thus, we have a new role for an old capital budgeting tool. When we calculate the PVI of an investment proposal whose value grows at a constant rate, we should defer investing if we find PVI is less than the trigger point $r/(r-g)$. On the other hand, if PVI equals or exceeds $r/(r-g)$, we should execute at once.

[4] Capital constraints are part of the reality of investment management. For an excellent exposition, see Richard Brealey and Stewart Myers, *Principles of Corporate Finance* (New York: McGraw-Hill, 1996).

[5] This role of PVI is examined in William T. Moore, "The Present Value Index and Optimal Timing of Investment," *Financial Practice and Education*, forthcoming.

Uncertain Growth in Value

Now let's consider uncertainty about the future value of a project's cash flow stream. Suppose V_t is *expected* to grow at rate g, but may deviate randomly according to a volatility parameter σ. This parameter is the standard deviation of the rate of growth in V_t.

Our goal is to maximize NPV_0 by undertaking an investment when marginal benefits equal marginal cost. There are now *two* sources of benefits, expected growth (g) and resolution of uncertainty (σ). Because V_t grows stochastically, we cannot use differential calculus to maximize NPV_0. Instead, we must employ stochastic dynamic programming, and fortunately the solution to this problem has been developed.[6]

Since V_t now varies stochastically, we cannot find the exact time (t^*) at which the investment should be undertaken. But we can easily determine the value of PVI at which investment should be triggered. To maximize NPV_0, we should wait to invest when PVI hits $b/(b-1)$, where

$$b = \sqrt{2r/\sigma^2 + (g/\sigma^2 - 0.5)^2} + 0.5 - g/\sigma^2 \qquad (8)$$

In equation (8), r represents the appropriate discount rate for the investment taking into account risk. Dixit and Pindyck develop a very similar solution without the need to specify the risk-adjusted discount rate.[7] Their alternative solution requires the risk-free rate instead, but we will proceed as if the appropriate discount rate is known.[8]

---

[6] See Robert L. McDonald and Daniel Siegel, "The Value of Waiting to Invest," *Quarterly Journal of Economics* (November 1986), pp. 707-728. An excellent exposition is in Dixit and Pindyck, *Investment Under Uncertainty*. McDonald and Siegel also consider the case where the investment outlay (I) grows stochastically.

[7] Dixit and Pindyck, *Investment Under Uncertainty*.

[8] They point out that specification of the risk-adjusted rate requires additional structure such as the assumptions needed to apply the capital asset pricing model (CAPM). But they also note that in order to avoid the need for specifying the risk adjustment and using the risk-free rate, a marketable asset must exist that is perfectly correlated with the project's value. This is to facilitate a no-arbitrage argument, as in F. Black and M. Scholes, "The Pricing of Options and Corporate Liabilities," *Journal of Political Economy* (May-June 1973), pp. 637-659, and is called *spanning*. The CAPM was published initially by William F. Sharpe in "Capital Asset Prices: A Theory of Market Equilibrium Under Conditions of Risk," *Journal of Finance* (September 1964), Vol. 19, pp. 425-442.

Suppose we continue our example where $r = 0.14$ and (expected) growth (g) is 0.02. Now let's add that uncertainty about the change in value is described by $\sigma = 0.10$, thus $\sigma^2 = 0.01$. Inserting these values in equation (8) gives $b = 4$. Thus, $b/(b - 1) = 4/3 = 1.333$. If we plan to wait until the project's value exceeds its cost by 33%, then NPV_0 will be maximized.

Recall that PVI based on immediate investment in our example is $V_0/I = 3.2/2.87 = 1.115$, thus we should wait. Recall also that when we ignored uncertainty ($\sigma = 0$), we found that we should commence the project when PVI rose to $r/(r - g) = 1.167$. But with σ greater than zero, we should be prepared to wait until PVI exceeds that trigger point (1.333 versus 1.667).

Why? With $\sigma = 0$, there is only a single benefit of waiting (g), whereas when σ exceeds 0, there are two benefits. Remember that we seek to equate marginal benefits and marginal costs. In our example with $\sigma = 0$, the marginal benefit of waiting exceeds the marginal cost initially. Thus we should wait until PVI grows to 1.167 from 1.115. But with $\sigma = 0.10$, the marginal benefits (due to g and σ) still exceed the marginal cost of waiting when PVI = 1.167. Only when PVI reaches 1.333 are marginal benefits and cost equated.

We can show that $b/(b - 1)$ is always greater than or equal to $r/(r - g)$. The two trigger points, $b/(b - 1)$ and $r/(r - g)$, are equal only when $\sigma = 0$. And if g and $\sigma = 0$ — that is, there is no benefit of waiting — then $r/(r - g) = 1$ and $b/(b - 1) = 1$. This means the decision rule reduces to accepting a project if PVI exceeds 1.0, the traditional rule. Thus, we see why the familiar edict, accept if NPV is positive, which implies PVI exceeds 1.0, may be the wrong prescription. The rule is optimal only when there are no valuable benefits to waiting, or if there are, the firm is somehow constrained to invest immediately.

The fact that managers may insist on IRR exceeding an "excessive" hurdle rate, or requiring PVI to exceed 1.0 by a substantial amount, does not necessarily mean they are investing inefficiently. As McDonald explains, their behavior may be closer to optimal than previously thought.[9]

---

[9] Robert L. McDonald, "Real Options and Rules of Thumb in Capital Budgeting."

It is suspected that managers may employ higher hurdle rates than appear justified because they believe risk-adjusted rates such as the CAPM miss some important risk. They are right in that the risk adjustment in the CAPM and similar models is due to *systematic* risk only, that which cannot be reduced by diversification. But as we now see, they should take *total* risk (systematic and diversifiable) into account when making the timing decision (i.e., σ in equation (8) represents total volatility). As the optimal timing rule implies, the greater σ, the higher the optimal PVI ($b/(b-1)$), thus requiring a higher cutoff than 1.0 does not necessarily mean that managers are focusing on the "wrong" risk.

Value of the Timing Option

Remember that NPV may be viewed as the sum of NPV* (ignoring optionality) and the value of flexibility. Denote NPV_0 conditioned on immediate investment as NPV*, and NPV_0 conditioned on deferring as NPV. The value of the timing option is then NPV − NPV*.

In our first example (with $\sigma = 0$), NPV_0 based on immediate execution was $V_0 - I = \$330,000$. This is NPV*. If we wait until $t^* = 2.27$ years, or equivalently when PVI = 1.167, then NPV_0 was found to be $348,300. This is NPV = NPV* + timing option value, thus the option to defer is worth $18,300.

In the second example, we expect the timing option to be worth even more. That is, the NPV found by executing the project when PVI = $b/(b-1)$ = 1.333 should exceed NPV*, the project's value without the timing option, which is $330,000. But what is NPV today if we plan to wait until PVI rises to 1.333?

It can be shown that the expected value of NPV today based on waiting to invest when PVI rises to $b/(b-1)$ is KV_0^b, where $V_0 = \$3.2$ million and $b = 4$ in our example.[10] To determine K, denote V^* as the optimal value of the project — that is, $V^*/I = b/(b-1)$. Then it can be shown that $K = (V^* - I)/V^{*b}$.

In our example, $V^* = (b/(b-1))I = (1.333)(2.87) = \$3.8267$ million. Given $I = \$2.87$ million and $b = 4$, we find

---

[10] This is derived by McDonald and Siegel, "The Value of Waiting to Invest." See Dixit and McDonald, *Investment Under Uncertainty*, pp. 140-142, for elaboration.

$$K = \frac{3.8267 - 2.87}{3.8267^4} = 0.00446 \qquad (9)$$

Thus NPV $= KV_0^b = 0.00446(3.2)^4 = \$467,700$. The value of the timing option, NPV $-$ NPV*, is \$467,700 $-$ \$330,000 = \$137,700. Compare this with the value of the option with $\sigma = 0$ (\$18,300).

Up to this point, you may be wondering what happens if project value is *not* expected to grow (hence $g = 0$), but will instead vary randomly over time according to the magnitude of σ. After all, this may be more representative of many investments (e.g., the price of crude oil may vary randomly with no predictable drift). The rule to invest when PVI approaches $b/(b-1)$ still holds when $g = 0$, and the parameter b in equation (8) becomes

$$b = \sqrt{2r/\sigma^2 + 0.25} + 0.5 \qquad (10)$$

Now the only benefit of waiting is due to volatility (σ), since $g = 0$. This means the firm should plan on investing at a lower PVI than when g is greater than zero. You can confirm this in our example with $r = 0.14$ and $\sigma = 0.10$. You should find that the firm should invest when PVI hits about 1.208. Recall that with $g = 0.02$ and $\sigma = 0.10$, we found that investment should be triggered at PVI = 1.333.

If you would like to know how much of the value of the timing option is due to expected growth at rate $g = 0.02$, just solve equation (9) using the value of b in equation (10) with g set equal to zero. Subtract this from the value of the option found with $\sigma = 0.10$ and $g = 0.02$ (i.e., \$137,700). You should now be able to say how much of the option value (\$137,700) is due to volatility ($\sigma = 0.10$) and how much is due to expected growth ($g = 0.02$).

TIMING IN PERSPECTIVE

Before leaving this chapter, let's form a rough picture of the effect of optimal timing on hurdle rates set by management to screen projects. Suppose we can invest \$10 (*I*) today in a project expected to generate annual cash flows of \$1.20 in perpetuity, and the firm's cost of capital is 12%. The value (V_0) today of projected cash flows is \$10 (\$1.20/0.12), thus PVI = 1.0, NPV is $V_0 - I$ = \$10 − \$10 = 0, and the internal rate of return (IRR) is 12%.

Now suppose we have the flexibility of delaying and that the benefits of waiting are such that PVI ($b/(b − 1)$) should be 1.25 before undertaking this project. This implies that in order to pass this screen now, expected annual cash flow must be at least \$1.50. This will give a present value (V_0) of \$12.50 (\$1.50/0.12), hence a PVI of 1.25 (V_0/I = \$12.50/\$10). This screen is equivalent to the firm requiring an IRR, or hurdle rate, of 15%, even though its cost of capital is only 12%.

If the benefits of waiting are greater, such that $b/(b − 1)$ is, say 1.5, the expected annual cash flow must be at least \$1.80. If you work this out, you'll find that this is equivalent to the firm requiring the project to meet a hurdle rate (IRR) of 18%. In Exhibit 10.1, we've plotted equivalent IRR values for levels of PVI ranging from 1.0 to 2.0. The plot is linear because we are assuming perpetual cash flows. Notice that doubling the PVI from 1.0 to 2.0 is equivalent to doubling the IRR from 12% to 24%. The slope of the plot is 0.12, the firm's cost of capital, and this is not a coincidence. In this example, an increase in the hurdle rate (IRR) of a given x% is equivalent to the same x% increase in PVI. In the case of a *perpetuity*, this will always be true — the plot of IRR versus PVI will be linear, and the slope of the plot will be the cost of capital. Thus for long-lived investments, an x% increase in $b/(b − 1)$, hence PVI, is approximately equivalent to an x% increase in the required hurdle rate.

As McDonald and Siegel show, and as you can see by inserting some numbers in equation (8), the optimal level of PVI ($b/(b − 1)$) well exceeds 1.0 for a wide range of plausible values.[11] Thus the practice of applying hurdle rates that are substantially higher than the cost of capital may be broadly consistent with value-maximizing behavior on the part of financial managers.

---

[11] McDonald and Siegel, "The Value of Waiting to Invest."

Exhibit 10.1: Internal Rate of Return

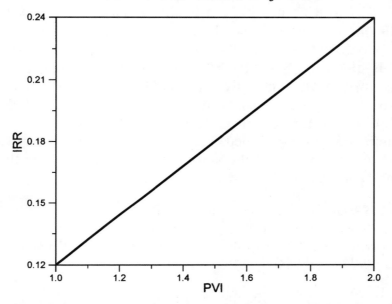

QUESTIONS AND PROBLEMS

1. Our firm is evaluating an investment proposal requiring an initial outlay of $55 million. If the project were undertaken immediately, the projected value of its cash flows would be about $60 million (in present value terms). The value of the project is expected to grow modestly over the next few years such that the projected cash flow value will advance at about 1.5% annually, continuously compounded. The firm's cost of capital for evaluating such proposals is 14% and we'll assume for now that the uncertainty about the growth rate (1.5%) is negligible.

   a. Clearly the project has positive NPV if undertaken immediately. The question is, should it be undertaken now, or should the firm plan on waiting? If you recommend waiting, how long should we defer?

   b. If the firm times the investment optimally, thus following your recommendation in part a, what will be the NPV in today's dollars?

   c. What is the present value index (PVI) of the project if we plan on undertaking it immediately? At what level of PVI do you recommend commencing the project?

   d. Suppose that the firm's cost of capital is 16% rather than 14%, but all the other parameters are the same. Speculate about the effect of this difference on optimal timing; i.e., how should it affect your recommendation in part a? Next, confirm your speculation analytically.

2. Now consider a modest amount of uncertainty about the growth rate such that volatility is estimated to be about 2%. The cost of capital is 14% and all other parameters are the same as in Question 1.

   a. Explain why the optimal PVI at which the project should be commenced will be different from that which you recommended in Question 1c.

b. Confirm your speculation analytically. At what level of PVI do you now recommend commencing the project. How does this compare with your answer in Question 1c.

3. As the volatility parameter in equation (8) of the Chapter approaches zero, it can be shown that the value of PVI at which investment should be commenced, $b/(b-1)$, converges to $r/(r-g)$. Explain why this should be the case.

Chapter 11

Real Calls and Puts

N ow we examine real options other than timing and we'll see that some of these may be valued using off-the-shelf pricing models developed for financial options. In other cases, the standard financial models can be tailored to fit the real investment setting, while in many cases we must resort to numerical solution methods.

Our first illustration involves a three-stage investment: (1) research, (2) development, and (3) commercial-scale production. As we recognize that the first stage (research) is a call option on the second (development), which is in turn a call on the third (commercial production), we encounter a *compound* option — an option on an option. Next, we examine a scale expansion option, a call option with a twist.

After a digression on volatility as it applies to real options, we will consider abandonment and will value this flexibility as a put option. We'll also see how to value the flexibility of switching from one production process to another. Finally, we'll describe a general modeling procedure that is suited to problems involving multiple options.

A RESEARCH AND DEVELOPMENT EXAMPLE

Here's our first story. We are considering a three-stage project whereby we commit $36 million today to establish a research program. This stage is expected to run for about three years during which we will spend more such that the present value of the expenditures based on the firm's 15% cost of capital is $19 million. To be consistent in our example, we will take the 15% as a continuously compounded rate.

In the second stage, we plan to develop the fruits of our research (an invention, perhaps a new chemical process) with an additional outlay estimated at $320 million. The development phase is expected to last about two years, then we may commence full scale commercial production for an outlay of $3.65 billion. Thus the commercial project may begin in five years, following three years of research, then two more years of development.

Based on our best estimates now, the full scale commercial project is expected to generate cash flows that have a value as of year 5 of about $3.5 billion. Given the expected outlay of $3.65 billion in that year, this means negative NPV in year 5 of −$150 million, and one might naturally wonder why we would further entertain such a project. According to this unappealing scenario, we would pay $36 million today, then another $19 million over three years for research, then launch a pilot project for yet another $320 million, and this gets us to a *negative* NPV investment in five years.

If the proposal is presented in essentially these terms to senior management for approval, one can only imagine the harsh words, evil looks, and tough questions we'll experience — and that may be the best part! There's not much point in calculating NPV, but for the record, if you discount the cash flows described in the scenario back to the current period using the continuous 15% discount rate, you'll get −$329.9 million.

But We Have a Call Option

The scenario we've just described would fit most R&D projects and most exploratory ventures such as petroleum and mineral extraction. Remember our description of the pharmaceutical drug development process we saw in Chapter 9. Given the long odds for success, and the massive time and costs involved, it's tough to imagine drug research projects with anything other than negative NPV.

Evidently we have missed something in our R&D example. The NPV of −$329.9 million is conditioned on what we know now, and committing now to the full five-year scenario. But we could view the costs of the research and development programs as the price of a call option on the commercial venture. Granted, from where we stand now it doesn't appear that we would proceed with the commercial stage, but we can make this decision in five years — after we determine the results of the pilot project. The fact that we don't have to commit now, before we acquire better information, should make the initial stages more appealing (hence more valuable).

What this means is the outlay for the research stage ($36 million), and the added $19 million in costs during the next three years, plus the present value (at 15%) of the $320 million development project, can be viewed as the price of a call option. This comes to about $259 million in present dollars. The call will have about five years of life and will be exercised only if the value of remaining cash flows assessed in year 5 exceeds the commercial outlay of $3.65 billion. If our uncertainty about the value of these cash flows as of year 5, which we now put at about $3.5 billion, is negligible, then this out-of-the money call option would command little value. In this case it would be impossible to justify the negative NPV of the research and development projects.

But suppose we're uncertain about the value of the commercial venture — say our uncertainty is described by a standard deviation (σ) of about 35%. That is, the percentage change in the cash flows from such commercial ventures is 35% annually. (We'll have more to say about σ later.) Let's say the rate on 5-year government debt instruments is 6%. Now we have the makings of a call option: the parameters are $X = \$3.65$ billion, $T = 5$ years, $\sigma = 35\%$, and $r = 6\%$.

How about the "stock price" (S)? In the option pricing models we've seen S is the current price of the underlying. So what exactly is the underlying in the present scenario? It is the value of cash flows to be generated during the lifetime of the commercial project, our third stage of the venture. Based on what we know now, the value of the commercial venture's projected cash flows is the present value of $3.5 billion. Using the continuous rate of 15% and $T = 5$ we find this is $1.6533 billion.

Now we calculate the value today of a 5-year call with $S = \$1.6533$ billion, $X = \$3.65$ billion, and so on. This is found by solving equation (12) in Chapter 3:

$$C = SN(d_1) - Xe^{-rT}N(d_2)$$

where

$$d_1 = (\ln(S/X) + (r + \sigma^2/2)T)/\sigma\sqrt{T}$$

and

$$d_2 = d_1 - \sigma\sqrt{T}$$

The call option is worth about $255 million today, and remember that our effective price of the call, the combined costs of the research and development programs, is $259 million. Thus we have a total NPV of about −$4 million, hence the research and development projects are unacceptable.

More Optionality

But this isn't the whole story. Shouldn't we regard the (first-stage) research project itself as a call option on the (second-stage) development project, and in turn view the development project as a call option on the (third stage) commercial venture? And if we do, will we arrive at a different NPV? Yes, and yes — we should view the three-stage project as a *compound* option, and we will almost surely get a different NPV.

The straight net present value, NPV*, of the *research* stage is −$55 million, the sum of the outlay (−$36 million) and the present value of 3-year cash flow projections (−$19 million). We may think of this expense as the price of a call option on the *development* stage, with an exercise price X_1 of $320 million, and an expected lifetime (T_1) of three years. The risk-free rate is 6%, and volatility is 35%, as in the case of the simple option we examined earlier. What is the underlying asset for the development stage option? It is the *option* to pursue the commercial venture, another call. Thus the first option is a call option on another option (i.e., a *compound* option). We will exercise the first option in three years only if the value of the option to proceed with the commercial stage exceeds $320 million.

The option on the stage-three commercial venture is a 5-year (T_2) option, and the risk-free rate appropriate for valuing this option is also assumed to be 6%. The exercise price is the outlay required to commence commercial-scale production, $3.65 billion. The underlying is the value of cash flows that will be generated by the commercial investment over its expected life. Based on what we know now, the value of these cash flows assessed as of year 5 is $3.5 billion, and given a continuous 15% discount rate, the value today of this projected value is $1.6533 billion.

To value the compound option, we must know at what point the first option will be exercised. Remember that this is the right to buy the option on the commercial venture for $320 million ($X_1$). Thus we need to know the value V^* of the commercial venture cash flows that will cause the exercise price ($320 million) to be equal to the value of the second option assessed at year 3.

At year 3, the second option will have a 2-year life ($T^* = T_2 - T_1$). To find V^*, the value of the commercial cash flows assessed as of year 3 that causes the second option to have value equal to $320 million ($X_1$), we must solve equation (1):

$$X_1 = VM(d_1) - X_2 e^{-rT^*} M(d_2) \tag{1}$$

where

$$d_1 = (\ln(V/V^*) + (r + \sigma^2/2)T^*)/\sigma\sqrt{T^*}$$
$$d_2 = d_1 - \sigma\sqrt{T^*}$$
$$V = \text{value of the underlying as of now}$$

and X_1, X_2 = exercise prices of the two options.

We can search for the value V^* which causes equation (1) to hold with the aid of a computer. In this case, X_2 = $3.65 billion, $T_2 - T_1 = T^* = 2$ years, $r = 0.06$, and $\sigma = 0.35$. The value V^* which forces this call option to be worth $320 million is found to be $2.64 billion.

Now we are prepared to solve for the value of the compound option — the call on a call. The solution is developed by Geske[1] and is given in general terms in equation (2):

$$C = VM(a_1, b_1, \sqrt{T_1/T_2}) - X_2 e^{-rT_2} M(a_2, b_2, \sqrt{T_1/T_2}) - X_1 e^{-rT_1} N(a_2) \tag{2}$$

where

$$a_1 = (\ln(V/V^*) + (r + \sigma^2/2)T_1)/\sigma\sqrt{T_1}$$
$$a_2 = a_1 - \sigma\sqrt{T_1}$$
$$b_1 = (\ln(V/X_2) + (r + \sigma^2/2)T_2)/\sigma\sqrt{T_2}$$
$$b_2 = a_1 - \sigma\sqrt{T_2}$$

---

[1] Robert Geske, "The Valuation of Compound Options," *Journal of Financial Economics* (March 1979), pp. 63- 81.

Exhibit 11.1: The Bivariate Standard Normal Density Function

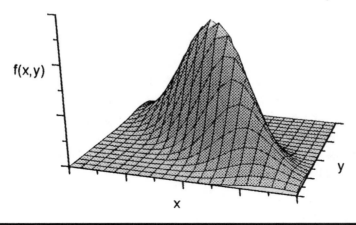

All the terms are familiar from the Black-Scholes development in Chapter 3 except $M(\ldots)$. This denotes the cumulative bivariate standard normal distribution and its value may be found in widely available statistical software routines. The function is:

$$f(x, y) = \frac{1}{2\pi\sqrt{1-\rho^2}}\exp\left\{-\frac{1}{2(1-\rho^2)}(x^2 - 2\rho xy + y^2)\right\} \qquad (3)$$

In equation (3), ρ is the correlation coefficient between the variables x and y. The correlation coefficient between the values of the two options is the square root of T_1/T_2, or 0.7746. The standard bivariate normal density function for a correlation of 0.7746 is plotted in Exhibit 11.1. The two values for $M(\ldots)$ in equation (3) are represented by the area under this figure for x less than a_1 and y less than b_1, and x less than a_2 and y less than b_2, respectively.

To solve equation (2) in the case at hand, we recognize that V = the value today of the projected cash flows from the commercial project, $1.6533 billion. Then X_2 = $3.65 billion, X_1 = $320 million, r = 0.06, T_2 = 5, and T_1 = 3. Using σ = 0.35, we find that a_1 = −0.1720, b_1 = −0.2373, a_2 = −0.7782, and b_2 = −1.0199. Recall that the correlation coefficient is 0.7746, the square root of 3/5. The value of $M(a_1,$ $b_1, \ldots)$ is determined from solving equation (3) to be 0.31187, and $M(a_2, b_2, \ldots)$ is 0.10997. Solving equation (2) using these values results in $281.5 million.

What does this mean? By committing to the research project (stage 1) for three years and −$55 million, we "purchase" the option to *develop* the research (for $320 million). We will exercise this option if $V = V^* = \$2.64$ billion at year 3, since this implies that the option to pursue the *commercial venture* will be worth $320 million. If we exercise the first option, we will then have an option to proceed commercially at an additional cost of $3.65 billion. The second option will be exercised in year 5 if the value of the commercial cash flow projections at that time exceeds $3.65 billion. The value today of the option to purchase the option is estimated from equation (2) at $281.5 million.

Now compare this with NPV* for the research stage, −$55 million. Clearly we have positive NPV of $226.5 million, thus the appropriate decision is to commence the research stage. Remember that in the previous section we treated the scenario as a simple option and found NPV of the two-stage research and development ensemble to be −$4 million. Where does the difference arise?

The project valued as a *compound* option should be worth more than the same project viewed as a *simple* option. The reason is that in the case of the simple option we assumed we would commit not only $55 million to the research stage, but also $320 million to the development stage, thus restricting flexibility. In the case of the compound option, we recognize that the firm will not commit the $320 million outlay for development unless the value of the second option exceeds this amount. We recognize greater flexibility in the case using the compound option, and that flexibility should be valued to the extent we face uncertainty as to whether the first option will be exercised.

Note that to the extent we are confident that the development option will be exercised, then this degree of flexibility is less valuable and the simple and compound approaches will converge. But to the extent we aren't sure, flexibility then has greater value. Perhaps unsurprisingly this example highlights a tradeoff. The more flexibility we take into account, the more complex the analysis can become. To the extent we assess a high probability that we would proceed to the development phase (stage 2) given completion of the research project (stage 1), then the first option would add little to

NPV at the margin. In this case we may be better served by treating the combined research and development phases as a simple option on the commercial venture, as we did in the example initially. In other words, the added complexity of modeling the problem as a compound option will be merited only to the extent that we have significant uncertainty as to whether both of the component options will be exercised. This is by now a familiar theme — uncertainty drives option value.

AN EXPANSION QUESTION

Here is another illustration of a call option, but with a twist. This illustration is designed to show how our basic understanding of option payoffs can be applied to find solutions that may not be obvious at first. The story is this. We are considering adding an ocean-going tug to our fleet in order to satisfy towing demand of one of our customers. The vessel we are evaluating is 15 years old and typically tugs of this type have an original useful life of about 30 years. This one may be bought and placed in service for about $3.2 million.

Based on current demand, we have projected annual net cash flows for each of the next 15 years, and these are given in Exhibit 11.2. In a typical year, we expect cash flow to be about $419,000, and every fifth year we reduce the projected amount due to periodic maintenance and overhaul. In the last year we will skip the overhaul and we believe the vessel could then be scrapped for about $400,000, thus cash flow in the terminal year is estimated at $819,000.

The firm's hurdle rate is 12% (continuously compounded), and if you discount the cash flows in Exhibit 11.2 to the present, then net out the outlay of $3.2 million, you should find NPV of −$480,000. If we stopped our analysis here, this would be an unacceptable investment. But suppose that demand for towing service is variable, and in the next few years it could grow to the point where our client would ask us to tow a larger barge. Given the size of the current barge, maximum projected cash flows are $440,000 annually, reduced to $335,000 every fifth year for maintenance. These are given in Exhibit 11.3.

Exhibit 11.2: Projected Annual Net Cash Flows

Year	Cash Flow	Year	Cash Flow
1	$419,000	9	$419,000
2	419,000	10	314,000
3	419,000	11	419,000
4	419,000	12	419,000
5	314,000	13	419,000
6	419,000	14	419,000
7	419,000	15	819,000
8	419,000		

If demand grows to a point where potential cash flows exceed those in Exhibit 11.3, the customer will shift to a larger barge, which in turn will require a tug with greater horsepower than the one we are considering. The firm could buy a larger tug to begin with, but demand growth is uncertain and we may not need the additional power and expense. But if we buy the tug currently under consideration, then find that demand rises to the point where more power is needed, the tug can be repowered with larger engines. Thus we can view the proposed tug as a tug plus an expansion option, then determine its NPV to make the investment decision.

We can buy larger engines on the secondary market, then install them for about $900,000. Let's value the expansion option. We'll assume a realistic timeframe is two years, and the risk-free rate is 6%. The uncertainty of our cash flow projections is measured by a standard deviation (σ) of, say 40%. What is the exercise price for the expansion option? It is tempting to say $900,000, the cost of repowering the tug. But will this be the trigger point that determines whether we expand in two years? In order to merit expansion, cash flows from years 3 through 15 must exceed the current barge capacity and these are given in Exhibit 11.3 Otherwise it would not make sense to spend $900,000 to expand towing capacity. In fact, once we get to year 2 we should project remaining cash flows for the remaining 13 years under conditions of demand at that time, then determine their value at that time. We should then compare this value to the sum of $900,00 and the value of the remaining 13 years of cash flows under maximum capacity (Exhibit 11.3).

Exhibit 11.3: Cash Flow Projections Under Maximum Capacity

Year	Cash Flow	Year	Cash Flow
1	$440,000	9	$440,000
2	440,000	10	335,000
3	440,000	11	440,000
4	440,000	12	440,000
5	335,000	13	440,000
6	440,000	14	440,000
7	440,000	15	840,000
8	440,000		

The value as of year 2 of the maximum capacity cash flows from year 3 to year 15 in Exhibit 11.3, using the firm's 12% (continuous) hurdle rate, is $2,121,116. Once we get to the end of year 2, we will forecast potential remaining cash flows in light of demand at that time, discount them to year 2 (call this V_2), then if V_2 exceeds $2,121,116, maximum capacity cash flow value at year 2, by more than $900,000, we should repower. The value of remaining cash flows under maximum capacity ($2,121,116) will be denoted by V_t^{MAX} in this case V_2^{MAX}. Thus the payoff on our option is

$$\max(V_2 - \Delta I - V_2^{MAX}, 0)$$

If V_2 exceeds

$$\Delta I + V_2^{MAX}$$

then we should repower. If not, we should continue operating as the vessel is currently powered. This is clearly a call option with exercise price (X) of

$$\Delta I + V_2^{MAX} = \$3,021,116$$

At this point, we have four parameters needed to value this call: X ($3,021,116), T (2 years), r (6%), and σ (40%). What is the value of the underlying in this case? Look once again at our payoffs,

$$\max(V_2 - \Delta I - V_2^{MAX}, 0)$$

and rewrite this as max($V_2 - X$, 0). The value today of the underlying is the present value of V_2. Based on information now, this means the present value of the cash flows from year 3 through year 15 in Exhibit 11.2. Using the firm's 12% rate, this comes to about $2,018,777.

Inserting the parameters in the call option model, equation (12) in Chapter 3, we find that the expansion option is worth approximately $254,800. Recall that NPV* for the tug is estimated at −$480,000, so the additional value of flexibility due to the repowering option is insufficient to merit the investment in this case.

Volatility and Other Sensitive Parameters

The volatility parameter (σ) is correctly interpreted as the annualized standard deviation of the continuously compounded rate of return on the underlying real asset. By now this surely sounds familiar. But where do we get σ for use in real options analysis? One way to find an estimate is to look to the financial markets. For instance, in the expansion question involving the tug, we need a measure of the volatility of the return on assets of this type. A few publicly traded companies specialize in this line of business — for example, Maritrans (listed on the NYSE) and Seabulk International (Nasdaq).

We could start by finding recent stock price histories for the sample of similar firms, then calculate continuously compounded rates of return on their respective equities. Once we estimate σ from each return series, we must then take into account financial leverage. The volatility parameter we need for real options analysis pertains to the firm's business or operating risk; that is, how uncertain is the return on assets. However, the return on equity has volatility that reflects business risk plus financial risk, the additional uncertainty in the equity return due to financial leverage such as debt and preferred stock financing.

It turns out that we can retrieve the volatility representing the business risk by appealing to an approximate relationship between levered and unlevered volatilities (σ_L and σ_U, respectively). The relationship is $\sigma_L = (1 + D/S)\sigma_U$, where D/S is the debt-equity ratio. By estimating volatility of common stock returns we arrive at σ_L, and this simple relation allows us to determine the implied σ_U, which is what we need for real options analysis.

Exhibit 11.4: NPV for Varying Volatility Estimates

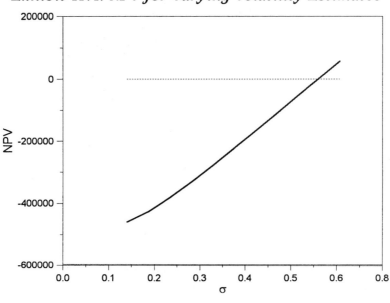

Another source of volatility assessments in the financial markets comes from the options markets. We can observe market prices of calls and puts on stocks in an industry related to the one at hand, and then solve for the implied standard deviation by inverting the Black-Scholes call and put pricing models from Chapter 3. But remember that these estimates also reflect financial leverage, hence we must "delever" the volatility estimates according to the relationship $\sigma_L = (1 + D/S)\sigma_U$

Still another way to approach the problem is to go around it. That is, we can examine the sensitivity of the real option value, hence NPV, to various assumptions about σ. For instance, in the expansion example we found that NPV was negative for volatility of 40%. But suppose we turn the question around — what range of volatility estimates delivers *positive* NPV? Then, Are these values plausible? In Exhibit 11.4, we have plotted NPV of the tug investment for levels of σ from 15% to 65%. For each level of σ in this range, we re-calculate the value of the call option, then add this to NPV*. For levels below about 55% the figure reveals that the investment has negative NPV. Thus, unless we are reasonably confident that σ exceeds 55%, the tug investment should not be undertaken.

Exhibit 11.5: NPV for Expansion Outlays from 400,000 to 1,500,000

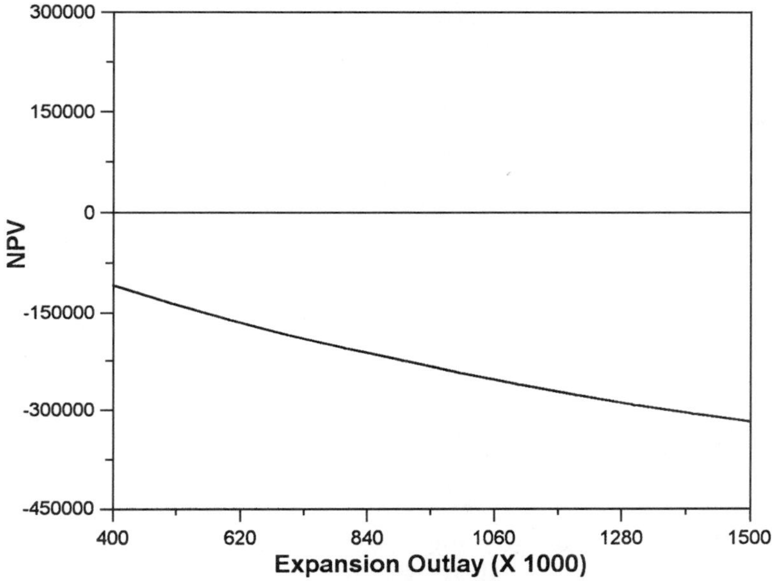

It is a good idea to check the sensitivity of the decision to any doubtful parameter. For instance, returning to the expansion example, suppose we're not terribly sure how much the repowering expenses will be. We estimate them now at $900,000, but let's explore a reasonable range of possible values to see if the decision is sensitive to the amount. In Exhibit 11.5, we plot NPV, which includes NPV* and the value of the call option, against levels of the expansion outlay ranging from $400,000 to $1,500,000. In this case, NPV is negative throughout this range, hence our decision is not sensitive to this estimate.

ABANDONMENT OPTIONS

In many cases the flexibility to discontinue an investment adds considerable value to a project. Recall our discussion of the put provision in many corporate bonds. In the event an investor wishes to disinvest in a putable bond, the provision is exercised usually for a preset cash amount. In the case of a real investment, the flexibility to discontinue is also viewed as a put option. This is not a new insight, but valuation of the abandonment option is easier given what we understand now about option pricing in general.[2]

To illustrate, we will assume the same setting we used earlier to explain the timing option in Chapter 10. Expected annual cash flows are assessed today to be $300,000 in perpetuity, based on a 50% probability that they will be $400,000, and a 50% chance they will be only $200,000. The outlay is $3.2 million and the firm's discount rate is 8%. If we discount the expected annual cash flow, $300,000, to the present we find that the perpetual series is worth $3.75 million. Given the outlay of $3.2 million, the NPV is $550,000.

Suppose that by the end of the first year we will have a much better picture of the cash flow series; that is, we'll know whether the level will be $400,000 or $200,000. Also suppose that at that time, if we choose to abandon, we may retrieve $2.7 million by liquidating our project which was originally worth $3.2 million. At the end of the first year ($t = 1$), if cash flows turn out to be $400,000 annually, we will continue the project. Why? At $t = 1$ the value of the remaining cash flows will be $5 million ($400,000/0.08), hence the project is worth more if we continue than if we abandon for $2.7 million.

If, at $t = 1$, the cash flows promise to be only $200,000 annually, we should abandon. The value at that time of the remaining cash flow stream is $2.5 million ($200,000/0.08), compared with $2.7 million if we discontinue — this is an easy choice. What is the project worth given the flexibility to abandon? What is the value of the abandonment option? If cash flows turn out to be $400,000, the value today of the project, net of the $3.2 million outlay, is $1.8 million, and recall that the probability of this event is 0.5. If cash flows turn out to be $200,000, we collect this amount at $t = 1$, then scrap the project for $2.7 million, so our total cash flow at $t = 1$ is $2.9 million. Discount this to $t = 0$ at 8%, then subtract the $3.2 million outlay, and you should get −$514,815. The expected NPV as of $t = 0$ is the probability weighted sum of $1.8 million and −$514,815, or

[2] See Stewart Myers and S. Majd, "Abandonment Value and Project Life," *Advances in Futures and Options Research*, Vol. 4 (1990), pp. 1-21.

about $642,593. The project is worth about $92,593 more ($642,593 − $550,000) given that we have the flexibility to abandon in one year for $2.7 million.

The "exercise price" for our put option is $2.7 million, and we can see that if the scrap value, hence the exercise price, is less than $2.5 million, the put will not be exercised because the value of the remaining cash flows as of $t = 1$ cannot be lower than $2.5 million in this setting. On the other hand, if the scrap value is, say $2.8 million, the flexibility to abandon will be worth even more than $92,593. If you work this out, you should find that the project's NPV taking into account abandonment at $t = 1$ for $2.8 million is $688,889, hence the option is then worth $138,889 ($688,889 − $550,000).

Suppose the uncertainty is greater such that cash flows may turn out to be $450,000 or only $150,000. You can easily confirm that the flexibility to abandon will be worth more than $92,593 given a scrap value of $2.7 million.

Here's an example where the Black-Scholes model may be applied. Suppose we are considering an investment which requires a $5.5 million outlay, and based on current projections we estimate annual cash flows to be $635,000 in perpetuity. The firm's cost of capital is 10%, and if we undertake the project now its NPV will be $850,000. At the end of a year we will reassess economic conditions, and if the value then (at $t = 1$) of the remaining cash flows is below the estimated salvage value of $4.4 million, then we will abandon. Suppose the one-year Treasury rate is 6%, and our uncertainty about the value of the cash flows is described by a volatility estimate (σ) of 30%.

In this case we have a put option with "exercise price" of $4.4 million, time to expiration (T) of 1 year, volatility of 30%, and exercise price (X) of $4.4 million. What is the value of the underlying? Based on our present knowledge (at $t = 0$), the cash flows from year 2 on are expected to be $635,000. Thus, as of year 1 the value of remaining cash flows is $6.35 million ($635,000/0.10), and today this is worth $5.7727 million.

If you solve the put pricing model with $X = \$4.4$ million, $S = \$5.7727$ million, and so on, you will find the value is about $98,900. Recall that the value of the project without considering flexibility

(NPV*) is $850,000, thus the combined NPV of the investment is about $948,900.

In many cases, realistic flexibility involves expansion or contraction, whereas purchase of a complete asset or total abandonment represent the respective extreme cases. The Black-Scholes model may not be well-suited to cases which lie outside these extremes. For example, we may wish to value the flexibility of abandoning part of an investment. In the Appendix to this chapter, we give a generalization of the Black-Scholes model and demonstrate how it can be used to value fractional expansion and contraction.

Of course, we restrict our analysis here and in the Appendix so that the option is European style — that is, we can exercise the put at $t = 1$ but not before and not after. If we could exercise at anytime before $t = 1$, it would be American style and would be worth more than $98,900 to the extent that early exercise is feasible. While no analytical solution to the problem of pricing American puts has been developed, numerical techniques involving binomial trees exist, and computer software for implementation is widely available. We will turn to this method later in this chapter.

OPTIONS TO SWITCH FACTORS OF PRODUCTION

The option to switch one risky asset for another is essentially a put and a call combined. We give up (put) one asset in exchange (call) for another. The option to switch one asset for another has a known analytical value derived by William Margrabe, and in this section, we adapt this model to a capital investment problem.[3]

Let V_1 represent the value of an asset we now have, and suppose we may exchange it for another asset with value V_2. The exercise price is V_2 and, unlike the case of options we've examined before, the exercise price is random.

Assume that the values of both assets follow Gauss-Wiener stochastic processes:

---

[3] William Margrabe, "The Value of an Option to Exchange One Asset for Another," *Journal of Finance* (March 1978), pp. 177-186.

$$dV_1/V_1 = \mu_1 dt + \sigma_1 dZ \tag{4}$$

and

$$dV_2/V_2 = \mu_2 dt + \sigma_2 dZ \tag{5}$$

The processes may be correlated according to the coefficient ρ, such that the appropriate volatility is the combination of the volatilities of the two assets:

$$\sigma^2 = \sigma_1^2 + \sigma_2^2 - 2\rho\sigma_1\sigma_2 \tag{6}$$

hence

$$\sigma = \sqrt{\sigma_1^2 + \sigma_2^2 - 2\rho\sigma_1\sigma_2} \tag{7}$$

As Margrabe shows, the value of the option to exchange asset 1 for asset 2 is

$$C = V_2 N(d_1) - V_1 N(d_2) \tag{8}$$

where

$$d_1 = (\ln(V_2/V_1) + T\sigma^2/2)/\sigma\sqrt{T}$$

and

$$d_2 = d_1 - \sigma\sqrt{T}$$

In equation (8), the volatility parameter σ is from equation (7). The switching option will be exercised if $V_2 > V_1$ at expiration, otherwise it will expire worthless.

Ordinarily in a real options context, we would bear some costs in switching from project 1 to project 2. For analytical convenience, let's suppose the cost of switching is a constant proportion of the value of the project we have initially (project 1). Let K represent the proportional cost, hence KV_1 is the dollar cost of switching. We will exercise the flexibility of switching only if $V_2 > (1 + K)V_1$. The model in equation (8) is easily modified as follows:

$$C_K = V_2 N(d_1) - (1 + K)V_1 N(d_2) \tag{9}$$

where

$$d_1 = (\ln(V_2/(1 + K)V_1) + T\sigma^2/2)/\sigma\sqrt{T}$$

and

$$d_2 = d_1 - \sigma\sqrt{T}$$

To illustrate, suppose we are considering investing in a project that requires a certain type of fuel such that the value today of cash flows from the project is $V_1 = \$33$ million. If we undertook the same project engineered for an alternative (and presently costlier) fuel type, the projected cash flows would have value $V_2 = \$26$ million.

The volatility of cash flows for project 1 is 30%, that for project 2 is 40%, and the correlation (ρ) between the fuel costs for the two projects is 0.8. The combined volatility is

$$\sigma^2 = \sigma_1^2 + \sigma_2^2 - 2\rho\sigma_1\sigma_2 = 0.058$$

hence $\sigma = 0.241$.

Suppose that our planning horizon is 2 years (T), and NPV* (ignoring optionality) for project 1 is $600,000. If we invest another $500,000 now in project 1, it can be engineered so that we can switch to the alternative fuel type. The cost of executing the switch is estimated at about 24% of cash flow value, hence the option would be exercised only if $V_2 > V_1(1 + K) = V_1(1.24)$.

Is this flexibility to switch fuel types worth an extra $500,000 invested today? By inserting the parameters $V_1 = \$33$ million, $V_2 = \$26$ million, $K = 0.24$, and so on in equation (9), we find that $C_K = \$900,000$. Thus the incremental investment adds $400,000 to the NPV* of the proposal, and NPV for the project including the switching option is $1,000,000 ($400,000 + $600,000).

THE ARBOREAL APPROACH

In some cases, we may approximate real option values with off-the-shelf pricing models — for example, the Black-Scholes and Merton call and put models discussed in Chapter 3, Geske's compound option formula discussed earlier in this chapter, and Margrabe's model of the option to exchange assets described earlier. In this section, we will illustrate a numerical valuation procedure that allows us to value options of virtually any stripe. We will adopt the pioneering approach of Cox, Ross, and Rubinstein whereby the underlying asset value follows a binomial branching process.[4] Reminiscent of our early treatment of calls and puts in Chapter 3, we will find probabilities that are implied if valuation is risk-neutral, and this will afford us the convenience of discounting at the risk-free rate.

The Underlying Tree

Suppose the value now ($t = 0$) of the cash flows of an investment is $5 million, denoted by V_0. If we undertake the venture an outlay of $5 million is required, thus the project is zero NPV. Let's say the volatility (σ) of the rate of change in V_0 is 25%. Each year the value of the cash flows may move up by amount u, or down by amount d, where $u = e^{\sigma} = 1.2840$, and $d = e^{-\sigma} = 1/u = 0.7788$. This means that at year 1 ($t = 1$), the cash flow value (V_1) will be either $6.42 million ($uV_0 = 1.284 \times \$5$ million), or $3.894 million ($dV_0 = 0.7788 \times \$5$ million). At year 2 ($t = 2$), project value (V_2) may be $8.2433 million ($uuV_0 = 1.284 \times 1.284 \times \$5$ million), $5 million ($udV_0 = duV_0 = V_0$), or $3.0326 million ($ddV_0 = 0.7788 \times 0.7788 \times \$5$ million). There are four possibilities in year 3 given by $uuuV_0$, $uudV_0$, $uddV_0$, and $dddV_0$.

The fully grown tree is depicted in Exhibit 11.6. We will stop the tree at the end of the third year ($t = 3$) because the options we will illustrate will have expired by that time even though the project will continue in existence beyond that.

To price options on the tree, we will exploit the pretense we made back in Chapter 3 — pretend that we are risk-neutral. Suppose the risk-free rate is 6%. What does this imply about the probability of an upward move (p_u), hence the probability of a downward move ($p_d = 1 - p_u$)? The expected value of the project at $t = 1$, denoted by $E(V_1)$ is p_u ($6.42 million) + p_d ($3.894 million). If we discount $E(V_1)$ at the risk-free rate ($r = 0.06$), what probabilities give a value of $5 million. This is answered by solving the following:

---

[4] J. Cox, S. Ross, and M. Rubinstein, "Option Pricing: A Simplified Approach," *Journal of Financial Economics* (October 1979), pp. 229-264.

$$\$5 \text{ million} = \frac{p_u(\$6.42 \text{ million}) + p_d(\$3.894 \text{ million})}{1.06}$$

Recognizing that $p_u = 1 - p_d$, we have one equation and one unknown. The solution is $p_u = 0.5566$ and $p_d = 0.4434$.

These risk-neutral probabilities are constant throughout the tree. For instance, at $t = 1$, suppose V_1 is $6.42 million. The next two possibilities in Exhibit 11.6 are an upward move to $8.2433 million, or a downward move to $5 million. If you take the expected value, $0.5566(\$8.2433 \text{ million}) + 0.4434 (\$5 \text{ million})$, then discount at 6%, you will get $6.42 million, consistent with the exhibit.

With a little algebra, we can find p_u and p_d for any tree constructed in this manner as

$$p_u = \frac{(1 + r_f) - d}{u - d} \tag{10}$$

and

$$p_d = \frac{u - (1 + r_f)}{u - d} \tag{11}$$

and you can readily see that these sum to 1.0.

The tree is already calibrated by virtue of the way we grew it. That is, if we begin at $t = 3$ and begin taking expected values of each pair of possibilities, then discount at 6% to find the values at $t = 2$, then repeat this process all the way back to $t = 0$, we will find $V_0 = \$5$ million.

Exhibit 11.6: Fully Grown Binomial Tree
(Values are in Millions of Dollars)

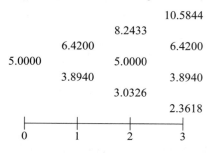

Exhibit 11.7: Binomial Tree with Abandonment Option
(Values are in millions of dollars)

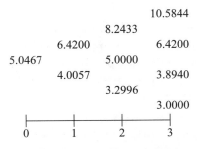

The value of the project reflecting the flexibility of abandon-

				10.5844
			8.2433	
		6.4200		6.4200
	5.0467		5.0000	
		4.0057		3.8940
			3.2996	
				3.0000

0	1	2	3

Two Simple Options

Now we are ready to value options. First, suppose we can abandon at *any* time for a salvage value (SV) of $3 million. As always, we begin at the end ($t = 3$) and work our way back assuming we act optimally throughout. From Exhibit 11.6, it is clear that we will abandon if V_3 turns out to be $2.3618 million. We then replace this value with $3 million (i.e., max($V_3$, SV) in general).

Next we take the expected value of $3.894 million and now $3 million; that is, 0.5566 ($3.894 million) + 0.4434 ($3 million), and discount to $t = 2$ at the 6% rate to get $3.2996 million. Because this amount exceeds $3 million (SV), we would not abandon at $t = 2$. To complete the tree reflecting the abandonment option, we discount the expected value of $5 million and $3.2996 million at 6% to get $4.0057 million at $t = 1$, and finally we discount the expected value of $6.42 million and $4.0057 million to $t = 0$ at 6%. The completed tree is shown in Exhibit 11.7.

The value of the project reflecting the flexibility of abandoning for $3 million at any time is determined to be $5.0467 million, thus the optionality adds about $46,700 to the NPV of the project. Given an outlay of $5 million, the NPV is now positive.

Notice that even though we have the flexibility to abandon anytime, the tree structure in Exhibit 11.7 implies that we will exercise that option only at $t = 3$ and not before. The reason is that this tree is rather coarse — we permit changes in project value only once each year according to the volatility (σ) of 25%. We could make the tree, hence the analysis, richer by allowing growth at a higher frequency. For instance, we could allow values to move up or down twice a year, every six months.

To do this, we must adjust the upward and downward amounts, u and d, to reflect the semi-annual volatility. Since $\sigma = 0.25$ is taken to be an annual volatility, the semi-annual amount is $0.25\sqrt{0.5} = 0.1768$, hence $u = e^{0.1768} = 1.1934$, and $d = e^{-0.1768} = 1/u = 0.8379$. Quarterly branching implies a quarterly volatility of $0.25\sqrt{0.25} = 0.125$, thus $u = e^{0.125} = 1.1331$, and $d = e^{-0.125} = 1/u = 0.8825$.

As we change the frequency of the branching process to semi-annual, quarterly, and so on, we must also calculate new risk-neutral probabilities. This is done easily by inserting the new values of u, d, and the risk-free rate (r_f) in equations (10) and (11). The risk-free rate for a semi-annual tree is

$$\sqrt{1.06} - 1 = 0.0296$$

roughly half the annual rate. The rate for a quarterly tree is

$$\sqrt[4]{1.06} - 1 = 0.0147$$

and so on.

If we were to increase the branching frequency to, say quarterly, we would find that abandonment before $t = 3$ would be optimal. The algorithm for valuing the option is the same — begin at $t = 3$ and work back toward $t = 0$, acting optimally all the way. If, for example, we find that abandonment at the end of the first quarter of year 2 ($t = 2.25$) is optimal, then we insert $3 million (SV) at that node, then insert zero at all remaining nodes that branch from that point.

To keep our analysis simple, let's continue with the tree described in Exhibit 11.6. Now we will consider another option, the flexibility of expanding the level of investment by 15%, and we will assume we can do this no earlier than year 3. The initial scale of the investment, $5 million, may thus be increased to $5.75 million, hence the incremental investment for the expansion option is $0.75 million.

Refer again to the fully grown tree in Exhibit 11.6. Suppose at $t = 3$, $V_3 = \$10.5844$ million; that is, the value has increased three consecutive years. If we invest an additional $0.75 million, an investment of 15%, suppose the value of the project's cash flows will increase by the same proportion. Thus, if 15% of $10.5844 million exceeds $0.75 million, we should exercise our expansion (call) option. In this case, we should expand since 15% of $10.5844 million is an increase in project value of $1.5877 million to $12.1721 million. The additional outlay of $0.75 million reduces this to $11.4221 million which exceeds $10.5844, so we should expand.

Suppose that project value is $6.42 million at $t = 3$, another possibility shown in Exhibit 11.6. If we expand by 15% ($0.75 million), project value will climb by $0.963 million (15% of $6.42 million), thus we should expand in this case as well. Accounting for the incremental outlay of $0.75 million, the value of this node will be $6.633 million.

In Exhibit 11.8, we show the tree reflecting *both* options, 15% expansion at $t = 3$ and abandon for $3 million anytime. We value the project by taking expected values of each pair of outcomes using p_u and p_d, then discount at 6%. Continue working back to the present and we find $V_0 = \$5.2171$ million.

Given an outlay of $5 million, our venture has positive NPV of about $217,000. Recall that in general, NPV = NPV* + option values, hence the abandonment and expansion options combined are worth $217,000 (since NPV* = 0). The put alone was worth about $47,000, so the flexibility to expand adds an additional $170,000 to project value.

Exhibit 11.8: Binomial Tree with Expansion and Abandonment Options
(Values are in millions of dollars)

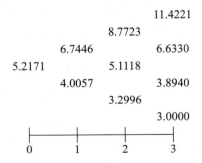

The option values are additive because they represent *simple* options. We could make the analysis richer (hence more complicated) by introducing interactions (i.e., the exercise of one option affects the value of another). Technically, our tree would become path dependent and valuation would grow more computer intensive.

From Trees to Forests

The binomial lattice we've just illustrated is quite versatile and can accommodate a variety of realistic scenarios (e.g., multiple options). This simple structure can handle even more complex settings such as changing parameter values. For instance, suppose expected salvage value is expected to decline over time. This is easily modeled once we have constructed a tree.

If the simple binomial lattice doesn't reflect reality sufficiently, we can extend to trinomial and even quadranomial lattices. A natural role for a quadranomial tree arises when there are two sources of uncertainty. For example, we may face technological uncertainty as well as product market uncertainty, hence a single binomial lattice will not serve us well.[5] We encountered these very circumstances in Chapter 8 in pricing bonds with options that depend upon interest rate dynamics as well as stock price processes.

It is also quite likely that sources of uncertainty will not be independent, hence multiple options will interact; the value of one option affects the value of another. This takes us to compound rainbow options — options on options with multiple sources of uncertainty. These are beyond the scope of this book.[6]

---

[5] For excellent examples, see T. Copeland and V. Antikarov, *Real Options — A Practitioner's Guide* (New York: TEXERE LLC, 2001), pp. 279-297.

[6] Lenos Trigeorgis has done pioneering work in interactive real options. See his book, *Real Options* (Cambridge, MA: MIT Press, 1996), Chapter 7.

APPENDIX

GENERALIZED CALL AND PUT PRICING MODELS

The Black-Scholes call and put option models can be derived by calculating expected payoffs assuming the underlying asset value is lognormally distributed, then invoking risk-neutrality and discounting at the risk-free rate (r). In the case of the call and put pricing models, the exercise price (X) is also the trigger point at which exercise occurs; that is, the payoff on a call is $S - X$ if $S > X$, and the payoff on a put is $X - S$ if $S < X$.

We may derive more general pricing models where the exercise price and trigger point are not the same, and as we shall illustrate, this more general framework permits valuation of scale reduction and expansion options. In an important contribution by Clifford Smith,[7] a general model is given for evaluating the partial expectation of a lognormally distributed random variable (e.g., the expected value of ($S - X$) conditioned on $S > X$). A general call option has payoffs at expiration (T):

$$C = \begin{cases} bS - cX & \text{if } aX \geq S > dX \\ 0 & \text{if } S \leq dX \end{cases} \tag{1A}$$

A standard call option payoff is equation (1A) with $a = \infty$, $b = 1$, $c = 1$, and $d = 1$. A general put has payoffs:

$$P = \begin{cases} 0 & \text{if } S \geq aX \\ bS - cX & \text{if } aX > S > dX \end{cases} \tag{2A}$$

A standard put payoff is equation (2A) with $a = 1$, $b = -1$, $c = -1$, and $d = 0$. If we take the expectation of C in equation (1A) or of P in equation (2A), then discount to the present at the continuous rate r, the resulting value is given by:

$$P \text{ or } C = bS[N(d_1) - N(d_3)] - cXe^{-rT}[N(d_2) - N(d_4)] \tag{3A}$$

---

[7] C.W. Smith, Jr., "Applications of Option Pricing Analysis," in *Handbook of Financial Economics*, J.L. Bicksler (ed.) (North-Holland Publishing Company, 1979), pp. 79-121.

where

$$d_1 = (\ln(S/dX) + (r + \sigma^2/2)T)/\sigma\sqrt{T}$$
$$d_2 = d_1 - \sigma\sqrt{T}$$
$$d_3 = (\ln(S/aX) + (r + \sigma^2/2)T)/\sigma\sqrt{T}$$
$$d_4 = d_3 - \sigma\sqrt{T}$$

For a standard call, the value of the payoff in equation (1A) is found by inserting $a = \infty$, $b = 1$, $c = 1$, and $d = 1$ in equation (3A) to get the familiar result:

$$C = SM(d_1) - Xe^{-rT}M(d_2)$$

For a standard put, the value is found by inserting $a = 1$, $b = -1$, $c = -1$, and $d = 0$ in equation (3A) to find:

$$P = Xe^{-rT}M(-d_4) - SM(-d_3)$$

where

$$d_3 = (\ln(S/X) + (r + \sigma^2/2)T)/\sigma\sqrt{T}$$

and

$$d_4 = d_3 - \sigma\sqrt{T}$$

In general, the exercise price for a call (cX) is not the same as the value of S which triggers exercise (dX), since c and d are not constrained to be 1. And the exercise price for a put (cX) is not generally the same as the trigger point (aX). This important generalization permits us to value options involving fractional payoffs and exercise prices, thus we may apply the general model in valuing scale reduction and scale expansion flexibility.

Let's illustrate using this simple story. We can liquidate one of our assembly plants for $24 million in two years, and this will reduce our capacity by 30%. Our multi-plant firm produces cash flows such that the total present value is $75 million. Suppose we have decided that if the total value falls below $60 million, we will liquidate the plant. What is this flexibility worth?

This is clearly a put, thus the payoff is described in equation (2A):

$$P = \begin{cases} 0 & \text{if } S \geq aX \\ bS - cX & \text{if } aX > S > dX \end{cases} \qquad (2A)$$

with $a = 2.5$, $X = \$24$ million (hence $aX = \$60$ million), $b = -0.3$, $c = -1$, and $d = 0$.

The value of the flexibility is found by solving equation (3A). Suppose $r = 0.05$ and $\sigma = 0.20$. Given that $S = \$75$ million, X $= \$24$ million, and $T = 2$, you can confirm that $d_1 = \infty$ and $d_2 = \infty$, hence $N(d_1) = N(d_2) = 1$. You will also find $d_3 = 1.2839$ and $d_4 = 1.0011$, hence $N(d_3) = 0.90041$ and $N(d_4) = 0.84161$. Insert all these values in equation (3A) and you'll find the flexibility is worth about $\$1.1988$ million.

QUESTIONS AND PROBLEMS

1. Our firm is evaluating a pilot project that will require expenditures over the next 18 months with a present value of $750,000. At the end of this period the firm will be in a position to invest another $18 million in full scale production. Based on current projections, the value of the cash flows of the full scale venture will be approximately $16 million at the time the venture is commenced (18 months from now). The firm's cost of capital is 10%, and the Treasury rate is 6%. Uncertainty about the value of the cash flows from the full scale venture is indicated by a volatility parameter of 25%. Should we undertake the pilot project?

2. We can expand our production capacity substantially with an incremental investment of $2 million. Let's use 3 years as the planning horizon for deciding whether to expand. We project the value of remaining cash flows as of year 3 to be $8 million at that time. Suppose that this value also represents production at maximum capacity (without expansion). Our firm's cost of capital is 15% and the Treasury rate is 6%.

   a. Assume a volatility parameter of 30% to assess the value today of the flexibility to expand in this case.

   b. What should be the effect on the value of the expansion flexibility you found in part a if the maximum capacity was $9 million rather than $8 million. Explain briefly, then confirm your conjecture analytically.

3. Suppose we are assessing an investment of $65 million and projected cash flows over the project's expected life of 20 years have a present value of $60.5 million. This assessment is based on the firm's 12% cost of capital and the assumption that the project will be continued through its 20-year lifetime. But suppose that management believes the project could be abandoned in a few years for a salvage value of about $40 million. Use 4 years as a planning horizon and suppose that the projected value of the

remaining cash flows as of that time will be about $52 million. The risk-free rate is 6%, and the uncertainty about the cash flow value indicates a volatility parameter of 40%.

a. Determine the value of the option to abandon the project.

b. Should the project be undertaken given your findings in part a?

4. Refer to the binomial tree in Exhibit 11.6 in the Chapter. The project values in the tree are based on a volatility parameter of 25%, hence u = 1.2840 and d = 0.7788. Valuation is done using a risk-free rate of 6%. The probability of an upward move was found to be 0.5566, and the probability of a downward move is therefore 0.4434.

a. Assuming the project may be abandoned for $3 million any-time during the project's life, determine the value today of the project. (You are confirming the solution found in the Chapter and depicted in Exhibit 11.7, thus you should find that the project is worth about $5.0467 million considering the aban-donment option.)

b. Now suppose the abandonment value is $3.5 million rather than $3 million. Determine the value of the project.

c. Suppose the Vice President for Finance wishes to have an assessment of the sensitivity of the value of the abandonment option to the estimated salvage value in this case? Explain how you would respond.

5. We have undertaken an investment which will allow us to exploit full scale production in about 1 year. The incremental investment will be about $40 million, but full scale production will not be commenced unless the value of the projected cash flows at that time exceeds $50 million. The risk-free rate is 6%, and the value today of projected cash flows from full scale operation is deter-mined to be $35 million. Assume a volatility parameter of 25%.

a. What is the value of the option to expand in this case?

b. How should the value you found in part a compare with the value of a call option that will be exercised at $40 million instead of $50 million? Confirm your intuition.

Chapter 12

Options in Risk Management

It seems natural to end our journey with a treatment of the uses of options in managing risk. Risk management is an expansive topic in its own right and several books have been devoted to it.[1] Our coverage will be less ambitious in that we shall focus on options rather than the full menu of derivative products. We will explore the use of options in managing the firm's *operating risk*, *interest rate risk*, and the risk exposure of equity portfolios. Our examination will include some exchange-traded options such as options on commodity futures and Treasury bonds, and it will take us into the vast over-the-counter market that has emerged to satisfy needs unmet by the standard exchange-listed options universe.

OPERATING RISK MANAGEMENT

Operating or *business risk* is the uncertainty the firm faces in its operating income, or earnings before interest and taxes. Steps taken to reduce uncertainty about revenues and operating expenses comprise operating risk management. In this section, we will consider standard exchange-traded options useful in managing operating risk, then we'll examine some of the *exotic* options — nonstandard options tailor-made by financial institutions and traded over-the-counter.

Options on Futures

We will illustrate the usefulness of options in operating risk management with two example firms. The first is a firm which extracts and sells crude oil. Suppose the firm has rights to extract four million barrels of oil, that it will take about four months to complete

---

[1] Two excellent examples are P. Jorion and S.J. Khoury, *Financial Risk Management* (Cambridge, MA: Blackwell Publishers, 1996), and S.E. Harrington and G.R. Niehaus, *Risk Management and Insurance* (New York: McGraw-Hill, 1998).

the extraction, and that it will sell the crude at the prevailing market price at that time. A helpful way of approaching this risk management problem is first to recognize that the firm now has a *long* position in the underlying (crude), hence its revenues will vary dollar for dollar with the price of crude prevailing in four months.

A simple way to eliminate the revenue uncertainty is to enter 4,000 short futures contracts on light sweet crude traded on the New York Mercantile Exchange. Each contract is for 1,000 barrels and expiration dates are standardized. In this way, we effectively lock in a selling price for our four million barrels of crude, hence the revenue risk is neutralized. In this case, we are protected against a *downturn* in oil prices, but we also forfeit additional profits that we would earn in the event of an *upturn*.

If we could buy a put option on crude oil, we would then create a floor effectively locking in a minimum selling price; this is a straightforward protective put strategy we saw in Chapter 2. In many cases, standard options on commodities themselves do not exist, but we have available a very close substitute — options on futures. Recall from Chapter 2 that we may enter into a *futures put option* which will pay a cash amount if exercised, and exercise will automatically place us in a *short* position in the underlying futures contract.

For example, suppose the futures price for December delivery of crude is $26 per barrel, and we plan to sell our four million barrels that month. Suppose we find that put options on crude futures with December expiration and $22 exercise price are trading on the New York Mercantile Exchange at $0.07 per barrel. Each put contract is for 1,000 barrels, hence the contract price is $70, and our outlay for 4,000 contracts would be $280,000.

As we approach the futures expiration date in December, the futures price will converge to the spot price of crude. If the spot price in December is, say $28 per barrel, the puts will expire out-of-the-money and our loss on the puts will be the full $280,000. However, relative to the $26 futures price today, we will gain $8 million when we sell our crude (4,000,000 × ($28 − $26)). On the other hand, if the spot price in December is only $20.50 per barrel, the puts will be exercised for a profit of $5,720,000 (4,000,000 × ($22 − $20.50) − $280,000). This helps cushion the loss of $22 million on the sale of crude in December at $20.50 rather than $26 per barrel. In fact, our combined losses on the crude oil relative to the current $26 futures price and the options are limited to $16.28 million.[2]

Now suppose our firm produces clothing and plans to purchase cotton soon. You may think of this as effectively a *short* position in cotton and a convenient way to lock in a future price is to enter a *long* futures contract traded on the New York Cotton Exchange.

But what if the price of cotton retreats by the time we must make the purchase? A long futures (or forward) contract will cause the firm to miss the opportunity to exploit a reduction in the cost of materials. How might we use options on futures to cap the price of cotton? Remember that we have a short position effectively, so a natural way to flatten out the profit graph is to enter *long call options* on cotton futures. You can confirm that this strategy places a floor on the firm's losses by plotting a short position in the underlying and a long call. The graph should resemble a long put position.

Pricing Standard Futures Options

Theoretical valuation of options on futures is no more complicated than pricing options on stocks. If the futures price (F) follows a Gauss-Wiener process we met back in Chapter 3, Black[3] has shown that the price of a European-style call on a futures contract is given by

$$C = FN(d_1) - XN(d_2) \tag{1}$$

where

$$d_1 = (\ln(F/X) + \sigma^2 T/2)/\sigma\sqrt{T}$$
$$d_2 = d_1 - \sigma\sqrt{T}$$
$$F = \text{current futures price}$$
$$X = \text{exercise price}$$
$$T = \text{time to expiration}$$
$$\sigma = \text{volatility of futures price}$$

---

[2] This "portfolio," long crude and long puts, is a familiar protective put position. If you sketch the profits and losses, you will find that we can lose no more than $4.07 per barrel no matter how low the price of crude drops. The maximum loss per barrel is the price of the put ($0.07) plus the difference between the futures price and exercise price ($26 − $22).

[3] F. Black, "The Pricing of Commodity Contracts," *Journal of Financial Economics* (March 1976), pp. 167-179.

The volatility parameter (σ) is the annualized standard deviation of the continuously compounded rate of change in the futures price. It may be estimated from a series of futures prices or inferred from observed futures options prices. Under fairly general conditions, the futures volatility will be very close to that of the underlying asset.[4]

The theoretical price of a put on futures is given by

$$P = XN(-d_2) - FN(-d_1) \qquad (2)$$

where d_1, d_2, and all other terms are as described in equation (1) for futures call options. To illustrate the call and put pricing models in equations (1) and (2), suppose crude oil futures for delivery in nine months are priced at $25.50 per barrel, and the volatility (σ) of oil futures is estimated at 23%. The exercise price (X) for 9-month option contracts on oil futures is $24. If you apply these parameters in the pricing models in equations (1) and (2), you will find $C =$ $2.80, the price of the call, and $P =$ $1.30, the price of the put per barrel. Thus the prices of 1,000 barrel contracts should be $2,800 and $1,300 for calls and puts, respectively.

Standardized futures options typically expire on the delivery dates of the futures contracts on which they are written; however, this need not be the case in order for equations (1) and (2) to make sense. What is needed is that the life of the option not exceed the life of the futures contract. Also, note that standard futures options are typically American-style, hence the models in equations (1) and (2) will tend to price low. An alternative to Black's model, which is easy to implement, is the binomial tree approach whereby the futures price process is modeled as we saw in Chapters 7 and 8 for interest rates and stock prices. This method will accommodate American-style options.

Nonstandard Options on Futures

Suppose our firm plans to buy crude oil in nine months. One way to lock in a price is to enter a *long forward* or *long futures contract*. Still another way is to synthesize a long forward position by *buying*

---

[4] See J.C. Hull, *Options, Futures, & Other Derivatives 4th Edition* (Upper Saddle River, NJ: Prentice-Hall, 2000), pp. 293-295.

a futures call option and *writing* a futures put for every 1,000 barrels we plan to buy. If the exercise price (*X*) in each option is $24, and the calls and puts are priced at $2.80 and $1.30, respectively, then our initial net outlay will be $1.50 per barrel. The firm has manufactured a long forward position, effectively locking in a price of $25.50 per barrel. Why $25.50? Suppose the price of crude in nine months is $24; both options expire at the money. We buy crude at the prevailing price, $24 per barrel, *and* we bought the call and wrote the put at an outlay of $1.50 thus our total cost is $25.50. On the other hand, if crude is at, say $25.50, we exercise the calls at $24 (*X*), but we had the net outlay of $1.50 for the options. The total outlay for oil will be $25.50, regardless of the spot price in nine months.

If we owned the crude and planned to sell it in nine months, we could lock in a price by manufacturing a *short futures position*. Simply write the call at $2.80 and buy the put at $1.30, for a net *inflow* of $1.50 per barrel. In this way, we lock in a selling price of $25.50 per barrel.

Now suppose that rather than locking in a price, the firm is content to lock in a *range* of possible prices. Recall that the 9-month oil futures put with exercise price (*X*) of $24 is worth $1.30. You can confirm that a 9-month *call* with exercise price of $27.30 is worth $1.30 from equation (1). Now note that the call (*X* = $27.30) is worth the same as the put (*X* = $24), $1.30 per barrel.

Let's say we *write* the call and *buy* the put for a net zero outlay. We have locked in a selling price for our oil in the range from $24 to $27.30. In this case, we can gain as much as $1.80 and lose no more than $1.50 per barrel. To see this, suppose oil climbs to $29. We gain $3.50 relative to its futures price of $25.50, but we lose $1.70 on the short call ($27.30 − $29), hence our profit is $1.80. You should confirm that for *any* price above $27.30, our profit is $1.80. Had the price of crude sunk to $22, we would have lost $3.50 on our oil and made $2 on the put ($24 − $22) for a net loss of $1.50. We can lose no more than $1.50 per barrel with this strategy. If you plot the gains and losses for oil prices of, say, $20 to $30, you should see a pattern we met in Chapter 2 — a *collar*.

Notice that in order to make this a zero net investment strategy, we need an option with a nonstandard exercise price, $27.30. Investment banks create and market *packages* of options tailored to risk management needs of their client firms. The example we just completed, writing the call ($X = \$27.30$) and buying the put ($X = \$24$), would ordinarily be available as a package called a *short range forward* contract. A *long range forward* simple reverses the option positions — buy the call and write the put, still for a net outlay of zero.[5] The theoretical price of a range forward contract in general is $C - P$ for a long position, or $P - C$ for a short position. Often the exercise prices are set so that $C = P$, hence they have zero net outlay.

MANAGING INTEREST RATE RISK

Suppose our firm has issued a floating-rate bond. Perhaps coupon payments are reset every 90 days based on the London interbank offer rate (LIBOR). Thus our firm's interest expense is uncertain, and if we were lending at a variable rate, our income would be uncertain. There are numerous ways to reduce or eliminate interest rate risk including *swapping* variable-rate bonds for fixed-rate instruments, hedging with exchange-traded *interest rate options*, and hedging with nonstandard *caps, floors*, and *collars*.

Interest Rate Options

If a firm wishes to hedge against an increase in interest rates, it can buy put options on bond futures (Chicago Board of Trade). As interest rates rise, bond futures prices decline, hence put values increase. To hedge against a decline in rates, calls on bond futures would be appropriate.

Options are also written on interest rates directly, and such *interest rate options* are traded over-the-counter. The exercise price (X) is the rate paid in the case of a long call, and the rate received in the case of a long put. The underlying is the market rate, often LIBOR. Thus the dollar payoff on an interest rate call is $\max(\text{LIBOR} - X, 0)$,

---

[5] Range forwards are *exotic* or *second-generation* options — nonstandard contracts traded over-the-counter, and they go by several names, including cylinder options, flexible forwards, and zero-cost collars. See Hull, *Options, Futures, & Other Derivatives*, p. 458 for more pseudonyms. For extensive treatment of exotics, see P. Zhang, *Exotic Options* (Singapore: World Scientific, 1997).

scaled by the principal amount, and adjusted to the length of time over which the particular LIBOR is defined. For instance, if the principal is \$1,000 and the underlying rate is the 90-day LIBOR, the payoff on a call is \$1,000 × [max(LIBOR − X, 0)] × (90/360), since the 90-day LIBOR is annualized using 360 days. For instance, suppose X = 9% and LIBOR = 10.3%. Exercise of an interest rate call with principal of \$1,000 will give a payoff of \$1,000 × [max(0.103 − 0.09, 0)] × (90/360) = \$3.25. The payoff on a corresponding put would be \$1,000 × [max (X − LIBOR, 0)] × (90/360).

A simple method for pricing an interest rate call is to adapt the Black model for futures options.[6] To illustrate, suppose we are interested in a call on the 90-day LIBOR, and the call expires in six months (T = 0.5). Suppose the exercise price (X) is 8%, and the 6-month Treasury rate (r) is 5.5%. To apply the Black model, we employ the forward LIBOR (f); in this case, the 6-month forward LIBOR for 90-day deposits. Let's say the annualized volatility (σ) of the 6-month forward LIBOR is estimated at 15%.

We now have the ingredients to determine the theoretical price of the interest rate call in equation (3):

$$C = e^{-rT}[fN(d_1) - XN(d_2)]e^{-fT^*} \qquad (3)$$

where

$$
\begin{aligned}
r &= \text{risk-free rate} \\
T &= \text{time to expiration} \\
f &= \text{forward rate} \\
X &= \text{strike price} \\
T^* &= n/360 \text{ for } n\text{-day LIBOR} \\
d_1 &= (\ln(f/X) + \sigma^2 T/2)/\sigma\sqrt{T} \\
d_2 &= d_1 - \sigma\sqrt{T} \\
\sigma &= \text{volatility of forward LIBOR}
\end{aligned}
$$

With r = 5.5%, T = 0.5, f = 9.3%, X = 8%, T^* = 0.25, and σ = 15%, the value of C in equation (3) is 0.01266. Remember this is scaled by the principal, say \$1,000, then weighted by 90/360 to give \$3.17.

---

[6] See D.M. Chance, *An Introduction to Derivatives 3rd Edition* (Forth Worth, TX: Dryden Press, 1995), Chapter 14.

To price an interest rate put using Black's model, we use equation (4):

$$P = e^{-rT}[XN(-d_2) - fN(-d_1)]e^{-fT*} \tag{4}$$

where all terms are as defined in equation (3). Using the same parameters as we did in our example, and assuming a $1,000 principal, the price of an interest rate put is about $0.30. The value of the put ($0.30) is substantially below that of the call ($3.17) because the call is in-the-money and the put is out.

Caps, Collars, and Floors

A firm may place an upper limit on its interest payments by purchasing a series of interest rate calls with expiration dates corresponding to coupon payment dates. Thus if interest rates, hence coupon payments on a floating rate bond, increase, the firm may exercise one or more of the series of calls, receiving cash payments that tend to offset the additional interest charges. Often such series of interest rate calls are packaged in *interest rate caps* by financial institutions. In this case, each call is known as a *caplet*.

Caps are straightforward to price because they are portfolios of interest rate calls, usually European-style. Let's illustrate using a simple 9-month note with quarterly interest paid at LIBOR. Suppose the principal is $100,000 and LIBOR is presently 9%. The firm's first coupon payment due in 90 days will then be $2,250 (= $0.09 \times \$100,000 \times 90/360$). If LIBOR increases to 11.5% as of the first payment date, the next coupon payment will be $2,875 (= $0.115 \times \$100,000 \times 90/360$). Then if LIBOR is 11.8% as of the second payment date, the third and final coupon payment will be $2,950.

If the 9-month bond had been priced originally at par, the effective annual rate would be the annualized value of i implied by the following:

$$\$100,000 = \frac{\$2,250}{1+i} + \frac{\$2,875}{(1+i)^2} + \frac{\$102,950}{(1+i)^3} \tag{5}$$

In this case, $i = 2.686\%$ and the annualized rate is $(1.02686)^4 - 1 = 0.1118$, or about 11.18%.

Exhibit 12.1: Loan Payments for $100,000 Floating Rate Bond and Interest Rate Cap with 9% Strike Price

Quarter	LIBOR	Cap Payment	Interest Paid	Net Cash Flow
0	9.0%	−$130	—	$99,870
1	11.5	0	$2,250	−$2,250
2	11.8	$625	$2,875	−$2,250
3	—	$700	$2,950	−$102,250

Now suppose the firm had purchased a cap with exercise price of 9%. This means the firm has a 3-month call and a 6-month call, each with an exercise price (X) of 9%. Note that if the 3-month call is exercised, it will pay off at the end of the following quarter, six months from now. If the 6-month call is struck, it will pay off nine months from now.

In this example, LIBOR is 11.5% as of the first quarter, hence the first call will be exercised for $100,000(0.115 − 0.09)(90/360) = $625, to be received six months from now. And because LIBOR rises to 11.8% as of the second payment, the second call will be exercised for $100,000(0.118 − 0.09)(90/360) = $700, received nine months from now. The cash flows are summarized in Exhibit 12.1.

The firm's net interest expense, interest paid less cap payment, is fixed at $2,250 each quarter. If the cap had zero cost, the firm's cost of debt would then be exactly 9%, the capped rate.[7] But suppose the firm had paid $130 for the cap, hence the initial net cash flow would have been $99,870 ($100,000 for the loan − $130 for the cap). The effective rate will then be a little higher than 9%, but substantially lower than the 11.18% without the cap.

Why is the cap worth $130? Recall that a cap is a series of caplets, hence the value of the cap is the sum of the prices of interest rate call options valued according to equation (3). Suppose the observed 90-day and 180-day forward LIBOR rates are 8.8% and 8.9%, respectively. The 3-month and 6-month Treasury rates are 5.6% and 5.8%, respectively, and the volatility of LIBOR is 15%. The parameters for the two caplets are summarized in Exhibit 12.2.

---

[7] In our example, LIBOR rises each period, thus the cost of debt is the capped rate. If rates declined during any period, the caplets would not be exercised and the firm's interest payments would be below $2,250 for that period. Thus the firm's cost of debt could be below 9%, but not above.

Exhibit 12.2: Price Computation for 9% LIBOR Caps

	1st caplet	2nd caplet
forward LIBOR (f)	0.088	0.089
risk-free rate (r)	0.056	0.058
exercise price (X)	0.090	0.090
volatility (σ)	0.15	0.15
time to expiration (T)	0.252	0.50
LIBOR term (T^*)	0.25	0.25
theoretical price	$43	$87

Cap value = $43 + $87 = $130

The price of each caplet in Exhibit 12.2 is from equation (3), scaled by the principal ($100,000), and weighted by 90/360. You can confirm that the caplet values are about $43 and $87, thus the cap is worth about $130. The firm's interest cost, taking into account the cost of the cap, is limited to about 9.5% (annualized). This is found by solving for i in the equation:

$$\$99,870 = \frac{\$2,250}{1+i} + \frac{\$2,250}{(1+i)^2} + \frac{\$102,250}{(1+i)^3} \tag{6}$$

We find that $i = 2.295\%$, thus $(1.0295)^4 - 1 = 0.095$. By purchasing the cap in this case, the firm's cost of debt will be no more than 9.5%, and if LIBOR declines, it may be less.

Just as a floating-rate borrower may wish to cap interest payments, a floating-rate lender might wish to establish a minimum. This is possible with an *interest-rate floor*, a series of *interest-rate puts*, or *floorlets*. A lender could establish a 9% floor on the same loan we analyzed in Exhibit 12.1. If the floor were costless, the lender's rate would be no less than 9%. Of course, a floor consists of puts valued according to equation (4), thus the lender's effective rate would have a minimum rate below 9% reflecting the cost of the floor.

Suppose a borrower is willing to accept a range of effective rates below a cap of, say, 10% and above a floor of, say, 8.5%. In this case, the borrower could *collar* the rates by buying a 10% cap and writing an 8.5% floor. On the other hand, a lender might collar by buying the 8.5% floor and writing the 10% cap. If the cap and floor rates are set just right, the value of the cap will equal that of the floor, hence the combined product will be a *zero cost collar*.

Swap Options

A firm paying fixed-rate interest payments may prefer a floating-rate arrangement, or vice versa, depending on circumstances. The firm may approach an intermediary such as an investment bank to identify a party with the opposite preference. These are the makings of a *swap*; that is, the two parties exchange obligations to pay interest on the same principal amount. Firms may also enter *currency swap* agreements whereby interest and principal payments in one currency are exchanged for these payments in another currency.

These two basic arrangements are "plain vanilla" swaps and there are seemingly countless variations and refinements.[8] There is also a market for options on swaps, known popularly as *swaptions*. The buyer of a *call swaption* pays a premium for the right either to pay or receive at a fixed-rate called the *strike rate*. The right to receive payments at the strike rate is a *receiver swaption*, whereas the right to pay at that rate is a *payer swaption*.

To see how these work, suppose a firm's treasurer fears that rates may rise, hence the firm's floating-rate interest payments will increase substantially. By purchasing a payer swaption, the treasurer secures the right to switch to a fixed (strike) rate in the event rates have risen.

EQUITY RISK MANAGEMENT

In this section, we will consider some of the more popular second-generation options useful in managing risks of common stocks and equity portfolios. A few of these, such as CAPS, are exchange-traded, while most are nonstandard contracts traded over-the-counter.

Barrier Options

A *CAP* is a call or a put on a stock index (the S&P 100 or S&P 500) that pays a fixed amount in the event the underlying index reaches a specified level at any time during the option's life. CAPS are traded on the Chicago Board Options Exchange (CBOE) and are standard-

---

[8] For an excellent survey, see Chance, *An Introduction to Derivatives*, pp. 515-516.

ized to pay \$30 per contract. If the index touches the specified level, the option is automatically and immediately exercised. A CAP is an example of a *barrier option*; that is, payoff is determined by the underlying price reaching a specified barrier.

Because the payoffs are capped, barrier options are appealing to some investors due to their lower costs relative to regular options. Barrier options in the over-the-counter market are classified as either *knock-in* or *knock-out*. A knock-in is *activated* only if (and when) the underlying touches a barrier, whereas a knock-out *ceases to exist* when a barrier is reached.

Call options may be *down-and-in* or *down-and-out*. If the underlying falls to a certain level below the initial price, a down-and-in call comes into existence, whereas a down-and-out call is terminated. Puts may be *up-and-in* or *up-and-out*. If the underlying rises to a specified level, an up-and-in put comes into being, while an up-and-out put is terminated. The down-and-in calls and up-and-in puts are examples of knock-in options, whereas down-and-out calls and up-and-out puts are knock-out options.

As you might expect, there are also *up-and-in calls* and *up-and-out calls*, and of course, *down-and-in puts* and *down-and-out puts*. The payoffs on all knock-in and knock-out options are capped and their lifetimes are truncated, hence their theoretical prices may be substantially below ordinary option values.

Binaries and Digitals

Cash-or-nothing calls and puts also feature capped payoffs. A cash-or-nothing call pays a fixed amount K if the underlying exceeds the exercise price (X), and zero otherwise, hence this is an example of a *binary* option. A cash-or-nothing put pays K if the underlying is less than X, and zero otherwise.

Unlike many of the second-generation or exotic options, binaries are easy to value. A cash-or-nothing call has theoretical price given by

$$C = Ke^{-rT}N(d_2) \qquad (7)$$

where $d_2 = (\ln(S/X) + (r - \sigma^2/2)T)/\sigma\sqrt{T}$, and the remaining terms are as defined previously. The normal probability $N(d_2)$ is the (risk-neutral) probability of exercise, thus equation (7) may be interpreted as the present value of the expected cash flow.

The value of a cash-or-nothing put is given by:

$$P = Ke^{-rT}N(-d_2) \qquad (8)$$

where the terms are the same as in equation (7). The probability $N(-d_2)$ is the (risk-neutral) probability that $S < X$, hence the put is exercised.

A *digital* call or put pays \$1 if exercised and zero otherwise, thus these are special cases of cash-or-nothing calls and puts. The values of digital calls and puts are given by:

$$C = e^{-rT}N(d_2) \qquad (9)$$

and

$$P = e^{-rT}N(-d_2) \qquad (10)$$

Another type of binary is an *asset-or-nothing option*. An asset-or-nothing call pays a cash amount equal to the underlying price if exercised ($S > K$), or zero if unexercised ($S \leq X$). An asset-or-nothing put pays cash amount S if $S < X$, and zero otherwise. The values of these binary options are:

$$C = Se^{-dT}N(d_1) \qquad (11)$$

and

$$P = Se^{-dT}N(-d_1) \qquad (12)$$

where $d_1 = (\ln(S/X) + (r + \sigma^2/2)T)/\sigma\sqrt{T}$. Equations (11) and (12) are the familiar components of the dividend-adjusted call and put option pricing models without the parts involving the exercise price, $Xe^{-rT}N(d_2)$ and $Xe^{-rT}N(-d_2)$, respectively.

Lookbacks and Average Price Options

Lookback options are interesting because their exercise prices are variable; indeed, the exercise prices are not known until expiration, hence the name. A *lookback call* pays the amount by which the final price exceeds the *minimum* stock price during the option's life. A *lookback put* pays the amount by which the *maximum* stock price exceeds the price at expiration. A lookback call allows the holder to buy the underlying at the lowest price achieved up to expiration, whereas a lookback put allows one to sell the underlying at its highest price.

Finally, *average price* options' payoffs are also determined by the behavior of the underlying during the option's life. These so-called *Asian* options have payoffs based on the average price of the underlying $(\bar{S})$, hence an Asian call pays $\max(S - \bar{S}, 0)$, and an Asian put pays $\max(\bar{S} - S, 0)$. For instance, suppose the average price $(\bar{S})$ of the underlying of an Asian call was \$43 during its life. At expiration, the underlying price (S) is, say, \$48. The call will be exercised and will pay $\max(S - \bar{S}, 0) = \max(\$48 - \$43, 0) = \$5$.

AND THERE'S MORE

Nonstandard options traded over the counter are plentiful. These include *chooser* options with the special feature that after a specified time period, the holder may determine whether the option is a put or a call. *Forward start* options are often used in employee compensation. As the name implies, the options are awarded now but are not activated until some point in the future. *Shout* options resemble lookbacks. These are European-style with the added feature that during their lives the holders may "shout" to the writers. Then, at expiration, the holder receives either the intrinsic value at the time of the shout or the usual payoff, whichever is greater.

We met options to exchange one asset for another in the context of real options in Chapter 11, and these may be formalized in contracts on financial assets and traded over-the-counter. We also discussed *rainbow* options in Chapter 8. These may involve multiple sources of risk, or they may be puts or calls on several assets.

Suppose an investor owns a bond issued by a firm and wishes to have some form of insurance in case the credit quality of the issuer declines. A *credit spread option* pays off a specified amount in the event the yield on the bond exceeds, say, the Treasury rate by a fixed number of basis points.

As you have seen, option contracts are often adapted to fit a wide variety of circumstances, and the ingenuity of the inventors is most impressive. Recently an insurance conglomerate, Swiss Re Group in Zurich, developed an insurance agreement that allows firms to tap capital in times when raising capital is difficult. These agreements are termed committed long-term capital solutions, or CLOCS. These call options may be exercised when certain economic conditions arise (e.g., a specified decline in a country's gross domestic product). It is interesting to note that CLOCS represent participation by an insurance firm in an endeavor traditionally within the exclusive domain of investment banks.

QUESTIONS AND PROBLEMS

1. Here's a straightforward valuation question concerning a put option on a futures contract on crude oil. Suppose the futures price for 6-month contracts is presently quoted at $24 per barrel, and the put has an exercise price of $22 per barrel. The volatility of oil futures is about 18%, and the option expires in six months. Based on the futures option pricing model in equation (2) of the chapter, what is the put contract worth?

2. Let's design a range forward contract using the futures put evaluated in Question 1, along with a futures call on crude oil. The call will have the same expiration as the put. What exercise price must be set for the call option in order to make this a zero cost package?

3. Our financial institution is assessing a risk management strategy involving interest rate puts. The 3-month forward LIBOR for 90-day deposits is 8.85%, and the volatility is estimated at 16%. The put expires in 3 months, and the 3-month Treasury rate is 6%. The strike price for the put we are evaluating is 7.75%. The principal amount to be specified in the contract is $600,000. What is the value of the option?

4. In addition to options on Treasury bond futures traded on the CBT, there are numerous tailored products for managing interest rate risk traded over the counter.

   a. What is an interest rate cap? An interest rate floor? A collar?

   b. What is an interest rate swaption?

5. Revisit Exhibit 12.2 in the chapter and confirm that the value of the first caplet is $43, and that of the second caplet is $87.

6. Our firm plans to write a binary put option on a stock priced at $65 per share. This is an asset-or-nothing put and the stock pays no dividend. The exercise price is $58, the put expires in six months, and the Treasury rate is 6%. The volatility of the underlying stock is estimated at 55%. What is the put worth?

7. Define the following exotic options.

    a. Forward start option

    b. Asian option

    c. Chooser option

    d. Up-and-in call option

    e. Down-and-in put option

    f. Credit spread option

Solutions to
Questions and Problems

CHAPTER 1

1. Calls and puts are rights to buy and sell specified assets. Forward contracts are bilateral obligations to buy and sell specified assets.

2.   A   (4)
           B   (1)
           C   (5)
           D   (2)
           E   (6)
           F   (3)

3. An index call (put) is the right to "buy" ("sell") an index scaled by a specified multiple. A call option holder may exercise by paying the exercise price, and will receive the cash value of the scaled index in return. A put holder exercises by paying the cash value of the scaled index and receiving the exercise price.

4. A futures call option holder receives (1) a long futures position, and (2) the cash difference between the exercise price and the futures price at exercise.

5. The number of common shares for which a convertible security may be exchanged. The conversion value is the conversion ratio multiplied by the common stock price.

6. A call is a contract between investors, whereas a warrant is a contract between a firm and an investor. As such, sale and exercise of warrants results in cash flow to issuing firms, and warrant

exercise increases the number of shares outstanding. None of these results are true of ordinary call options.

7. No, it is in-the-money; i.e., if expiration is imminent, it will be exercised regardless of the price that had been paid for it. If the stock price remains at $57, the call will be exercised for a rate of return of −50% (= ($57 − $55 − $4)/$4). If the call is not exercised in this case, the rate will be −100%.

8. Yes, exercise, even though your rate of return will be 0% (= ($0.94 − $0.91 − $0.03)/$0.03).

9. Conversion value = 1.250 × $44 = $55.

10. Yes, they will convert into common shares worth $55 rather than surrender their preferred shares for $50.

CHAPTER 2

1. a. long underlying, short call
   b. long underlying, long put
   c. short call
   d. long call, long put, exercise price of call > exercise price of put
   e. short call, short put, equal exercise prices
   f. long call, short call, exercise price of long < exercise price of short
   g. long underlying, long put, short call, equal exercise price

2. Covered call: long stock, short call.
   Profits per share will be:

	$48	$33
long stock	+8	−7
short call	−3	+5
net profit	+5	−2

If the stock price rises, we make more with the long stock position ($8) than with the covered call position ($5). If the stock falls, we lose more with the long stock ($7) than with the covered call ($2). The covered call is more conservative.

3. Riskless hedge: long stock, long put, short call
   Profits per share will be:

	$50	$28
long stock	+10	−12
long put	−4	+8
short call	−5	+5
net profit	+1	+1

Net investment = stock (40) + put (4) − call (5) = $39
Rate of return = profit/investment = $1/$39 = 0.0256
Annualized, this is a little over 5.12%.

4. Buy call with $X = \$25$ for $12, buy call with $X = \$35$ for $4, and write 2 calls with $X = \$30$ for $8 each. Calculate net profits for a range of stock prices:

	$20	$30	$40
long call (X=25)	−12	−7	+3
2 short calls (X=30)	+16	+16	−4
long call (X=35)	−6	−6	−1
net profit	−2	3	−2

Maximum profit = $3 and maximum loss is $2.

5. Buy put with $X = \$25$, buy put with $X = \$35$, and write 2 puts with $X = \$30$.
   For a range of prices, calculate net profits:

	$20	$30	$40
long put (X=25)	+1	−4	−4
2 short puts (X=30)	−6	+14	+14
long put (X=35)	+4	−6	−11
net profit	−1	+5	−1

Maximum profit = $5 and maximum loss = $1.

CHAPTER 3

1. Delta is the amount by which the price of an option will change in response to a unit change in the price of the underlying asset. Thus if delta for a call option on stock is 0.70, then an increase in the stock price of, say $0.10, should lead to an increase in the call's price of about $0.07.

2. A short position in a bond; i.e., borrowing.

3. Delta shares of the underlying stock.

4. Re-arrange equation (15) so that PUT appears on one side and CALL, STOCK and $PV(X)$ appear on the opposite, then examine the signs. You should see that CALL has positive sign, STOCK is negative and $PV(X)$ is positive. This means you should execute a short position in the stock, buy a call and lend the present value of the exercise price to synthesize a put option.

5. a. If you use Excel to determine the cumulative normal densities, you should find the value of the call to be about $2.42 on a per share basis.

   b. The put will be worth about $6.89 on a per share basis. Note that the put is worth considerably more than the call in this case because the call is out of the money, and the put is in.

   c. Your net investment in this riskless hedge position is $55 for the stock, $6.89 for the put and −$2.42 for the call, or about $59.47 per share.

   d. Since this is a riskless hedge, and the exercise price for each option is $60, we know that the portfolio will be worth $60 at exercise regardless of the price of the stock at that time. If we invest $59.47 today and it grows to $60 in 8 weeks (0.1538 years), the continuously compounded rate of return is about 0.88725%. Annualize this by scaling by 52/8 to get an implied rate of roughly 5.77%. The small difference between this and the Treasury rate (5.8%) is due to rounding the option prices.

e. Put-call parity implies CALL – PUT = STOCK – $PV(X)$ from equation (15). The present value of the exercise price using continuous compounding is about $59.47 (sound familiar?). Thus the question is whether $2.42 – $6.89 is equal to $55 – $59.47. It is, thus our Black-Scholes-Merton model values in this case are consistent with parity.

f. Delta for the call was about 0.3742, while that for the put was –0.6258. If the stock price advances by, say $0.10, we would expect the call price to increase by $0.037, or roughly 4 cents. The put should decline by about $0.063, or 6 cents.

CHAPTER 4

1. a. Using equation (2) and an accurate value of the cumulative normal density you should get about $2.35 for the call price. This is a little lower than that with dividends ignored ($2.42), exactly as we would have expected.

   b. With equation (3) you should find the price of the put to be about $7.00. This is a little higher than the price with dividends ignored, as we would have expected.

2. Delta for the call option is about 0.3664. If the stock price falls by $0.25, the call price should decline by about $0.09 to $2.26.

3. We need delta shares per call and we have 10,000 shares. This means we need to write calls using the reciprocal of delta to determine the hedge ratio. Since delta is 0.3664, this means we need about 27,293 short calls, or about 273 contracts.

4. Gamma is 0.03627. Delta should change by about 0.0091, and since the stock price increased we need to increase delta by this

amount to about 0.3755. If we rebalanced our delta hedge portfolio subsequent to the stock price change, we would need more shares per call written, or fewer calls given that we have 10,000 shares.

5. Designate the $60 exercise price call as call number 1, and the $55 exercise price call as number 2. Delta and gamma for call number 1 are 0.3664 and 0.03627, respectively. Delta and gamma for call number 2 are 0.5475 and 0.038111, respectively. The number of shares (n) is fixed at 10,000. Insert the delta and gamma values into equations (18) and (19) in the Chapter, then solve by substitution! You should get about 64,651 for call number 1 and −61,531 for call number 2. This means the delta-gamma neutral portfolio will consist of 10,000 shares, about 647 long calls with $60 exercise price, and about 615 short calls with $55 exercise price.

6. Vega for the first call is determined to be 8.10, thus a change in volatility of +2% implies an increase in call value of about $0.16.

7. The prices and continuously compounded returns are given below. Using equation (23) in the Chapter we find that the estimated variance of the weekly returns is 0.000711, and this is annualized to 0.036972 by scaling by 52. Taking the square root we find the volatility is 0.19228, a little over 19%.

Week	Price ($)	Return
1	92.05	—
2	91.35	−0.00763
3	88.75	−0.02887
4	86.50	−0.02568
5	87.85	0.01549
6	88.65	0.00907
7	84.90	−0.04322
8	83.85	−0.01244
9	85.55	0.02007
10	88.95	0.03897

CHAPTER 5

1. The "underlying" is the firm itself. This means all of the assets of the corporation. The exercise price is the promised payment to the creditors. The stockholders essentially have the right, under limited liability, to "buy" the firm's assets by paying the promised payment to the bondholders.

2. The put is short. The higher the value of the put, the lower the value of the debt. The exercise price is the promised payment to the bondholders.

3. If the policy change increases asset volatility, then both the call and put option values increase. The call option of the stockholders is long, hence their wealth is improved. The bondholders' put is short, thus their wealth declines.

4. This comes back to changes in volatility. Due to the portfolio effect, when two or more operating divisions are housed in the firm, the firm's operating volatility is lower than the average of the volatilities of the respective divisions. This represents the effect of diversifying away some of the unique or unsystematic risk of each division while it is housed in the firm. When we experience a divestiture of any type (spin-off, carve-out, etc.), the risk that has been diversified away is restored. This leads to an increase in asset volatility and we know the effect this has on stock and bond values.

5. Creditors anticipate these kinds of problems and impose various restrictions in response. In a bond indenture these will be codified as restrictive covenants. These may and often do constrain the firm's capital structure, investment policy, dividend policy, and any other aspect of the firm's operations that may be altered in such a way as to expropriate value from the bondholders. Other defensive measures might include conversion terms or warrant attachment, or the requirement that collateral be specified.

6. a. From equation (1) you should get about $22.387 million for S.

 b. The put is worth $4.167 million, and the risk-free equivalent debt is worth the present value of the $24 million payment over 5 years at the 6% rate, or $17.78 million. Thus the debt (D) has a value of $13.613 million. A quick way to check this is to add S ($22.387 million) and D ($13.613 million), and you should get the firm's total value (V) of $36 million.

 c. The value of the put option in the debt will increase to $5.749 million, and the risk-free equivalent remains $17.78 million. Thus the value of the debt (D) will fall to $12.031 million. Clearly the value of the equity (S) in equation (1) will climb. In this case it will increase to $23.969 million. It is easy to check that the value lost by bondholders is value gained by stockholders. You can see why this must be so by recalling an important aspect of vega which we met in Chapter 3. Recall that vega is the amount by which an option price changes in response to a unit change in volatility. And you may remember that vega for a call is the same as the vega for a corresponding put. Hence the put and call values change by the same amount because the two options have the same parameters.

CHAPTER 6

1. Financial managers have reported in various surveys that they issue warrants to "sweeten" debt and preferred issues; i.e., to make them easier to sell to investors at reasonable rates. In addition, managers say they use warrants as "delayed equity financing" devices. This means that they prefer to raise capital by issuance of stock, but they perceive the market environment is not favorable for a stock issue at that time. Thus they issue warrants along with senior securities such as bonds, then as the market environment becomes favorable, the warrants will be exercised. The firm eventually attains its goal of financing with equity, but on a delayed basis.

2. Hard protection is absolute. For example, an issue may not be callable under any circumstances until a specified date has passed. Soft protection is conditional usually on stock price performance. For instance, an issue may not be called until and unless the firm's common stock price has exceeded the warrant exercise price by at least 50% for a specified number of days.

3. When firms issue straight debt there is essentially no measurable effect on stock price. The market evidently shrugs these announcements off as benign events, or perhaps they were expected and the stock price has already reflected the issuance decision by the time it is announced. But when warrants are added to bond issues, those announcements are met by an average stock price decline of between 1% and 2%. This may not sound like much, but bear in mind that this is 1 - 2% of the entire equity value of the issuing firm. When firms call and force exercise of warrants, the stock price reaction is more severe. Studies have shown that average declines of 4% to 6% are typical. This could be because of the dilutive effect, but it could also be because the announcement to force exercise, hence raise equity capital, reveals that the firm is not doing well and needs cash. Either way, the stock price reaction to calls of warrants is negative and severe. Add to this the market's reaction to issuance announcements and you can see that warrants are by no means a cheap source of financing.

4. This is a rights offer. Current stockholders often have a preemptive right to participate in new security issues. They are said to "subscribe" to the issue when they exercise their rights, hence the term, privileged subscription.

5. Often rights offerings are underwritten. This means the firm secures an investment bank to stand ready to buy and exercise unexercised rights. The standby fee is the flat rate charged for standing ready to exercise the rights. The take-up fee is the price charged by the underwriter for each right it is called upon to exercise. It is reflected in a reduction in the subscription price.

6. The ex-rights price should be about $43.82. This is determined from the formula $(nS + X)/(n + 1)$, where S = rights-on price ($44), X = subscription price ($42), and n = the number of shares needed to exercise one right (10). A stockholder who exercises or sells the rights will not suffer financially. This is because the right is worth $0.18 in this case, determined from the formula $(S - X)/(n + 1)$. An investor who owns the stock at $42 before the rights offer will have a stock worth $43.82 ex-rights and could have sold the right for $0.18 or exercised it. The only investors who are harmed are those who neglect to exercise or to sell their rights.

7. a. With some trial and error you should get about $18.64 for the warrant price (W).

   b. If there are more shares outstanding, with the same stock price, then the firm's equity value is greater. This means the underlying value claimed by warrant holders is greater, hence W should be higher. Also, the dilutive effect is less severe in this case. The proportion of shares claimed by warrant holders will be lower given more outstanding common shares initially. If you solve equation (4) with $N = 9$ million shares, you should find that convergence is achieved when $W = \$18.70$, a little higher than before ($18.64), as expected.

CHAPTER 7

1. Since this is an annual tree, and the 14% volatility is an annual amount, we merely calculate $\exp(0.14) = 1.1503$. Multiply this by $R(1,L) = 4.891\%$ to get 5.6261%.

2. Calibrating a tree is done by backward induction. To build and calibrate an annual tree, we begin with a two-year bond with an observed price. We have a one-year spot rate, $R(0)$, and we guess the first one-year rate in year 1, $R(1,L)$. Then given an assessment of rate volatility, we determine $R(1,H)$ as in Question 1. Next we discount the cash flows (face value plus final coupon

interest payment) from period 2 back to period 1 using $R(1,H)$ and $R(1,L)$, then using probabilities (often 0.5), we discount the expected value of the bond back to the initial period. If the resulting value happens to equal the observed bond price, the tree is calibrated up to the two-year horizon. Otherwise we must guess another value of $R(1,L)$, then $R(1,H)$, and repeat the process. We continue until the calculated value at the initial period equals the bond's observed price. Next we find a 3-year bond, then guess the lower one-year rate for period 2, $R(2,LL)$. Then we use the volatility parameter to calculate $R(2,HL)$ and $R(2,HH)$. We then discount the final cash flows of the three-year bond to period 2 using $R(2,LL)$, $R(2,HL)$ and $R(2,HH)$, then discount the resulting values at period 2 back to period 1 using the rates from the calibration of the two-year tree. Finally, we discount expected values at period 1 back to the current period, and compare with the observed price of the 3-year bond. If these are equal, the 3-year tree is calibrated. Otherwise...guess again and keep modifying the guess of $R(2,LL)$, hence $R(2,HL)$ and $R(2,HH)$, until convergence. For practical problems a computer is invaluable!

3. a. This will increase the theoretical value of the bond above $98.65 because the call option will be worth less. Remember that the call is short in the bond, thus a reduction in the value of the call provision makes the bond more valuable.

   b. This will bring the bond's theoretical price down below $98.65. The call option will be more valuable because it can be exercised earlier, hence the bond will be worth less.

   c. Of course, this is a put feature and this option will increase the value of the bond.

   d. This will make the put feature more valuable, hence the bond's theoretical price will increase.

4. The OAS is a constant amount added to (subtracted from) the rates at each node in a tree that will force the theoretical price of

a bond relative to a particular interest rate tree to equal its observed market price. The two prices, theoretical and market, may differ for a number of reasons including differences in credit risk, liquidity, and so on. It is important to note that the OAS reflects all features except optionality, hence the name. That is, the OAS reflects differences in prices due to credit risk, liquidity and tax status, but not callability, putability, etc.

CHAPTER 8

1. Compare the conversion value with the effective call price. The conversion value is the product of the conversion rate and the stock price. The effective call price includes accrued interest and the nominal call price. If conversion value exceeds the call price, the issue is in the money. Otherwise it is out of the money. If a firm calls an in-the-money convertible, investors should convert. This is termed "forced conversion."

2. The conversion factor is 0.1228 (= (350,000)/(350,000 + 2,500,000)), and the firm's equity value (V) is $97.5 million. The promised payment (B) is $17.5 million (= $1,000 × 17,500 bonds). Given the volatility (40%), risk-free rate (6%) and 5-year term (T), the value of the conversion option for the entire issue is $3,825,846 from equation (2). This means about $219 per bond, and combined with the straight value of $900, the bonds should sell at about $1,119.

3. The conversion ratio (CR) for this bond issue is 20 (= 350,000/ 17,500), and the straight bond value (SBV) is given in Question 2 ($900). The call price ($K$) is $1,000. Using $T = 3$, $r = 6\%$ and a volatility of 40%, the value of the conversion option (W) in equation (10) is about $9.72, or about $194 per bond. Combined with SBV, the issue should be fairly priced at about $1,094. Note that this is a little lower than the noncallable price we got in Question 2.

4. a. You should find that $u = 1.4191$ and $d = 0.7047$.

b. First find that $k = \exp(0.06) = 1.0618$. Then $p = (k - d)/(u - d)$ = 0.4999, or about 0.5. Thus $1 - p = 0.5$, the probability of a downward move.

c. The prices will be either $68.12 in an upward move, or $33.83 in a downward move.

d. If the stock price moves down, the bond's conversion value will be only $845.75, hence investors will not convert. They will collect $1,000 instead. If the price moves up the conversion value will be $1,703, hence they will convert.

e. The discount rate for the upward move is 6%, the risk-free rate. For the downward move we should use 12%, appropriate for the bond. By discounting the probability-weighted values to the present you should get about $1,245.40 for the value of the convertible bond.

5. a. LYONS are securities designed by Merrill Lynch. They are notes with conversion features, put provisions, and they are callable.

b. DECS are mandatory convertible preferred securities with absolute limits on upside participation.

c. PRIDES are mandatory convertible preferred securities with restrictions, but not absolute limits, on upside participation.

d. The coupon rate for a step-up bond will be automatically adjusted upward on specified dates.

e. Mandatory reset convertibles are redeemable for specified cash amounts in the event the underlying stock prices fall below stated levels.

Chapter 9

1. There are at least two ways to approach this. First, we must be careful to define NPV (or IRR, or PVI) as a measure which takes into account all the optionality of an investment. Thus we are discussing the post-modern definition rather than the neoclassical. Clearly the neoclassical rule is not reliable; e.g., rejecting a project with negative NPV in the neoclassical sense may well be the wrong decision. It may have sufficiently rich optionality to render it a valuable and worthwhile investment. Second, the three decision rules are often stated in the absence of a time dimension, hence it is assumed that we mean NPV, IRR or PVI at this time. As we will see in Chapter 10, a negative NPV based on immediate execution may be the incorrect reason to reject because NPV may be expected to grow over time. Also, a positive NPV project should not necessarily be commenced now. If we are in a position to wait, we may capture even greater NPV by executing in the future.

2. Financial options are much more clearly defined because of their contractual nature, and the parameters which influence option value are far less ambiguous for financial options than for real options. For instance, a firm's flexibility of abandoning a project at some point in the future may be viewed as a put option, and in a few cases this right may be established by contract with another party. But most often this "right" arises from the nature of the investment, thus key parameters such as the "exercise price" and "expiration" are quite nebulous and difficult to pin down.

3. Sensitivity analysis involves manipulation of parameter values, one at a time, to identify those to which the project's value, hence the decision, is most sensitive. For instance, once we have calculated NPV using our best information and identifying all relevant optionality, we disturb a parameter such as the volatility estimate by altering it within plausible bounds. If NPV changes sign for volatility estimates which lie within the plausible range, the decision is sensitive to this estimate and the analysis suggests we need to endeavor to refine our estimate to improve its precision and reliability.

4. It is both! As we will see in Chapter 11 such an option to exchange one risky asset for another can be valued theoretically using a straightforward model. Such options are calls in that they represent the right or flexibility to claim a risky asset, and they are puts in that they allow the holder to forfeit a risky asset.

5. An example could be a multistage research and development project. Investment in the initial phase gives the firm flexibility to exploit a subsequent development stage, which may ultimately result in execution of a commercial project. You could view the initial phase as a call on a call; i.e., the flexibility to acquire still more flexibility in the future. In Chapter 11 we will meet such compound options. They may be calls on calls, calls on puts, puts on puts or puts on calls.

CHAPTER 10

1. a. If you insert the parameter values in equation (4) in the Chapter, you should find the optimal time for executing the investment (t^*) is about 1.75. Thus you should recommend that the firm not execute immediately.

   b. If the project is undertaken now, NPV is $5 million. However, if it defers investment until about 1.75 years from now, NPV (in today's terms) will be a little higher, about $5.163 million. The firm will be worth about $163,000 more by following your advice!

   c. The PVI if undertaken now is 1.091 (= $60/$55 million). The firm should wait until PVI has grown to 1.12 (= $r/(r-g)$). You should confirm that at $t = 1.75$, the PVI of the project will be 1.12.

   d. Recall that an obvious cost of waiting is the opportunity cost of capital. The longer we defer a positive NPV investment, the lower its value to the firm in today's dollars. So given a higher cost of capital, you should expect the optimal time for execution (t^*) to be less than 1.75. You can confirm by solving equation (4). You will get $t^* = 0.762$; i.e., the firm should plan on delaying about 9 months.

2. a. Uncertainty represents a benefit of waiting, and now that we have introduced even a modest amount, it should manifest itself in a higher target value of PVI. This may not be obvious from the expression for b (equation (8)), hence $b/(b-1)$, but as the volatility parameter is increased, b grows larger, thus $b/(b-1)$ increases This means that the firm should hold off on the project until PVI has grown past 1.12.

   b. As expected, if you insert the parameters in equation (8) and solve for b you will get about 8.49. Then find $b/(b-1)$ to be 1.33. This is a little higher that 1.12, the value found in Question 1c with uncertainty ignored.

3. The expression for b in equation (8) reflects three effects on optimal timing. The cost of waiting is measured by the cost of capital, while the benefits of waiting are measured by the expected growth rate in project value, as well as the level of uncertainty about that rate. Consequently, for a given set of parameters the value $b/(b-1)$ will be higher as (1) uncertainty increases, or (2) the rate of growth increases, and it will be lower as the cost of capital increases. As volatility approaches zero, the only benefit of waiting is the growth rate in project value. This is the sole benefit accounted for in the expression $r/(r-g)$, the level of PVI at which a project should be commenced when uncertainty is negligible.

CHAPTER 11

1. By now this is an easy one. The expansion flexibility may be evaluated as a call option with 1.5-year life. The value of the underlying is the present value, at 10%, of the $16 million assessed at $t = 1.5$, or about $13.87 million. The exercise price is $18 million, so the call is out of the money significantly. Using a

volatility of 25% and risk-free rate of 6% you should find that the option is worth about $830,500. Should we undertake the pilot project? Given that it costs only $750,000, yes. Viewed as a call option, the pilot project has positive NPV.

2. a. This is a call option, but with a slight twist. The "exercise price" is the incremental investment ($2 million) plus the value at year 3 of the remaining cash flows under maximum capacity ($8 million), or $X = \$10$ million. Given the cost of capital of 15%, the value today of the projected $8 million project value in year 3 is $5.26 million. Using a risk-free rate of 6% and volatility of 30%, the call is worth about $0.345 million.

   b. If the maximum capacity is greater than $8 million, the effective exercise price in the call option will be higher, thus the option's value must decline. This is easy to confirm. Just repeat the steps in part a but use an exercise price of $11 million instead of $10 million.

3. a. This is a straightforward put option with exercise price of $40 million. Given the firm's 12% cost of capital, the project's $52 million in 4 years is now worth $33.05 million. Using a volatility of 40% and a risk-free rate of 6%, you should find that the abandonment option is worth $9.25 million.

   b. The NPV of the project ignoring the abandonment flexibility is −$4.5 million. But the flexibility more than compensates, so yes, the project should be undertaken.

4. a. Refer to the Chapter and the discussion of Exhibit 11.7 to confirm that the project's value at $t = 0$ is $5.0467 million, hence the put is worth $46,700.

   b. If the salvage value is $3.5 million, the firm will abandon in the third year if project value drops to $2.3618 million (in Exhibit 11.6), assuming it has not abandoned before then. Working backward to year 2, you should find that the expected project value in the lowest node in that year will be \$3.5088 million, compared to \$\$3.2296 million in Exhibit 11.7. Since salvage value is \$3.5 million, the project will be continued in year 2. Now work backwards to year 1 and you should find the expected project value to be \$4.0932 million (compare with \$4.0057 million in Exhibit 11.7). Now discount the expected value of the project back to the initial period ($t = 0$) and you should get about \$5.0833 million, hence the value of the abandonment flexibility is worth \$83,300. One simple way to respond to the Vice President is to point out that an increase in salvage value of \$.5 million changes the value of the flexibility by only \$36,600, thus the decision does not appear to be terribly sensitive to the estimated salvage value. The reason this is so in this case is that the put option is significantly out of the money; i.e., the project is worth \$5 million initially even without the put, and a salvage value of \$3 million, or \$3.5 million, isn't likely to influence the decision very much.

5. a. By reviewing the Appendix to the Chapter, in particular equation (1A), you will see how to price this modified call. The payoff on the call in general will be $bS - cX$ if exercised, and it will be exercised if S exceeds dX. In this case, c is not equal to d. Let a = infinity, $b = 1$, $c = 1$, and $d = 1.25$. Let $X = \$40$ million. Then the payoff will be $S - \$40$ million if S exceeds \$50 million (= $dX = 1.25 \times \$40$). Now examine equation (3A) in the Appendix and insert the values for a, b, c, and d. Use $S = \$35$ million, $r = 0.06$, $T = 1$, and a volatility of 25%. If you work through the calculations you'll find that the call is worth about \$1.9084 million.

   b. The value of the modified call will be lower than that of the ordinary call with $X = \$40$ million. You should get about \$2.4335 million compared to \$1.9084 million, reflecting the fact that the call will be exercised with a greater probability if the trigger point is only \$40 million.

CHAPTER 12

1. Inserting the parameters in the futures put pricing model in equation (2) you should find the put is worth about $0.429 per barrel. These contracts are standardized so that the underlying futures contract is for 1,000 barrels of crude, thus the put contract should be worth about $429.

2. The put with $22 exercise price was found to be worth $0.429 in Question 1, and in order for a corresponding call to have the same price, its exercise price must be higher than $22. Some trial and error reveals that if the exercise price is set at $26.36, the 6-month call will be worth about $0.429, thus the package (range forward contract, or cylinder option) should require an initial outlay of zero since it involves a long call and a short put (or vice versa). Note that the exercise price of $26.36 is not standard, hence the package must be tailored by an intermediary such as an investment bank.

3. Solve equation (4) in the Chapter, using $f = 0.0885$, $X = 0.0775$, $r = 0.06$, $T = T^* = 0.25$, and volatility $= 0.16$, then scale the result by $600,000, the principal. You should find that the put contract is worth about $77.29.

4. a. An interest rate cap is a portfolio of European-style interest rate calls known as caplets. The caplets have different expiration dates corresponding to a schedule that matches interest rate payment dates. A floor is a portfolio of European-style interest rate puts known as floorlets, and an interest rate collar is a portfolio of floorlets and caplets such that payoffs each period are constrained to lie within bounds defined by the exercise prices in the caplets and floorlets.

   b. An interest rate swap is a bilateral agreement for two parties to exchange obligations to pay or rights to receive interest payments. One party has a fixed-rate position, and the other has a floating-rate position. A swaption may be a call in which the holder buys the right to pay or receive at a fixed (strike) rate.

The holder receives the payments at the strike rate in a receiver swaption, and pays at the strike rate in a payer swaption.

5. Inserting the parameters for the 1st caplet in equation (3), then scaling by the principal amount of $100,000, you should find $C =$ $43. All but three of the parameters for the 1st caplet are the same as for the first; i.e., change T to 0.50, f to 0.089 and r to 0.058, then solve equation (2), scale by $100,000, and you should get about $87 for the 2nd caplet. Thus the LIBOR cap is worth $130.

6. Using equation (12) in the Chapter you should find that the binary put is worth about $18.60 on a per share basis. Note that the put is well out of the money, yet it commands a relatively high price. The reason is that in a binary option no exercise price is paid by the holder at exercise.

7. a. These are usually call options granted in employee compensation packages. They are fairly ordinary calls except that they are not effective immediately.

b. Asian-style calls and puts have payoffs determined by the average price of the underlying during the lives of the options. These are also known as average price options.

c. A chooser option is truly exotic! It is either a put or a call at the choice of the holder, and the choice is not made until expiration.

d. An up-and-in call is a call which becomes effective if an upper barrier is reached. That is, the underlying price must touch a specified upper bound in order for the up-and-in call to become effective.

e. A down-and-in put doesn't become effective until and unless the underlying drops below a specified barrier.

f. These options pay a specified amount to the holder in the event the yield on a particular bond issue exceeds a benchmark. Often the benchmark is the Treasury rate plus a certain number of basis points.

Index